With Innoc

With Innocence and Hope

Michael Williams

YOUCAXTON PUBLICATIONS
OXFORD & SHREWSBURY

This book is dedicated to the memory of the thousands of young men who went, 'In Innocence and Hope', to fight in 'The Great War', only to pay with their lives in a quarrel not of their own making.

Acknowledgements

J.M. Gregory, Assistance and Support
P.A. Williams, Military Research, Kew
N.D. Williams, Front Cover Design
Freda Benson, Walter's daughter, who kindly gave permission to use the photographs in this book and on the cover

Contents

LEST WE FORGET

Walter's Story
1914 – 1918

'Here dead lie we
Because we did not choose
To stay, and shame the land
From which we sprung.
Life to be sure is nothing much to lose,
But young men think it is
And we were young'

Introduction

April 1998

Rain, cold and cruel as bayonets struck the bent black figures that followed the coffin through the lychgate and out into the lane, where sandy water, red as blood, raced and gurgled into the overflowing drains.

At the head of the procession, tugged by the wind, the vicar's cloak whipped the coffin, tossing petals from the solitary wreath fluttering like confetti above the mourner's heads, some to be swept away on the wind, others drowned in the whirlpool of a drain unable to cope with this sudden downpour.

As if encouraged by the wind, the British Legion flag, a solitary flash of colour on this melancholy day, snatched and snapped at its staff as though intent on hurling itself from the grasp of its ancient Standard Bearer.

Huddled together both for warmth and comfort, family and friends watched in silence as the coffin was lowered into the streaming ground and, while the vicar intoned the solemn words of internment, an ancient bugler, his lips blue with cold, did his best to sound a tremulous but barely recognisable version of the last post.

Walter's passing was marked with these tributes as a veteran of the Great War and, apart from those terrible years, he had spent the greater part of his life within a rifles shot of this quiet place where he now lay. Finally, only two short years from his one hundredth birthday, in his passing he had exchanged a bloody trench for a peaceful grave, little difference in some men's eyes, for both contain dead men.

Like countless other fresh faced country boys, still barely sixteen and having known only the simple pattern of life in the tiny hamlet of Kenstone in North Shropshire he volunteered to fight in the filth and horror of what would become known as the war to end all wars, which, after four agonising years of bloody conflict, meant that an entire generation, the flower of British youth, would not come home.

Walter was one of 'the lucky ones' who, although badly wounded, managed to survive, only to find that life as he had known it could never be the same again.

Soon after the outbreak of war, like so many other impressionable young men he lied about his age and joined the army to 'do his bit for King and Country'. This book is a tribute not only to Walter who, although badly wounded, managed to somehow survive to tell the tale, but to those tens of thousands of other nameless young men who went 'In Innocence and Hope' to offer their lives in a quarrel not of their own making.

This book is dedicated to them.

J. M. Gregory

WALTER AGED 89 WEARING BOTH HIS CAMPAIGN MEDALS AND TWO
OTHERS AWARDED BY THE FRENCH GOVERNMENT TO VETERANS WHO
FOUGHT IN THE WAR . HE IS ALSO HOLDING BOTH A CERTIFICATE
AWARDING HIM THE CROIX DU COMBATTANT DE L'EUROPE AND A
CITATION OF MERIT ASSOCIATED WITH THE AWARD OF THE ALLIES MEDAL

WALTER AGED 16 AT THE TIME HE ENLISTED IN THE KSLI.
LOOKING AT HIS PICTURE, IT IS HARD TO IMAGINE HOW HE
WAS ACCEPTED AS BEING 18.

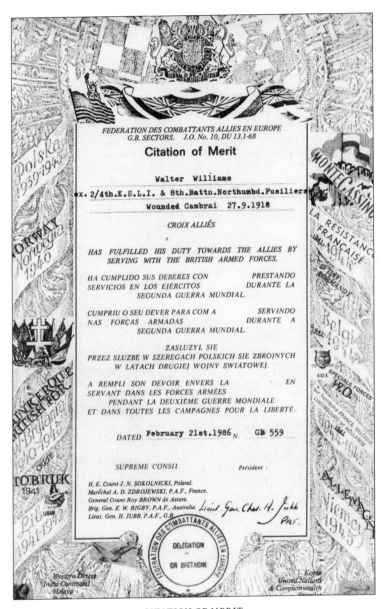

CITATION OF MERIT.

OTE—This Certificate is to be issued without any altera-
N.F 5061 tions in the manuscript.

Certificate of discharge of No. 5.4.8.0.0 Rank......*P te.*

Name..................*Williams..............Walter.*
Surname.   Christian Names in full.

Unit*
and
Regiment or Corps **NORTHUMBERLAND FUSILIERS.**
from which discharged

* The unit of the Regiment or Corps such as Field Co. R.E., H.T., or M.T., A.S.C., etc.,
is invariably to be stated.

Regiment or Corps to which first posted *No. Shrop. Lt. Infty.*

Also previously served in *Machine Gun Corps.*
...... *Army Cyclist Corps.*
...... *N.F.*

Only Regiments or Corps in which the soldier served since August 4th, 1914, are to be
stated. If inapplicable this space is to be ruled through in ink and initialled.

. Specialist Qualifications (Military)..................*Nil.*

Medals, Clasps,   *Two Blue Chevrons*
Decorations and   .... *Nil.*   Wound Stripes*...*One.*
Mentions in dispatches   To be inserted in words.

Has served Overseas on Active Service†

Enlisted a. *Shrewsbury*................on *29 - 3 -*......1915.
*Each space is to be filled in and the word "nil" inserted where necessary.
†To be struck out in ink if not applicable.

He is discharged in consequence of *being surplus to military*
requirements (having suffered impairment since
entry into the Service Para 392 XV. 1 a. IX IB.:
after serving*....*Three*....years*....*315*............days with the Colours, a

*....*Nil*....years*....*nil*............days in the   Army Reserve } Strike out
                                        or   } whichever
                                        Territorial Force† } inapplicable.
*Each space is to be filled in and the word "nil" inserted where necessary; number of
                      years to be written in words.
†Service with Territorial Force to be shown only in cases of soldiers serving on a
                      T.F. attestation.

Date of discharge.....*6 - 2 - 1919.*   Signature
                                                 and
                                                 Rank.

Jn. Officer i/c *Infantry*......Records.
                                         (Place)

A COPY OF WALTERS DISCHARGE CERTIFICATE.

6

WALTER WITH NURSES AND OTHER WOUNDED SOLDIERS AT THE
HOSPITAL AT BOULOGNE IN FRANCE.

IN DECEMBER MY NEW PLATOON, ALL PROSPECTIVE
MACHINE-GUNNERS, WAS POSTED TO TENBY.

WALTER AS A LANCE CORPORAL IN THE NORTHUMBERLAND FUSILIERS.

WALTER IN TRAINING FOR THE BRIGADE BOXING CHAMPIONSHIPS

Chapter 1

Taking the King's Shilling - November 1914

Into Battle

The naked earth is warm with Spring,
And with green grass and bursting trees,
Leans to the sun's gaze glorying,
And quivers in the sunny breeze.
And life is colour and warmth and light,
And striving ever more for these;
And he is dead who will not fight;
And who dies fighting has increase.

Grenfell

It was the late summer of 1914 and with the leaves on the trees already turning to autumn shades of brown, there were still many acres of standing corn still waiting to be cut and carried.

For once the delay was not because of the weather but due to the desperate shortage of manpower available to do the work now that so many of the more able bodied men had gone to swell the ranks of regular soldiers already fighting in France. Now there were only the old men and boys left to harvest the crops, many acres of which had been planted in the early spring at a time when no thought had been given as to how and by whom this might be achieved. As a result, goaded on by a bailiff anxious to please his master, on the large farm where I worked it had been left to Old Harry and me, a lad barely sixteen years old, assisted by a motley collection of men too old to fight and the wives of those who had already gone, to get as much of the job done as we could before the winter rains turned the corn rotten on the stalks. So it was, as we were nearing the end of another backbreaking day carrying corn from the bottom twenty acres, that we first heard the distant ring of horses' hooves on the Weston turnpike and looking back, saw the figures of three horseman coming our way. As they grew closer we could see that the trio consisted of an officer and two troopers, each dressed in scarlet uniforms and mounted on fine, thoroughbred horses. More accustomed to seeing such magnificent animals ridden by the county squire and his guests, perhaps accompanied by a pack of baying hounds, we all stopped to stare, even the women from the village who had reluctantly lent a hand with the harvest in return for a few days gleaning, straightening their backs, standing, hands on hips, to watch them ride by. But having already passed the gate into the field where we were working, to our surprise they suddenly reined their mounts to a halt and after a brief conversation, wheeled round and rode back into the field where we stood. Without speaking, the two troopers dismounted and, completely ignoring our curious stares, walked over to the loaded cart and began to examine the two horses still harnessed into its shafts. Then, signalled by a nod of approval from one of the troopers, the officer called Old Harry over and curtly explained to him that he had the authority to requisition any horses that were considered suitable for war work and as ours fitted that description, they should be unhitched from the cart and made ready to leave immediately. Horses were already being shipped overseas in their hundreds and with hunting suspended by Parliament lest it gave the impression that the gentry were still enjoying their sport while lesser mortals were dying for their country, with his reluctant approval, most of the Squires riding stock had already gone. Now it seemed that any horse could be taken without a by-your-leave and at a moment's notice, by those members of the forces who were authorized to do so. This was all too much for Old Harry who suddenly burst into tears and violently wringing his cap watched while I unhitched the horses from the cart and handed them over to the two troopers.

Within minutes they had gone, the silence only broken by the excited chattering of the women and the sobs of Old Harry whose spontaneous show of emotion was, I suspected, in some part due to the loss of his horses but, more importantly, the realisation that he faced almost certain dismissal once the bailiff learned what he had allowed to happen.

For my part, what I had just witnessed had a much more profound effect than the loss of the horses. Just to see the immaculate scarlet uniforms worn by the troopers as well as the magnificent horses they rode, not to mention the air of authority and superiority they possessed was all it took to finally convince me that I too should join the army.

My two older brothers Jack and Tom were already fighting in France. Both regular soldiers and veterans of the Boer War, they had joined the colours before I was born so that I scarcely knew them, seeing them more as visiting uncles rather than older brothers. Even so, as I grew up there had been times when one or both of them had come home on leave, big, confident, fighting men, outrageously flirting with the ladies who listened, spellbound, to dramatic accounts of their adventures while serving in Africa, adventures that had me itching to join them just as soon as I was able.

That however would not be so easy to accomplish, the main obstacle being that as I was still only sixteen and as the minimum age to enlist was eighteen and to serve overseas nineteen, it would be more than two years before I could do so legitimately, by which time the war might well be over.

Determined to succeed but knowing that my only chance of doing this was to convince the relevant authorities that I was much older than I appeared to be, I decided that I would try my luck the next time one of the now frequently held recruiting rallies was staged in the area.

Fortunately, I did not have long to wait as only a few weeks later the recruiting sergeant and his assistants opened for business using a makeshift stage set up in the yard of the Bear Hotel. That evening I joined the small crowd that had gathered and watched as several young men urged on by a mixture of a sense of duty and the encouraging cries of the ladies, happily signed away their lives for the price of the King's shilling. Caught up on a wave of patriotic fervour, I joined the queue waiting to volunteer, only to be turned away by the recruiting sergeant, his mocking advice to "come back once you have started shaving, laddie", only serving to make me more determined to join.

Without telling anybody of my intensions I bided my time so that when some months later another recruiting team visited the small town of Wem some ten miles away, confident that I would not be known there I once more mingled with the crowd, all the time watching the recruiting procedure and what was needed to improve my chances of success. After confidently being predicted by the Government that the war would all be over by Christmas but that celebration having come and gone, with the hastily assembled British Expeditionary Force still smarting from its ignominious withdrawal from Mons inflicted by the superior numbers and better trained forces of a well equipped enemy, the importance of recruiting had been upgraded to the point where it was now deemed essential that every community should supply their quota of men to assist in the war effort. At Wem, this was emphasised by the presence of our local MP, Beville Stanier, as well as the Mayor and Mayoress, both in full regalia, all doing their bit to persuade those still reluctant souls who had not yet done so to take the plunge and sign on. For some reason the stationmaster had also considered it his duty to be there and the vicar, wearing black polished gaiters and a stove pipe hat, was doing his best to swell the ranks, even if actively assisting in persuading young men to throw their lives away was playing on his conscience!

Having witnessed the casual manner in which previous applicants had been accepted, this time I was better prepared and with burnt wood ash rubbed into my chin to resemble stubble and my cap pulled well down over my face, felt that I stood a good chance. However, to my dismay when it was my turn it appeared at first that this might not be the case after the recruiting sergeant seemed to take a special interest in my declaration that I was eighteen years old, instantly questioning this and why I seemed to be in such a hurry to join the army. Fortunately, in answering his question I mentioned that my two brothers were already fighting overseas, information which turned out to be to my advantage, especially when the recruiting sergeant explained that he not only knew Jack but had served with him in Africa. From then on his demeanour became more relaxed so that after a little more gentle persuasion and a lot of pleading I was able to convince a somewhat doubtful recruiter that I was older than I was. Perhaps, without my birth certificate and with no other way of confirming my age he had no option. Although the registering of children had been made compulsory since 1837, purchasing the birth certificate had not and because very few people had this official document proving their true age, rather than lose good men who legitimately qualified by age but could not prove it, the military had issued an order that recruiters should not make the production of birth certificates compulsory. Furthermore, here was a lad with serving members of the military in his family who was determined to join his brothers in France. If he didn't succeed here, he would probably enjoy more success elsewhere, perhaps with another regiment. What was even more significant, as recruiting figures were rapidly on the decline helped in no short way by the growing lists of causalities appearing in the press on a daily basis, both recruiting sergeants and doctors acting as medical examiners were now being paid two shillings and sixpence for every man they could persuade to sign on. So, to my delight and surprise, at the tender age of fifteen I was accepted into the British army and by taking the King's shilling in recognition of that fact, I sold my life away for the princely sum of less than one day's wages!

Chapter 2

Early Days in the Army - March 1915

Lads You're Wanted
Lads you're wanted over there,
Shiver in the morning dew.
More poor devils like yourself,
Waiting to be killed by you!
Macmillan

It was still dark when Father shook me gently awake from what at best had been a night of fitful sleep. Instinct told me that it was still very early and a quick glance at the luminous hands of the clock beside my bed confirmed that it was barely half past four. For a moment I panicked, thinking I had overslept, then, realising what day it was, was confused as to why he was rousing me so early. Usually, by this time we would have set off on the long walk to work, going together as far as Paradise before taking our separate routes, Father turning right to the Hall while I took the road to the left and on to Weston Farm. Today, for the first time for many months I could lie abed, for there was no urgency for me to be up at this ungodly hour. Today I was joining the army!

Now, in the darkness of the room, I could just make out his familiar, stocky figure, framed against the lighter shape that was the window.

"I'll be off to work now son, the horses feeding can't wait for heroes!" he said in his half joking, half mocking way.

"I just wanted to say good luck and God bless before I left. I don't have to tell you that both your Mam and me are proud of you, even if we don't understand or maybe agree with what you're doing. You aren't the first young 'un and I'll wager you won't be the last by many a mile to spread his wings and seek a bit of excitement beyond the parish and until you've been and seen for yourself, you'll never be content staying around here. All I ask is that you don't do anything silly. Try to remember what our Jack always says, never volunteer,

17

and he's managed to survive a few scrapes and live to tell the tale during his time in the army! If you have to go to France, and I hope to God you don't, you can be certain that all the family will be praying for you to come home safe and sound".

For a moment he paused as if lost for words, not knowing or perhaps uncertain what else there was to say. Then, once more withdrawing back into the private shell he used to protect himself from the outside world, almost as an afterthought and as practical as ever "Try not to wake your Mother too early, she's been pacing the room most of the night and only lately fallen asleep. I keep telling her you're going no farther than Shrewsbury but it won't settle her mind. Having both our Jack and Bill out there in the thick of it, it's more than she can bear to see you going too. If we lose any of you lads I reckon it will be the end of her."

All the time he was talking he had been absent-mindedly kneading my shoulder and suddenly, for the first time in my life, I experienced an overwhelming feeling of love tinged with pity for this man who saw emotion only as a sign of weakness. Now, as he turned away, he ruffled my hair in what for him was a rare show of affection. He had no need to worry for I understood that there were so many things he wanted to say but couldn't find the words to say them.

At the door he stopped.

"Try to write to your Mother whenever you get a chance, you know how much she enjoys receiving a line or two from the other lads."

Then I was alone with only his familiar smell, his pipe, his horses and the quiet tread of his footsteps on the stairs. As he went, was it my imagination or did I hear a stifled sob reaching out towards me from the darkness?

After Father had gone, abandoning any idea of further sleep, I crept downstairs to wash at the kitchen pump. It had been another bitter night and the ice on the frosty slopstone glistened in the flickering light of the candle lighting my way.

There was no need for caution. In the kitchen I found Mother, already up and dressed, once more repacking my few belongings while she waited for the freshly kindled fire to gain sufficient heat both to boil the kettle and take the chill out of the room. My shirts and other things might be well worn but nobody could point a finger at them when it came to their whiteness or criticise the creases in my only pair of decent trousers!

Soon she had some breakfast on the table, hovering around the kitchen while I ate, all the time making no fuss nor challenging why I was going. All those questions had been asked and answered a hundred times before and were all behind us now so that she had finally reluctantly accepted that for me there was no turning back. Now, although it was breaking her heart, realising that I was determined to go she would not stand in my way.

When I had finished eating, Mother remarked that it would be nice to be out, so we walked together arm in arm into the breaking day. It was early March and the long winter was still upon us so as we climbed the path to the top of the hill, the frozen ground crackled beneath our feet and the bitterly cold air caught at our hands and faces in spite of the warm layer of clothing we had on. As we reached the top a lightening in the sky beyond the Hawkstone Ridge heralded the arrival of another day and soon the orange rim of a pale, wintry sun painted the tops of the hills with its scarlet hues. I recalled another day, a dozen years before, when we watched the same sun rise above familiar hills. Then, like now, we had been up before the dawn to start out on a journey to a new life at this place we had grown to love and call our home.

There were less of us now than in those heady, eager days of yesterday. Then the future had been full of hope and expectation, now, with the country at war, there was an uncertainty of life no one had ever imagined or experienced before.

Already there were many families in the parish who had relatives fighting in Europe and ours was no exception. Of our scattered family, as well as myself, one of fourteen brothers and sisters, there was my brother Jack, a regular soldier since leaving school and a sergeant in the Shropshire Pals who was in the line near Ypres, while Bill, also a regular, had been in France from the start. They would soon be followed by Dai and Tom. My brother George had died the year we came to Daneswell[1] and Fred, Edward, William and my sister Mildred had also gone, emigrating to Canada to start a fresh life in the newly opened territories.[2] Now it was my turn to leave our swiftly dwindling band. Despite my lack of years I now felt grown enough to make my way in life and ever since I could remember had harboured a burning ambition to follow my elder brothers into soldiering.

They had both visited us whenever they had leave. Both were tall and straight from a lifetime in the military and their scarlet uniforms and shining belts and badges had made a lasting impression on the younger members of the community, especially the ladies. Both had seen action in the Boer War and told us wonderful tales of their adventures, no doubt spiced up a bit in the telling for our benefit, so that I couldn't wait to be part of it myself.

As the frosty morning air caught at our throats, Mother and I snuggled together, oblivious to the cold. As the sky got lighter neither of us spoke, each buried in our own private thoughts as one by one the orange glow of oil lamps in our neighbours' cottages paled and then went out. Soon, sweet smelling wood smoke began to rise from chimneys as housewives lit their fires, got the breakfast prepared and their husbands off to work. All around us I recognised familiar sights and sounds as our small community awoke and went about the business of yet another ordinary day. Cattle in the field next to ours mooed impatiently, their steaming breath hanging above them like veils in the frozen air, eager to be brought in from the cold for milking. Clear on the morning air, from across the frozen fields came the metallic clanking of milk churns and the tinkling laughter of a milkmaid, soon followed by the strident voice of a cowhand calling in his herd.

"Come up, come up, cush, cush my lovely ladies", he called in the sing song voice known only to his profession and faintly I heard the gentle lowing of the cattle, the slam of a door and rattle of chains as they followed him obediently into the milking parlour.

That was the unmistakable bark of Floss, the Grass's dog, signalling an early success in her all consuming passion for hunting and unrolling indignant hedgehogs, still fast asleep in their winter hibernation. I laughed to myself! However much he tried, old Ted would never break her of that habit.

"Leave Floss, leave you silly bugger", angrily. Then, "I'll skin that stupid hound alive one of these days Missus, you mark my words if I don't, if she doesn't leave them blooming hogs alone", this to his wife Minny who must have left the warmth of her kitchen to see what all the commotion was about.

In the distance Eddy the postman was starting his round, his familiar tuneless whistle competing with other early birds singing their dawn chorus from the leafless hedges and frost white fields. All of these things I had taken for granted in the past, now, this morning, they took on a new significance and I longed to reach out and touch them, to gather them into my arms and take them with me when I left. I drank in each familiar sight and sound and, for a fleeting moment, was jealous of the honest, hard working people for whom this was just another working day.

The spell was finally broken when my brother Joe, stumbling sleepily downstairs, found himself alone in the house. With no breakfast on the table and an empty kitchen, he wandered indignantly outside in search of Mother and an explanation as to what was going on.

Joe had left school at Christmas and in spite of Father's misgivings had taken a job as an apprentice ganger on the railway, a career he would follow for the rest of his working life. My youngest brother Alec would soon need rousing too and started on his reluctant way to school less his tardiness be rewarded with the usual frantic lashings from our village schoolmaster Mr Gillibrand.

As we made our way back to the house I again begged Mother not to accompany me to the station, but to say her goodbyes in the privacy of our home. She would have none of it! The spectre of tearful farewells and matronly hugs witnessed by and to the amusement of the rest of the draft, sent shivers of embarrassment coursing down my spine. I knew I was wasting my breath, she was coming and that was that. As she indignantly informed me,

"I don't know what the worlds coming to when a mother can't see her soldier son off to war and shed a few tears doing it without causing mirth and merriment to his mates and comrades!"

Once again I reminded her that Shrewsbury Barracks, my destination, was hardly "off to war", mouthing a silent prayer to the

Saint of all departing soldiers, whoever he was, that my leave taking would proceed as smoothly and with the least embarrassment to me as possible. Many years later I would regret my selfishness at even suggesting she should not accompany me, but in my defence I was just a callow youth, young and self-indulgent, too full of myself to consider the feelings of others.

The goodbyes to my two younger brothers were perfunctory and without emotion. Joe, a country boy moulded in the image of my Father, would never wish to experience life beyond the stifling confines of the village. Content to play the hand that life had dealt him, he could never comprehend, even to the point of resentment, my urge to get away. Alec, on the other hand, was too young to understand the full implications of what I was doing and saw the whole thing as some huge adventure. It was 1915, still a year before the mass slaughter in the fertile water meadows of the Somme which would eventually lead to the introduction and implementation of conscription. Few of his classmates, if any, could boast of having two brothers fighting in France, now a third Williams would be added to the growing column of names hanging in pride of place next to the picture of the King, listing those who had already volunteered from the parish.

Left alone together, Mother and I whiled away the remaining hours with meaningless talk punctuated by long periods of silence so it came as a relief when the dawdling clock finally signalled it was time to climb aboard the trap for the journey to the station.

In such a small community everybody knew that I was leaving today and as we clattered along the frost hard road through Paradise, despite the cold, whole families were waiting at their doors or in their gardens to send me on my way. To my amazement some of the children even waved Union flags, making me feel very important! Enjoying every moment of my hour of fame I waved regally back, imitating the King who I had seen on the newsreels when the travelling picture shows came to the parish hall. I shouted back my thanks for their good wishes to each family as we passed, embarrassing Mother and spooking Bob our new horse into the bargain, for all this kindness and goodwill was too much for her. And so she rode the trap, staring straight ahead, only nodding and smiling to those she knew well, afraid that their genuine concern might be too much for her pent up emotions and unleash the flood of tears she struggled so hard to keep in check.

On reaching the station I was surprised to find a small crowd of well wishers had gathered. I knew that my friends Eddie Pye and Bill Capper were going and recognised a couple of other lads who had come in from Peplow. To my great relief my reservations regarding Mother proved unfounded. Family and friends of all the volunteers had turned out to see us on our way and already the handkerchiefs were out in force! I was surprised and a little concerned to see that the estate agent was there in polished gaiters and black hard hat, stamping his feet and blowing on his hands against the cold. He was standing with the vicar and for a moment I was afraid one of them might give the game away about my true age. I need not have worried. They either didn't know or didn't care so that when the train finally huffed and puffed into the station I was the first to scramble aboard and seek anonymity among the rest of the passengers. By the time I had stowed my case and found a place by the window there was only time to call out one last goodbye to Mother, who took the opportunity to press a package of sandwiches into my reluctant hands just before the train got under way, obscuring the small knot of well wishers behind a cloud of dripping steam. By the time it had cleared we were gathering speed and hanging from the window at first I was unable to see Mother until I saw that she had left the platform and climbed the embankment for a better view. There she was, standing alone, knee deep in the brown winter grasses. She was no longer waving, but her hand, still clutching a handkerchief, was frozen in space almost as if she was beckoning me back. All at once I felt a sudden urge to jump from the train, to run back and throw myself into her arms. Determined not to embarrass me, true to her word she had not shed a single tear since the time when the two of us had shared the sunrise several hours before. Those would come later on the lonely drive home.

At a bend in the line, first the station and then the rest of the village disappeared from view while for a fleeting moment I saw the familiar outline of the Hall through a break in the trees, then it too was gone and with it that part of my life forever.

The train wound its way through the countryside, stopping from time to time to pick up more people. These were mostly ordinary passengers, some carrying produce and other goods into the market at Wellington, but at nearly every stop the little knot of well wishers, the earnest, embarrassed young men and their tearful, flustered families, indicated the departure of more volunteers on their way to enlist. Occasionally there were men in uniform, going back off leave carrying rifles and kitbags, some wearing battered caps with the rim band removed, evidence that they had already served at the front.

After about an hour the train pulled into the larger station of Wellington where a porter walked the length of the train calling, "All change for Shrewsbury, change here for Shrewsbury" and we tumbled off in some confusion, clattering over the iron bridge to the other platform where our connection was already waiting. This train had come in from Birmingham and young men crowded at every window, shouting encouragement as we ran. Suddenly I felt that the mood had changed as the sadness of leaving was forgotten and a new sense of adventure lifted everyone's spirits. Now, when the train stopped at a halt, there was a crowd of faces at every window, ready to shout advice to the little knots of passengers saying their awkward goodbyes. Some of it was bawdy, some funny, but all was given in good humour. I found myself joining in, enjoying the carnival atmosphere which seemed to have developed with the arrival of the lads from Birmingham.

"Give her a kiss from me old lad. Blimey, what a smasher" or "You shouldn't have joined if you can't take a joke old son", echoed down the train, to the odd one who took offence. Already what few doubts I had about enlisting were all forgotten.

Once we were under way I had a chance to look around and see what sort of people were travelling with me. There were men from all walks of life, some young, others not so young, but everyone a volunteer and on the face of each and every one of them I saw a look of eager expectation, a desire to get the job done, and in each one I recognised a kindred spirit. Some were bundled up against the cold in warm overcoats and carried leather suitcases, others came in what they stood up in, their meagre belongings, perhaps a second shirt and worn pair of boots, wrapped in brown paper and carried by a loop in the string.

I took to the city lads straight away. They seemed to be so much more confident and mature than us country boys, each equipped with a sharp or witty remark for every occasion.

In no time at all we were steaming into Shrewsbury where a sergeant major paced up and down, his scarlet sash and polished pace stick sure evidence that the time for fun was over and the serious business of becoming a soldier had already began. True to the tradition of his rank, the train had hardly stopped before he began roaring meaningless orders, his waxed moustache bristling with indignation if we failed to comprehend or comply with their meaning. Assisted by two equally officious corporals, he eventually got us fell in into three columns and on his command we marched briskly from the station and out into the town. I use the word "marched" loosely! Out of the forty or so who fell in, there seemed hardly any who were able to keep step, a fact not lost on the gang of urchins who skipped and danced alongside us, mimicking our efforts, as we made our way across the station yard and out into the town. All this was too much for the R.S.M. who bellowed curses, slashing at the air with his pace stick, his face turning redder with every mistake we made. It was still early in the war and patriotism in the town was still very much alive. As we stepped out for Coleham Barracks, our cases and packages, not rifles, clutched in our hands, several bystanders stopped to give us a clap and a cheer. Once, as we passed a flower shop, a young girl ran out and tossed some blooms amongst us. This was more like it! This was what we had all joined for! Suddenly backs became straighter, arms began swinging in unison and our ragged marching picked up, encouraged by one of the corporals who started calling the step.

"Left, left, left, right, left!" so that by the time we wheeled in through the impressive gates guarding the entrance to Coleham Drill hall even the R.S.M. had calmed down to the point where he no longer looked as if he was about to explode. We were fallen out for a smoke and I took the opportunity to open the bag of sandwiches Mother had given me. It had been a long day with nothing to eat since breakfast .Others got their rations out too, and we shared their contents with those who had none. Without realising it we were already forging that bond of friendship unique to generations of serving men, an unwritten code that no matter what befalls you, you will share both the good and bad times together.

The rest of the day was just a blur. There were kit issues, haircuts, injections and the thousand and one things that go together to convert what in the morning had been forty odd individuals into that many servicemen.

My platoon was put under the command of Sergeant Beasley, a tall, angular man in his mid-forties whose uniform never quite seemed to fit him. However his medal ribbons told a different story, recording the fact that he had fought through several campaigns in India and in the more recent Boer War and was very much a regular soldier and a veteran who, during our training period, we got to know as a stern but fair taskmaster. I discovered that he knew my brother Jack, they had fought together in the Boer War and when we were off duty, in lighter moments he liked to reminisce about those heady days, describing many a scrape he and Jack had somehow survived. It became plain that he felt an acute embarrassment at still serving in a training camp while many of his contemporaries, albeit much younger than himself, were already in the thick of it. Despite his age, when his chance came he grabbed it with both hands, only to be killed just a month after landing in France, leading a night raid on an enemy trench. He was a regular soldier, one of Kitchener's Old Contemptibles, who gave me my first taste of soldiering and I remember him with respect and affection from all those years ago.

Coleham Barracks, headquarters of the 2/4th KSLI, was filled to over flowing so that many troops had to be billeted out in the town. On my first night, four of us were sent to the home of a Mr Harry Wright at Bishops Street were we would stay until April. The four included me, Ernie Pye, a lad from Newport and another from Welshpool called Evans. We were to become firm friends for the duration of our training and for the rest of our lives for the two of us lucky enough to survive.

Mr Wright and his family were kind and generous and our rooms were always warm and dry. We were at the end of one of the worst winters in recent years and it was a great comfort to return after a freezing day on the firing range or parade ground to be greeted with a warm meal and roaring fire.

Each day in training was the same as the last. At six thirty each morning we would report to the Barracks. From there we would march in double time up to Monkmore Race course for a day of extended order drill, PT, bayonet practice, or whatever took the instructor's fancy. On one occasion we were made to swim across the river Severn, a task made harder by the fact that hardly any of us could swim. Somehow everyone got across, many using pieces of wood or anything else which would float, to help them. After that our instructors never tried it again, perhaps fearing that the next time they would not be so lucky. Some mornings we went via the quarry where we did physical exercises in the Dingle. At midday we would form up and march back to Coleham for a meal served in the mess hall before returning in the afternoon to our labours on the Racecourse. At first I found it hard going although I was pretty fit, certainly a lot fitter than most of the town lads anyway, many of whom struggled right from the start, particularly with the route marches and obstacle courses. Soon I grew to relish each new challenge that was put before me and thoroughly enjoyed this early phase of training. On the rifle range I found I had the natural ability to be a better than average shot, both with the Lee Enfield rifle and later with the Vickers machine gun. Never tested before, this natural born talent would stand me in good stead throughout my service career.

In April we were ordered to pack our kit and the whole company formed up and marched to Park Hall camp in Oswestry, a journey that took most of the day. All the other ranks were on foot in extended order; the officers were mounted on splendid horses, riding up and down the toiling columns of men ensuring everybody kept up and gave a good account of themselves. The CO, Lt-Colonel Cunliffe, a very grand and remote character mounted on a high stepping charger came too, glaring about him through the monocle he always seem to wear. Predictably, just like the officers at Balaclava, having reached his destination he dismounted and was driven back to Shrewsbury in a staff car accompanied by most of his staff!. Later he would move with his headquarters to Pembroke Docks which had been the home of the 9th Battalion KSLI since November 1914. We were never told why! Only the military could make a decision to station the Shropshire Light Infantry in darkest Wales! Later in the war they must have had a change of heart when the regiment returned to the County to be stationed at Prees Heath near Whitchurch under the command of Colonel Ransom. Here they would stay for the duration of hostilities.

The CO left us under the command of Captain Sparrow and the two Lieutenants Hazard, I'm not sure if they were related, the Regimental Sergeant Major and his NCOs. We were billeted under canvas on very boggy ground and from the onsett it was pretty obvious things were going to be tough. Nearly all the tents rained in and there was never anywhere to dry our clothes or blankets. Fortunately the people from the town rallied round to ease our discomfort, the Ladies of Oswestry YMCA co-operated by making and mending clothes and taking in washing, while a hospital, manned by nuns from the Red Cross, was set up in the town workhouse. They were soon in business! By now we had been joined by men from the Welsh Border Infantry Brigade and with nearly five thousand troops living under canvas in primitive conditions, it was soon full to over flowing.

After only a few days at Oswestry I was sent for by messenger and told to report immediately to the orderly room. Assuming I was in trouble for something I'd done, I was alarmed to see not only Sergeant Beasley waiting for me but also my divisional officer, Captain Sparrow. On arriving I was paraded in front of the Captain before being stood at ease.

"I'm afraid I'm the bearer of very grave news, Williams", he told me, "We have just received the latest regimental casualty figures and I regret to inform you that they include the name of your brother,

Sergeant Jack Williams, who has died of wounds sustained in action near the Ypres Salient earlier this month. While informing you of this very sad news I would like you to know that both Sergeant Beasley and myself have known and served with your brother for many years. He was a good, steady soldier, loyal to the regiment and the men of his company. He will be sorely missed by everyone who was privileged to know him. I'm so very, very sorry for both you and your family."

With that he turned and walked away, leaving me alone with my thoughts. The news hit me like a sledge hammer and for a moment I stood there in a daze, not knowing what to do or say. Our Jack dead! I just couldn't believe it. I recalled the last time he'd been on leave, remembering his cheery and devil-may-care manner. He'd been teasing the girls, hiding the presents he'd brought and roaring with laughter at their efforts to find them. As soon as he was through the door he'd swept Mother up in his arms and, despite her half hearted screams of protest, swung her round and round until both collapsed in a laughing heap on the kitchen floor. This was the man who had survived the African campaign without a scratch, riding with the mounted rifles against the elusive Boers. Both he and my brother Bill had fought through many a skirmish, including the relief of Ladysmith. They had brought trophies back from Africa which Mr Rutter the landlord of the Bear Hotel at Hodnet had given pride of place above the bar. Now the news of Jack's death seemed impossible to comprehend for he had always seemed so confident, and one of life's survivors. Now he was dead, cut down in the muddy fields of Picardy by an enemy he probably never even saw. It all seemed so unfair![3]

Sergeant Beasley, as practical but as caring as he always was with all his charges, had arranged a forty eight hour pass enabling me to go home. Although obviously upset himself at the death of a friend, in true military fashion he refused to show it. In time I would learn to adopt the same philosophy for both life and death. "Stiff upper lip old lad, old soldiers don't blub at the death of a mate. Drink to his memory when you get the chance but get on with the job at all costs!"

In a daze I returned to the tent line, fighting back the tears stinging my eyes. Quickly changing into my best uniform I set off for home, glad to be away from my mates who were curious to know what was going on. A carrier's cart gave me a lift as far as Wem and from there a Waggoner with an empty cart returning from the railway goods yards, took me on to Weston and the three short miles to home. Night was drawing in by the time I climbed the steep road through Kenstone. Curtains were already drawn in many of the houses as I passed. I knew that they would have been drawn all day out of respect for our bereavement. Several families in Hodnet and the surrounding areas had already lost loved ones in the war but Jack's was the first death from within our small community.

On reaching home there was no cheery welcome as I raised the latch and went inside. Even Bess the sheepdog seemed to sense that things were not as they should be, hardly finding time to greet me before returning to her place behind Father's chair. Most of the family who could get there were gathered around the fire in the darkened room. Mother hardly spoke but gathered me in her arms and hugged me to her breast, afraid perhaps that I could be the next to go and this her last chance to say goodbye. Father acknowledged my presence briefly before returning to his thoughts, staring gravely into the fire. My bothers Alec and Joe tried their best to assume the solemn faces of their elders but without the same conviction. You couldn't blame them. Jack had been many years older than them, and me too for that matter so that we had looked on him more as an uncle than a brother, a larger-than-life character who periodically joined our company for short periods of leave at which time he would briefly enter our lives like a brilliant, shooting star, only to be gone soon after as if he had never existed. Dressed in his scarlet uniform and golden stripes, his buttons and badges gleaming in the sun, he had brightened our humdrum days for brief moments before disappearing as suddenly as he had come.

I stayed for the next two days but there was nothing to be done and I longed to be back with my mates at camp. There was no funeral to be arranged, Jack had been buried at the clearing station where he had been taken before he died, neither was there a service to attend as his name would be added to the growing roll of honour and read out, with those of others from the parish that had died, at future Sunday services.

Mother took the loss badly, never ever being quite the same again, while Father retreated further into his shell, still unable to express himself in anything but silence. For the rest of us, the world went on as we returned to our various endeavours. Perhaps, as young men do, I made a secret pact to avenge my brother's death but if I did, I can't remember doing it. The news of Jack's death came as a reminder of what I had let myself in for and taught me the important and fundamental lesson that nobody is immortal so that after his passing I returned to the rigours of training an older and much wiser young man.

By November the winter rains had turned the camp into a sea of mud, a taste of things to come in France! Cases of rheumatic fever were reported and after the first fatality efforts were made to improve our living quarters when as many as possible were moved into a number of hastily constructed but as yet unfinished huts, where we stayed for a further two weeks. On Saturday 20th November the complete company was paraded in full kit and marched back to Shrewsbury! People must have known we were coming for at every village we passed, ladies were there with baskets of apples, cakes and buns which they pressed into our hands as we marched by. The local paper of the time reported, "The streets were densely thronged with civilians who lustily cheered the soldiers and sang patriotic songs as they passed!" but I think we should put that down to a bit of editorial licence for as I stumbled wearily along, I have no recollection of hearing any patriotic songs or seeing huge crowds that day!

It was dark when we reached Shrewsbury and once again I was billeted out, this time with a Mrs Knight and her daughter July at number 1, Moreton Terrace, Coleham where I would stay until Christmas. The routine was the same as before. After breakfast we had PT in the quarry followed by drill and manoeuvres at the race course for the rest of the day. My skill as a marksman was getting me noticed and I spent more and more time on the firing range. This was before the Machine Gun Corps had been formed as an independent unit when each regiment provided their own teams of six men to man the Vickers machine guns and it was at about this time that I was selected to train as a machine gunner, an opportunity that I grasped with both hands.

All the time I was at Shrewsbury, a steady trickle of volunteers were arriving but now the euphoria of the previous year was forgotten as the growing lists of casualties appeared in the local newspapers. In a concerted effort to replace the dead with new recruits, Lord Kitchener began putting demands on landlords to release their workers to the cause and even encouraged firms to provide volunteers by offering a bounty of five pounds for every worker they persuaded to sign on. Prisoners were even being released from prison on their promise that they would join and I remember a father and his three sons called Hughes who were all serving prison sentences with hard labour for poaching, who "volunteered" and did their training at the same time as me. I don't know if they all survived but I bet there came a time when they wished they'd stayed where they were in prison! To add to this motley bunch, three tramps came in from Llyanfylin having been recruited by the master of the workhouse there. Thus the standard of volunteers was deteriorating to the point where in February 1916, when all young men over the age of nineteen were advised to report to their nearest barracks, the British public would be introduced to an unfamiliar word never used before in their vocabulary. From now on only those with reserved occupations would be excused from signing on. The new word and the process it described would become known as 'conscription'![4]

With almost six months service, from our superior position as "old sweats", we observed these goings on with haughty disdain, advising any new recruits who crossed our path to "get some time in." As Ernie Pye declared, glaring at us through a hole made by his fingers representing a monocle, "If I'd have known the class of fellow I was expected to serve with, I'd have jolly well signed for the Guards!"

Perhaps we were too hard on them, having forgotten the debacle of our own arrival and the jeers and laughter of the then established Coleham trainees. To be fair, regardless of their background, they came just as we had, armed with the two most essential assets needed by somebody about to kill or be killed. In the coming months and years, although for many of us both would be lost forever, those assets would be the staff on which we all would learn to lean. The two assets which we clung to were innocence and hope.

In December my new platoon, all prospective machine gunners, was posted to Tenby near Pembroke Dock where I stayed for three months.

Each machine gun unit was manned by six men and the policy was to mould each team into an efficient fighting unit, entirely dependent on each other, and to that end we always trained and were billeted together. If for some reason a person didn't fit into a team he was replaced by another before being sent back to his regiment, so it was looked on as a distinction first to get through the initial selection process and then become a permanent member of one of the teams. Although only the 'number one' actually fired the gun, all the rest were expected to be crack shots. To operate the gun, each team was made up and operated in the following manner. For as long as he was able, number one was always in command. He set up, selected the target and fired the gun. In action he always carried the heavy tripod on which the gun was mounted so was usually the strongest. Number two carried the gun, taking up a position to the right of number one from where he would load and feed in the ammunition belt from a box carried by number three who would have taken up a position on the left of number one where he could clear the belt through the gun. Numbers four, five and six carried more boxes of ammunition, spare parts for the gun and a can of water for its cooling jacket. Each member was trained to man any position in the team but in action the number one would always take control regardless of his seniority.

We spent about three months at different machine gun schools sited in South Wales, learning to fire and service both the Lewis and Vickers machine guns. Soon we were joined by many other platoons from different regiments, all of us completing our training at Swansea. After a full passing out parade we were informed by the CO that all of us would be transferred to the newly formed Machine Gun Corps which had recently become an independent unit. With some regrets but a great deal of pride I exchanged the horned cap badge of the Shropshires for the coveted crossed guns of the Machine Gun Corps. At the same time I exchanged my old friend the Lee Enfield .303 rifle for a holstered .45 revolver. In April, a year almost to the day since the news of Jack's death, the whole company entrained for Harrowby Camp at Grantham in Yorkshire. This had been set up on the vast estate of Lord Brownlow and was to become the headquarters of the Machine Gun Corps. It was just like going home![5]

Chapter 3

First Days in France - May 1916

A Rendezvous with Death
I have a rendezvous with death,
On some disputed barricade.
When Spring comes back with rustling shade,
And apple blossoms fill the air,
I have a rendezvous with death,
When Spring brings back blue days and fair.
Seeger

During the several weeks that I was billeted at the Machine Gun school at Grantham, the days were filled with training both on the Vickers machine gun and with rifles. We also carried out complicated manoeuvres attacking invisible enemies concealed in the woods and fields around the camp. By now we were all very fit, accepting and meeting each challenge put before us head on. As members of a newly formed regiment with each of us handpicked for our individual skills, we truly considered ourselves to be superior to any other regiment, a belief fostered and encouraged by our officers and NCOs. In training exercises we always defeated the enemy, advancing in well ordered files, destroying with bullet and bayonet every "German" that crossed our path. We practised in the day and at night until we could carry out each manoeuvre, stripping down and reassembling our weapons, blindfold. As one of the lads remarked, "Those blooming Jerries had better look out when we get amongst them, they'll have their hands full dealing with us lot of handy buggers and no mistake!" Oh the confidence of youth! If we had only known then what real war was going to be like!

The word was out that the big push was not far away, adding an extra urgency to everything we did. During the last few days of training, a rapid fire rifle competition was held for individual shots which I was lucky enough to win. The £1 prize was a lot of money when compared with the one shilling per day we were paid as machine gunners. In order to win I managed to fire twelve rounds into a target 200 yards away in one minute. Our glum faced weapons instructors were quick to point out that before the war, by the end of a similar course recruits were expected to fire fifteen rounds per minute into a target at 300 yards, while marksmen often managed thirty! Slowly it began to dawn on us that maybe we weren't the top class soldiers we thought we were and that perhaps our training had been too little and by now was possibly too late.

One morning in mid-May I was told to report to the orderly room. Only the day before, I'd applied for a forty eight hours pass, so it came as a bit of a shock when the orderly sergeant took great delight in informing me that "the bad news is that your request for leave has been denied, while the good news is that you've been posted to France!" Having recovered my composure, on reading my orders I was relieved to see that I was to transfer to the 20th Division to which the 6th Battalion the Shropshire Light Infantry was also attached. This was just what I'd been waiting for and I ran through the billet, shouting the news to anyone who was prepared to listen. The 6th Shropshires, that would do very nicely thank you! My older brother Jack had been killed, fighting with the 5th Battalion near Ypres, so I saw this as a chance to get out there and settle a few old scores on his behalf. I also hoped to meet some of the mates I'd left behind in Shrewsbury as, owing to my transfer to the Machine Gun Corps and the extra training involved, it was possible that they had already been out here for some time.

Throughout the day more orders came in and my good news became tinged with regret when I learned that none of the friends I'd made during my stay at Grantham were posted to the same division as me. The night before I left, all of us went down to a pub in the town and drowned our sorrows in several pints of the local ale and as the evening wore on and we got more and more tipsy, swore undying friendship to each other, even making plans to meet after the war for a reunion and a few beers. How many servicemen in how many conflicts have made the same promises and how many times have they been kept? We never met again. Of the twelve of us who sat drinking in that smoky bar in Grantham, our faces red from too much beer and too much laughter, only myself and one other would survive the war. After a while I came to accept this as a part of military life, both in peace time and in war. Good friends made today could be gone tomorrow, often never seen or heard of again. I'll never forget those earnest young men with their smiling, honest faces, whose laughter and friendship I shared on that last night at Grantham. We planned together for the future with the confidence born of youth, for none of us ever doubted our own immortality.

Those of us drafted to France went by rail to Dover the next day, most of my friends coming to the station to see me on my way. Once more I was alone and feeling pretty sorry for myself. The train was crowded with soldiers and their equipment, crammed in ten to a carriage, so most of us had to stand. Next to me was a young squaddy about my age that I recognised from my stay at Grantham.

"You're Walter Williams aren't you?", he asked, "I watched you boxing in the Brigade championships. Thought you were robbed incidentally, never had a snowballs chance in hell of getting that decision, him being an officer and all. I reckon you'd have had to knock him out to get a draw! I'm Jim Rogers by the way, but most people call me Nobby."

I smiled to myself. I'd always been keen to put the gloves on and on that occasion had lost on points in the Brigade finals. "I reckon you could be right," I replied, "Hope you enjoyed the scrap anyway." I didn't crack on to Nobby but the chap I'd fought might have been an officer but he'd been a good sort, sharing his prize money with me. We talked together for the rest of the journey and by the time we reached our destination we were firm friends. Our backgrounds couldn't have been more different. He had never known his parents, having lived in an orphanage until he was thirteen when he was put out to fend for himself. Where my playground had been the fields and woods around Kenstone, his had been the slums and back streets of Manchester. He told me about days without food and nights spent huddled in doorways or by factory ventilation shafts, the hot polluted air offering some comfort from the winter's cold. Unable to find a steady job he had fallen in with the wrong crowd, resorting to petty crime to exist. Eventually he'd been caught by the police and taken before a magistrate who had given him two options. Either he went to prison with hard labour or he signed on for the militia!

"I said to myself, Nobby old lad, you've got yourself half way between the devil and the deep blue sea here and no easy way out. So you better weigh up the odds and pretty quick about it! At least if you sign on the dotted line you'll be getting three squares a day and a place to lay your head, whereas, if you go to the poky, you'll have to break rocks for your crust."

So that was it. He'd joined the Lancashire Fusiliers and, like me, had been transferred to the Machine Gun Corps then drafted to Grantham. Nobby was streetwise and sharp and I reckoned he'd be the right one to have on your side in a scrap. I told him about my parents and the names of my brothers and sisters and how close we were as a family. Finally I found myself inviting him to spend some time with us when he was next on leave. By the time we reached Dover it was as if we had known each other all our lives.

It was drizzling when we disembarked off the train and by the time we had collected our kit, formed up, and marched the short distance to the docks, we were soaking wet and thoroughly miserable. Blimey, I'd had this romantic image in my mind that our departure to France would somehow involve bands playing and beautiful women shedding buckets of tears as they saw us off. Instead, only a handful of curt officials, anxious to get back to the warmth of their offices and out of the rain, unceremoniously herded us on board the troopship like so many wet, bedraggled and very confused sheep. Worse still, once on board any thoughts of a cosy billet were soon forgotten when a number of us were posted on deck with loaded rifles, as lookouts for submarines. These, we were assured, we would identify by their periscopes!

"What's a bloody periscope look like?" somebody asked. "Do we shoot the bugger if we see one?"

"Just you keep your gobs shut and your eyes open", growled the sergeant, "You'll know one when you see one." It never occurred to us that he, like the rest of us, came from a land locked county and probably wouldn't have recognised a periscope if he'd tripped over one!

By the time we left the shelter of the harbour a heavy sea was running and we were sailing straight into the teeth of a gale. Huge brown swells ran down the length of the ship, the wind whipping the spume into our faces like icy needles. I stuck at my post, feeling more sea sick by the minute, earnestly scanning the mountainous waves for what I thought a periscope might look like. If there was one out there then I never saw it, neither did anybody else for that matter. If we had known anything at all about submarine warfare we would have realised that there was no chance that one would carry out an attack in weather like that. Any submarines in the Channel that day would have long since dived deep to avoid the storm and as we became progressively more sick searching for them, their crews would be sitting it out below us, oblivious of our discomfort in the angry seas above. Although those of us on deck felt hard done by, conditions were even worse for the troops battened down below decks. Not so long before, they had laughed at those of us detailed as lookouts, now they would have given anything to join us up in the fresh air. Soon people began to be sick where they lay, unable to escape from the prison where they found themselves battered and thrown about with every roll and pitch of the ship. The ones nearest to the great steel watertight doors beat on them with their fists, pleading to be released, but the ships company were stood to at action stations in these dangerous waters so their pleas went either unanswered or ignored. On deck things were not much better. I had long since lost interest in searching for the illusive periscope and even found myself wishing a submarine would appear and put us out of our misery. I also thanked God I hadn't joined the navy! At the start of the journey I was afraid I was going to die; by the end I was afraid I wasn't![1]

At last, to every ones relief the coast of France was sighted and we entered the peaceful waters of the harbour at Calais. Disembarking in a heavy thunder storm, we marched the mile or so to the local railway station, the relentless rain running in rivulets from the rubber groundsheets draped round our heads and shoulders. When the train eventually arrived we were packed, cold, wet and hungry, into what appeared to have once been a number of luggage vans and cattle trucks and after what seemed like hours while we waited shivering in our wet clothes, the train finally moved off. After about an hour the word was passed from carriage to carriage telling us that due to an error in the organisation, no messing facilities and therefore no hot food would be available until the morning so we should open our iron rations of hard biscuits and bully beef and make do with that. Although desperately trying but failing even to chew let alone digest either commodity, by now absolutely starving, wet, cold, and thoroughly fed up, huddling together for what warmth we could find, we bedded down as best we could in the cold and draughty carriages. As some disgruntled soul acidly remarked "What a bloody way to run an army!" I had to agree that, all things being considered, it was not a very auspicious start to my first day on foreign soil!

The train moved slowly through the night, stopping every now and then to pick up more troops before starting again with much shunting and banging of couplings making any thought of sleep impossible. We travelled for what seemed like hours, never going faster than walking pace throughout the journey. At day break the train stopped and we were allowed off to stretch our legs and relieve ourselves, taking the chance to eat some porridge and lukewarm stew cooked on field kitchens hastily set up alongside the track. We filled our pockets with half ripe apples and pears from nearby orchards, angering the owners in the process. In the fields and farms the workers went about their tasks, apparently oblivious of the war that was going on around them. Some tossed apples to us through the windows and open grills of the carriages but for the most part they chose to ignore our shouts of greeting as if resentful of our intrusion into their country. Many of the girls stopped what they were doing and leant on their implements, some even adopting suggestive poses, watching the train go by. This raised a chorus of wolf whistles and bawdy remarks from its passengers and angry stares and gestures from the farmers.

"Ungrateful bastards!" we yelled, "You should be fighting your own bloody war, not expecting us to do it for you!"

The reason for our low opinion of them was because it had been said that some French farmers were actually demanding compensation for damage done to their crops during military exercises in preparation for the expected big push. Of course, at that time we hadn't heard of the thousands of casualties the French were suffering at Verdun or perhaps we'd have been less critical of them. Even so, throughout the war whenever we came in contact with French troops, there always seemed to be an element of mistrust between the two sides, a situation rather controversially summed up after the war by an old soldier friend of mine when he remarked, "Walter old lad, in my opinion we killed the wrong pig", going on to suggest that instead of going to the aid of the French, Britain should have joined forces with the Germans, first defeating Russia and then France in that order!

At last the train stopped at a small station on the outskirts of the city of Amiens and to everyone's relief we were ordered to collect our kit and weapons and disembark. Painfully climbing down from the cramped and by now extremely smelly confines of the carriage, the scene that greeted us was incredible. Everywhere we looked there was a bustle of activity. In nearby fields row upon row of tents had been pitched, every fourth row served by a makeshift field kitchen where cooks could be seen preparing meals for the thousands of troops billeted there and medical tents, marked with big red crosses, had been erected at a discrete distance from the lines. Cavalry and pack horses in their hundreds, chafed on their bits where they were tied on pickets or penned in makeshift corrals while guns and mortars of all shapes and sizes were parked in the fields all around. The station where we stopped and the buildings that surrounded it had been taken over by the military and every house, cellar, barn and even the church had been used to billet soldiers or pressed into use as orderly rooms and offices. Everywhere the air buzzed with excitement and expectation.

"It looks like the rumours were right," said Nobby, "They don't mass troops like this for a blooming picnic; this has got to be the big break out everyone's been talking about."

For several months now, in the fertile water meadows that lay between the river Somme and the smaller river Ancre, British and German troops, dug in in a maze of trench systems, had faced each other across a morass of broken ground known to both sides as No

Man's Land. Apart from brief excursions into each other's territory, usually resolutely rebuffed by the defenders, a stalemate had existed throughout the previous winter and early spring. Now, if the rumours were right, it looked as if the time had come to mount an attack on the enemy in huge numbers, driving them from their trenches to eventual defeat. This was the big push that Nobby was referring to. He had to be right. Even the old sweats amongst us, veterans of the earlier bloody battles at Mons and Ypres, admitted they'd never seen such concentrations of troops before.

Each platoon was allocated a tent with each one expected to sleep ten men although they were only designed to sleep six. The canvas was old and in many cases leaked whenever it rained, which was quite often, so there never seemed to be a time when our kit, our bedding or both were not wet through.

For the next few weeks we were employed as labourers hauling guns and equipment from the many trains which arrived at the station. Occasionally we took part in exercises in the surrounding fields with white tape marking the outlines of the German trenches, copied from aerial photographs, but for the most part it was the daily drudgery of stacking shells or cleaning equipment which occupied our days.

It was almost a relief then that in the first week in June, my section was ordered up nearer the front. This time we travelled by road on the much shorter journey to the town of Albert. The French pronunciation of this was Al'bair but we would always know it as Albert, just like the cartoon character we had sung about when we were kids.

The town was in ruins, shot to pieces by the German batteries which occupied the high ground overlooking it. The whole area seethed with activity, all visible to the enemy observation posts who directed their artillery with such devastating effect. New railways had been built, old bridges strengthened or rebuilt, while vast dumps of ammunition and stores concealed in surrounding woods was in constant danger of being found by the enemy guns. As we fell in and marched from the station, shells were falling on the town. The whoosh and thump as they passed overhead to strike some unseen target was the nearest we had been to active service and for the first time I experienced the urge to dive for cover every time one approached. Our route out of the town took us past the ruined tower of the Church of Notre Dame de Brebiere with the gilded statue of the Virgin and child hanging at a crazy angle from its tower. The body of the church had been decimated by gunfire, now only its tower survived and by some miracle, the gilded statue of the Virgin at its summit had been hit and displaced but had not fallen. Now she hung at a crazy angle over the town, her golden arms reaching out in supplication to all who passed below. A legend had been born on both sides that when she fell the war would end, which even before we had seen any action, couldn't come too soon as far as most of us were concerned. In reality and much less romantically, she only stayed aloft because French engineers had secured her up there with wires, perhaps a silly thing to do under the circumstances! Known to tommies as the Leaning Virgin, she became a major land mark in the town as well as a firing point for the German artillery! We were a superstitious lot and I for one gave up a silent prayer begging her to fall. Some of my mates were less discreet. "Why don't you fall and let us get out of this stinking mess you golden bitch?" shouted an old sweat obviously not of the Catholic faith. If she heard him she took no heed, hanging in that precarious position until 1918 when both the church and Virgin were blown to smithereens by British artillery after the Germans had retaken the town. As the legend predicted, the war ended soon after ![(2)]

Leaving the ruined town behind we marched out into the unspoilt countryside, only occasionally scarred by old rain-filled shell craters.

This time we were billeted in the grounds of an old farmhouse and for the first time since arriving in France were able to enjoy a few home comforts. Once again the town and surrounding fields were teeming with troops and for the first time we mixed with men who had seen action in the trenches and were enjoying a few days relief behind the lines. Their harrowing stories of life under fire filled us with fear and, like a condemned man, I found myself longing for the day to come when I could get my first experience over with.

On the 8th of June all work stopped and we were ordered to

parade in a large field on the outskirts of the town. A grim faced commander read out the news of the death of Lord Kitchener three days before, drowned off the Orkneys when H.M.S. Hampshire was sunk under mysterious circumstances. He implored us "not to be dismayed" by this news but to fight on as the great man would have wished. Dismayed! It took a conscious effort by some of the veterans of Ypres who had fought with and witnessed the death of an army caused to a great extent by Kitchener's mismanagement, to stop from whooping with glee. Never before could such tragic news have been greeted with such a show of hilarity.

"Drowning was too good for the murdering bastard," growled a veteran of that debacle, a thought echoed by us untried soldiers who had only heard stories of the carnage in the killing fields of Picardy.

At last the day came when we were to go up to the front for the first time and looking round I could see the nervous tension showing in everybody's face. None of us had slept much the night before, choosing to sit up in our tents, talking in hushed whispers, and gaining comfort from each other's company. We had all heard the harrowing tales told by the old sweats and now it was our turn to experience it ourselves. With dawn already breaking we finally fell into exhausted sleep, the silence of the night often interrupted by the nightmare cries of our dreams so it came as a relief when reveille roused us from our individual torment. In the mess tent the thick porridge served as breakfast stuck in dry throats.

"Get it down you lads" joshed the sergeant cook, "might be your last meal this side of the Pearly gates."

We laughed nervously trying to put on brave faces but for my part it took a conscious effort not to throw the whole lot up again!

"Who called the cook a bastard?" someone shouted from the back of the mess hall.

"Who called the bastard a cook?" we all roared back, glad of the excuse to break the tension and hide our apprehension. Was everybody as scared as I was, if they were they didn't show it? I wondered if my brave smile and nonchalant manner hid the fear that gripped my stomach like a steel band, hoping it wouldn't let me down when it mattered most, when we came under fire. Thinking back I was probably more afraid of being a coward and letting everybody down than I was of dying!

After mess call we fell in, dressed in full battle dress, carrying arms, and were issued mess rations and ammunition to last a week. Next we were given a form to fill in detailing our next of kin and an address where any personal mail could be directed. Green as ever, as I wasn't expecting any mail that needed redirecting, I expressed my surprise at this!

"Bloody telegram address," somebody muttered, "I wonder how many of our folks will be getting one of them before the weeks out?"

So that was it! I thought of Mum and Dad and my brothers and sisters. I imagined them sitting round the table eating breakfast, seeing a shadow pass the window, becoming aware of the telegram boy then hearing his knock on the door. My parents would exchange glances, the colour drained from their faces. They would go together to answer the door, just as I'm sure they had when the telegram arrived about my brother Jack. On the door step the sad faced messenger would hand over the brown envelope containing the news. With two boys fighting in France, which one would it be?

"We regret to inform you of the death of Private Walter Williams..." Mother would read out loud, her voice breaking with emotion.

The sergeant's command to come to attention woke me from my reverie. "What the hell am I doing here?" I asked myself, cursing my stupidity for signing on for the umpteenth time since I landed in France.

A mounted officer rode into the yard, the sun gleaming from his polished buttons and Sam brown belt.

"You fellows are going up to the front today, many of you for the first time, and I expect you all to do your duty for both your King and your country", he said grandly.

"Thinks he's bloody Horatio Nelson", came a voice from the ranks, raising a titter of nervous laughter.

"Although I'm sure it will not happen, I don't have to tell you that any form of subordination or show of funk while you are up there will be severely dealt with", he continued, ignoring the remark, "Now good luck and good hunting."

Returning the salute thrown up by the sergeant, he clattered away across the cobbles, no doubt to return to the leisurely breakfast he had so generously interrupted to send us on our way!

Now it was the padres turn to say a few words, his polished carpet slippers appearing incongruously from beneath his starched white surplice.

"Are you coming with us your Holiness?" somebody inquired, tongue in cheek, knowing full well what the answer would be.

"I'm afraid that's not possible my son, but be sure that I'll be with you in spirit during your hardships and here to give you comfort when you return."

"Never mind the comfort and hardships, give us a ticket to Blighty on a blooming troopship", quipped the same voice.

My mate Nobby Rogers nudged me in the back. "Did you know Walter that it's not considered good policy to send the God botherers up to the front because they reckon if one of 'em stopped one it would be bad for our moral? If a bloke in daily touch with the Almighty ain't safe, what chance has the rest of us bloody sinners got? I don't expect it affects old Daddy Haig's moral very much when one of us bloody cannon fodder buys one"

The sergeant called us to attention, turned us right and marched us in single file past the padre who blessed us as we passed, taking the opportunity to collect the forms bearing our "telegram" addresses as we went.

As we marched out from that quiet French courtyard you wouldn't have thought that less than five miles away men would soon be dying in their thousands. Everything around us seemed to be at peace. Apples ripened in the orchards, hay turned yellow in the warm summer sun and overhead, larks filled the sky with their singing. We were young men and as we marched we forgot for a moment the fear that knotted and rumbled in our stomachs. Our hearts and heads were filled with thoughts of adventure and heroic deeds and each one of us felt ourselves invincible. We were not to know that our lives would never be the same again. If that same padre had offered to save our souls six months later, we could have been excused from asking, "Which God would want to save our souls after the horrors we have seen and taken part in?" Had it happened, I don't think he would have had an answer!

In a short time we had left the village and were out in the countryside where to our amazement we saw farmers working in the fields just as if the war didn't exist. Some of us even managed to produce enough spit from dry lips and throats to whistle a ragged chorus of Colonel Bogey as we marched along.

After about three miles we were directed off the road by a military policeman, onto a lane sunken between high hedges. There were still no signs of action. Now we entered a wood and here the rutted track was cut up by the hooves of many horses and the tracks of heavy machinery. I couldn't know at the time that this insignificant two or three acres of scrub and trees, now in full leaf and echoing to the sound of bird song, would, in the next few years, gain a name synonymous with evil. Although the maps of that time mark it as Authuille Wood, military historians would name it from a fortified village close by and behind the German lines. The village was called Thiepval. It seemed right then to call this nondescript stand of timber, Thiepval Wood!

As we advanced further we saw trees blown apart by shellfire and we came across our first casualties. To the side of the track a gun carriage lay at a crazy angle its wheels smashed beyond recognition. Still in the harness where they had died lay the team of horses that had pulled it, their extended, bloated bodies putrefying in the summer sun. The sergeant poked one of them with his boot. At his touch the body burst open releasing a flood of putrid black liquid. The stench was appalling.

"Jesus Christ!".

Somewhere in the ranks a soldier retched. Another staggered out of line to be sick at the edge of the track, the grey of his recently eaten porridge staining the front of his uniform and surrounding undergrowth.

"Got dicky digestions have we lads, must be somethin' you ate?" smirked the sergeant, "After a couple of weeks at the front, that's if you ain't goners, you'll be cutting steaks off the likes of these beauties and thinking it a luxury!"

We marched on through the wood, pale faced and sweating, giving the fallen horses as wide a berth as possible on the narrow track. Many of us were country lads, used to working with horses as part of our jobs. In a long lonely day at the plough or on the road, a horse would often be our only companion, a trusting friend who would give his best without complaint, only asking for a warm stall and feed at the end of a long days work. How could we be treating these gentle creatures this way? What terrors must these poor horses and many more like them have experienced before they died in such hideous circumstances for a quarrel not of their making or understanding? I thought of Father and his great love for animals and was glad he would not see what I had just seen for I'm sure it would have broken his heart.[3]

As we progressed the trees showed further signs of action. Great swathes of undergrowth had been on fire and the ground was black with ashes where we walked. Few of the trees were intact and those which had escaped the fire had broken branches or were split apart as if hit by some giant axe.

Only our occasional nervous whispers and the crunch of our feet in the charred branches broke the silence.

Crack!

A rifle went off some distance away to our right in the ruined trees. Instinctively, we all dived for cover, grovelling in the charred earth for any protection we could find. Only the sergeant remained standing, nonchalantly rolling a cigarette.

"Sniper", he remarked, barely hiding his scorn at our blackened, frightened faces. "One of ours, probably been waiting all day for that one shot. Let's hope he got the bugger".

"Christ, Walter", whispered Nobby, his voice shaking with fear, "I thought we were under fire, I almost messed myself". He wasn't alone! As he spoke a dozen hands furtively felt the back of their trousers for tell tale signs of moisture! We clambered self consciously to our feet, our faces and uniforms black from the ash we had grovelled in. As we recovered the weapons and baggage discarded in our panic, the tat-tat-tat of a machine gun opened up a long distance away.

"That's Jerry returning his fire, firing blind hoping to hit him on the move. Don't you fret, he's too smart for that. He'll be face down in his scrape, probably fast asleep by now, waiting for dark before taking up a new position. Soulless bastards them snipers, got to be to pick their target like that then shoot him in cold blood. Not a job for anyone who thinks too much. I was thinking. I was remembering the dark nights I had spent with my friend Eli on our nocturnal poaching sessions when we would sometimes lie in hiding for hours, waiting for the pheasants to roost in the high branches before taking them without a sound. In an instant I realised that this was poaching on a much grander scale. This time the quarry was human!

As we came to the edge of the wood, I saw the battle ground for the first time, laid out before me. Everywhere I looked I saw devastation. What had once been fertile fields and orchards was now a churned up mass of broken ground and wire, intersected with the snowy white spoil of countless trenches. As far as the eye could see, the chalky soil looked like drifts of snow where it had been blown apart by shell fire or by digging. As we watched, the guns on both sides opened up and once again we ducked for cover at the sound of shells passing overhead in both directions. About a mile away across the ruined countryside we watched as our shells began to fall behind the enemies lines on what had once been a village. Now the houses were gone and the orchards levelled by shellfire. Over the fields buzzed a tiny silver aircraft sweeping in narrow circles as it observed and laid the fall of shot for the gunners. I could see a wood to the left and a small copse to the right, partly visible over the shoulders of some low hills shrouded in smoke. From one of these a column of black smoke went curling up, spreading like a huge umbrella in the sky, at its base an impromptu firework display of exploding ammunition. Even at this great distance, the earth shook and trembled with the explosions and the scorched trees, behind which we sheltered, trembled with the detonations.

One of our aircraft was in the air now attacking the plane we had first seen. We watched them weave and dive like two silver, angry gnats, too far away by now to hear their engines. The silent fight continued for some minutes until one of the planes peeled off, smoke and flames marking its fatal passage to the ground. We were too far away to know which side had been the victor.

Chapter 4

Early Experiences of Trench Warfare - June 1916

Salvoes

At the noon of the dreadful day
Our trench and deaths is of a sudden storm.
With huge and shattering salvoes, the clay dances
In founts of clods around the concrete sties.
Where still the brain devises some last armour
To live out the poor limbs.

Blunden

The sergeant led us to where the entrance to the trench system began in ground out of sight of the enemy. Here he fell us out and formed us into platoons, giving orders to each platoon commander as he did so. As we moved through the trenches, platoons were dropped off until only mine was left.

"This is as far as I'm going, take your platoon through to the firing lines and report for duty to the senior NCO when you get there", he said.

I suddenly realised he was talking to me! The day before, our corporal had been kicked by one of the cavalry horses which he had tried to befriend and had been evacuated back to Amiens with a broken leg, ironically, his being the first "war wound" to be sustained by our section! Because I was number one on the gun, in his absence I had become the senior trooper present and therefore, with nobody being more senior, platoon commander.

As directed by the sergeant, I led the platoon cautiously along a series of communication trenches and after passing both the reserve and support lines, eventually came to the forward firing positions where we would be stationed for the next few days. Even here, the last bastion between us and the enemy, it was obvious from all the frantic activity that something big was coming off. Most of the experienced front line infantry had been withdrawn; we had met the last of them going in the opposite direction as we entered the trenches. They had filed past us in silence, hardly seeming to notice us as we pressed against the sides of the dripping trench to give them right of way, their shuffling half stooped posture testified to the length of time they had spent at the front and their gaunt, dirty faces mirrored the fatigue they were suffering. Many months later I would learn that these were men of the Ulster Division whose courage and determination would lead to their name becoming synonymous with the terrible carnage and huge loss of life associated with the battle to take and hold Thiepval Wood.[1]

Not being very tall, I felt confident enough to walk upright in the deeper trenches, taller men facing the constant hazard of snipers should even part of their heads appear above the parapet. To counter this most people adopted a forward stoop, their hands and arms hanging apelike in front of them as they moved up and down the lines, a posture which anyone who had spent time there would immediately recognise as 'the front line shuffle'.

Looking around me I was surprised to see the basic construction and poor condition of the trench in which I found myself. During exercises outside Albert we had been shown a replica of a typical German trench modelled on a real one captured intact by the French. It had deep dugouts many feet below the ground, entered by concrete steps and protected by blast proof doors. There were bunks and cooking facilities for the men and a forced air ventilation system, the whole structure being designed to give lasting protection from artillery fire while offering some comfort to its occupants. In comparison our trench was little more than a crude, open ditch, its sides bolstered here and there by sticks woven into rafts held up by rough stakes and rotting sandbags. Along its length, small hollows had been gouged out of the chalky clay which stained the sides white and made the thin layer of mud covering the trench bottom the colour and texture of porridge. Most were open to the elements, only the larger ones boasting ragged pieces of canvas or sacking held up by spent cartridge cases pushed into the clay covering their entrances. These were the dugouts in which off duty soldiers would try to snatch a few hours sleep, an almost impossible task because their feet, sticking out onto the duckboards, were in constant danger of being trodden on by working parties or others moving up and down the lines.[2]

Soon our faces, hands and uniform were stained white with the chalk, making each of us look like ghosts as we huddled below the forward parapet, waiting for our instructions. Leaving them there I moved gingerly along the trench, looking for somebody in authority to report to. I found it strange that out here in the firing line with nothing but the broken ground of no man's land between us and the enemy, that everything was so amazingly quiet. Only the occasional weary lookout, fighting sleep, manned the firing step, while from the dugouts, the smell of freshly fried bacon and the snores of their sleeping occupants filled the air, painting a far different picture to the one I had expected.

As I stood wondering what to do, the canvas from one of the dugouts was suddenly pulled aside and a sergeant scrambled out into the trench, almost knocking me over as he did so. His face was covered in shaving soap while in one hand he held a piece of broken mirror and with the other brandished an open razor.

"Machine gun platoon awaiting orders" I blurted, standing stiffly to attention, "Who should we report to sergeant?".

By the look on his face I'm not sure which of us was the most surprised but after a moment he regained his composure enough to take stock of the situation.

"You're not a very big chap private", he barked, "But you'll be reporting to Saint Peter himself if you don't get your bloody head down. Jerry's got snipers trained on these forward trenches twenty-four hours a day and one of them will give you a better parting in your hair than your dear old mother ever dreamed of !"

Suddenly his face cracked into a friendly smile, not the sort of thing we'd been used to seeing while in training!

"I guess that this is your first time in the line young 'un, there's a first time for everyone, and I know exactly how you're feeling. We don't stand on ceremony here lad, stand at ease and I'll put you all in the picture.

I'm Sergeant Jenkins and you'll take your orders from me while you're in this section of the trench. You'll meet the CO, Lieutenant

Ridgeway later. He's only a lad himself, still wet behind the ears, but I daresay we'll make soldiers out of the lot of you if Jerry doesn't get you first"

He explained that the front line regiments had been withdrawn for relief, leaving only a skeleton core of newly arrived troops to act as forward observers and gas guards. Our job would be to provide cover for the several mine platoons and other Field Company personnel who were bringing ammunition and stores into the firing lines or digging mines and saps that would eventually reach out far below the enemy trenches. Leaving the cover of the wood I had seen the great mounds of white clay lying like snowdrifts in the summer sun and now I realised where all the earth had come from.[3]

Our job would be to man the Vickers and Lewis machine guns already in place, and reporting any movement we saw through crude periscopes set at intervals along the trench. We were each provided with a whistle and several rocket flares to alert the fresh troops held behind us in reserve, should the enemy show any signs of attacking.

When my turn came, I took my place on the firing step, the man I was relieving only stopping long enough to report that all was quiet before scuttling back to the support trenches and the comparative safety of a dugout and some well earned rest. Putting my eye to the periscope I was able to see the enemy lines for the first time and what I saw sent a shiver of both fear and excitement rushing through my body. They were so close! Across a space of broken earth, pock marked with the craters of many shells, I could clearly make out the line of the German trenches, only two or three hundred yards away. From my position the ground rose gently upwards and I was alarmed to realise that so far as I could see, the enemy held the high ground along the complete front. From this vantage point it must have been possible for them to look down into our lines, observing our every move! In between, suspended on rusty steel pickets there was coil upon coil of rusting wire both ours and theirs, sometimes thirty or forty yards deep,. Surprisingly, the mounds of earth which marked the enemy lines were over grown with a mass of green weed covered with bright yellow flowers and in the broken ground beyond, clouds of crimson poppies were in bloom. Everything was quiet. All along the enemy lines small columns of smoke rose lazily on the still air for it was mid-morning, when both sides observed an unofficial truce, making it possible to eat some breakfast, cooked over little fires lit in the bottom of the trench. It was also a chance to carry out rudimentary ablutions, although water was always scarce and what little was available had to be hauled up by working parties from behind the lines, a backbreaking task carried out under cover of darkness. At best there would be enough to have a wash and shave (although I wasn't shaving yet) before cleaning your teeth, carried out in that order and using the same ration of water! The routine was always the same. Nights were the busiest time when officers would take the opportunity to send raiding parties out into No Man's Land to reconnoitre the enemy positions, to repair or lay our own wire or try to cut theirs. This was dangerous work. The Germans were doing the same and it was not uncommon for raiders to stumble across each other in the darkness and for a hand to hand fight to the death to break out, the desperate struggle lit by the eerie silver light of star shells. Weapons were trench clubs or bayonets with no quarter expected or given.

If not on a working or raiding party or detailed as a lookout, we tried to snatch a few minutes sleep, huddled under canvas sheets on the slimy duckboards lining the floor of the trench or crouching in the body sized dugouts scraped from its sides by previous occupants. Only the senior NCOs and officers enjoyed the comparative comfort of the few room sized dugouts and even these were only holes in the ground, shored up with pit props, a rough piece of timber or corrugated iron covering the entrance.

We were shaken awake several times throughout the night to take our turn as lookout on the firing step so after only a few days and nights in the line it became progressively harder to stay awake. To be caught asleep on duty was a serious offence which could result in courts martial and in some cases death by firing squad or at the very least, number one field punishment. It was always a relief at first light when the bugle sounded stand-to and we were able to ease cramped and aching limbs as we manned the firing steps ready to repel any dawn raid the enemy might attempt. We could hear them doing exactly the same on the other side of No Man's Land, adding a touch of farce to the whole procedure. As a rule neither side left their trenches, each firing a few speculative rounds with rifle and machine gun, a procedure we called "Sending the Jerries a bit of hate mail", before settling down to the rest of the morning and a chance to grab some sleep now that the sun had taken the chill from the cold, wet trenches.

Another blessing was that the huge number of rats which infested the battle area seemed to decrease with day break, perhaps, like ourselves, taking the opportunity to grab a few moments sleep! It was a relief not to have them scurrying over us as we tried to sleep, or steal the food from our dixies as we ate our meals. The biggest, fattest rats I'd ever seen and almost entirely carnivorous, these were the grim undertakers of the uncollected dead. Grown fat on the carrion meat of No Man's Land, neither the greatest barrage nor strongest gas attack seemed ever to reduce their numbers. They were everywhere. I was once alarmed to see what I thought was a rotting skull, sticking from the base of a crater, winking at me! On closer inspection I found that what I'd seen was the face of a rat peering out at me through the gaping eye socket of the skull in which he'd made his home.

Strangely enough, in the early years of the war neither food nor ammunition ever seemed to be scarce so that some of the old sweats were able to amuse themselves by baiting their bayonet with cheese and pointing their rifle over the parapet. Soon a number of rats would be nibbling at the bait, only to be blown to kingdom come when their tormentor pulled the trigger!

Each trench was constructed in a zigzag pattern, running from right to left. This was to reduce the damage from shell bursts or shots fired down its length. The spaces in between were called bays and each of these was manned by a platoon of men. After a couple of nights, as soon as I was relieved from my stint of lookout duties I made my way along the trench to look for Nobby and the rest of my friends who were not in my platoon. I found them squatting around an upturned ammunition box, playing cards.

"Cut me in lads I shouted, I'm here to take your money off you".

"You might as well have it Walter" retorted Taffy Edwardss, as pessimistic as ever, "There ain't no pockets in shrouds and as far as I can see we'll be lucky to get out of this place in one piece."

"Don't take any notice of Taffy, he had a bit of a scare in No Man's Land last night, and he's really got the wind up", laughed Nobby. He explained that the two of them had been detailed off as part of a raiding party to report on the strength of the enemy's wire.

"We'd got almost half way over when a star shell lit the whole blooming scene up, bright as day, and Jerry opened up with a machine gun", he said, "Lucky for us he was firing in enfilade so most of us had time to dive for cover in a shell hole. The only one hit was poor old Corporal Johnstone who stopped a burst right in the chest. Killed him stone dead it did. His body fell straight on top of Taffy who was face down in the mud calling for his mother. He thought it was Fritz jumping in on top of him and we could hear him pleading for mercy from three shell holes away. We managed to get up to their wire eventually and report back with no further casualties but it's really knocked the stuffing out of all of us. They're asking for volunteers to go back tonight to try to recover the Corps body."

I had known Corporal Johnstone, a married man with three small children, since we were in training together and the news of his death, killed in his first week at the front, brought home the awful reality of the situation I'd got myself into. I decided then and there that if I could I would be the first to volunteer to bring his body back that night.

Later that day a Royal Artillery officer took up a position on the firing step and soon after the artillery positioned behind our lines began to shell the enemy positions.

As a forward observer his job was to lay, or direct, the fall of shot so that the guns had the exact range of the enemy lines. By using a field telephone, he was able to tell the gunners where their shells were landing, enabling them to make the necessary adjustments to the elevation of their sights. Within a short time the Germans began to retaliate, firing round after round of explosive shells at our positions. I dived for cover with the rest and we cowered together in the bottom of the trench, praying that one of the shells would not find us. I had heard veterans of the battles around Ypres describing what it was like to be under an artillery bombardment but nothing I had heard could have prepared me for what I was experiencing now. The whole world seemed to be exploding all around me as shells burst in geysers of black smoke and upflung debris. I covered my ears with my hands in a vain attempt to cut out the deafening roar of the detonations while at my feet the duckboards leapt and danced in a frenzy at every explosion and the air was full of flying shrapnel, bursting in handfuls of spiralling smoke from which darted the spinning trails of deadly metal like a multitude of uncoiling heads. The eerie, whistling sound as it flew overhead belied the awful injuries suffered by anybody unlucky enough to be in its path. Soon the trench filled with dense black smoke and the acrid smell of cordite made breathing difficult. In the bottom of the trench, I pressed my face into the grey mud and found myself pleading with God to make it stop. Every shell as it roared overhead, sounded like an express train approaching so that I was convinced that each one would be my last. The mud which I clawed at for protection, smelled of urine and vomit, and the smoking earth, raining down on us from the bursting shells, blinding our eyes and filling our mouths, tasted and smelled of gunpowder, cordite and worst of all, rotting flesh. Most of all, it smelled of fear. Soon I felt a warm trickle of blood running down my face and was alarmed to think I had been hit but it was only my nose bleeding from the force of the detonations. Farther up the trench they had taken a direct hit and I could hear the screams of the wounded above the noise of the shells.

"Medics, medics, for God's sake bring stretchers", the cry went up, and I was aware of running feet on the duckboards beside me.

Many of the medics were men whose religious beliefs did not allow them to carry arms, who, in training had been the butt of our barrack room jokes. Now, when the chips were down, they were going about their job in a calm orderly fashion while I and many other erstwhile heroes, cowered in the bottom of the trench like frightened children, too petrified to move. All at once I felt a sense of shame and guilt at the lack of respect I had previously shown them.

A grizzled old private from one of the mining sections was

sheltering beside me and seeing my distress, put a protective arm around my shoulder.

"Just keep your head down, young 'un and think of better times. There's nothing you can do but pray that one of them big beggars hasn't got your name on it and if it has you'll probably never know it."

As if to take my mind off the hurricane of fire bursting around us he began to explain, shouting to make himself heard above the din, how to distinguish between the different types of shell the German artillery were firing. The ones coming in now made a loud shriek and an equally loud explosion when they hit.

"Hear that one?", said the miner, "That's an eighteen pounder, one of their bigger ones, probably fired by artillery sited in one of them ruined villages behind their lines. We call them Coal Boxes because they go off with a hell of an explosion and clouds of black smoke. The smaller and more dangerous ones we call whiz-bangs because they have a flat trajectory and you don't hear the beggars coming 'till they're on you. Old Fritz has got his dander up because that silly beggar was ranging our guns on him. Between the two of them they'll get somebody killed if they're not careful!"

Even though I was shaking with fear I had to laugh at his dry sense of humour and I made a point of thanking him when at last the barrage lifted and we scrambled to our feet to survey the damage.

"Don't worry about it son, you'll never get used to it but in time you'll learn to cope," he said, "I've got a lad your age back in Blighty but if he was here I'm sure your Dad would do the same for him if he found himself in this hell hole. Remember, I was just as scared as you, I've just learned not to show it."

I would always be grateful for the comfort and understanding of a man, who, before the bombardment had been just another tired and dirty face in the crowd. When I needed a steadying hand, he was there to help me through despite his own fear. These were the type of men that life in the trenches bred. The constant danger and deprivation fused them together into a bond of friendship, only understood by those who shared the terror, hardships and occasional moments of light relief on those fearful early days on the Western Front.

Passing down the trench we found that one of the bays had

received two direct hits and the scene that greeted us was of total destruction. First a high powered shell had hit the parapet and exploded amongst the men taking cover below. Almost immediately, a shrapnel shell had exploded directly above the already stricken trench, sending its deadly cargo of jagged metal crashing into the tangled mass of dead and wounded men lying where the first explosion had thrown them. Nobody had escaped unscathed. Men from the adjoining bays rushed to help the medics already at work doing what they could to save those not mortally wounded. I never had time to think, joining the others frantically trying to untangle the bodies, some living, others obviously dead, from the gruesome pile where they had been blown by the force of the explosions. The screams and groans of the wounded and the blood that quickly soaked my uniform was something I had not prepared myself for but somehow I kept going and did the best I could to offer some comfort and consolation to those who, even to my untrained eye, were obviously not going to make it. At least by doing so it enabled the medics to treat the less critically injured.

Finally, when the wounds of the injured had been dressed and they had been carried by stretcher bearers and volunteers back through the lines and on their way to a casualty clearing station, it was time to bury the dead. Most of the bodies were blown apart so badly it was impossible to identify them, others, probably killed by blast, bore no marks or wounds at all and seemed only to be sleeping. Of the nine who had been killed, I recognised one as a man who had marched so confidently with me only a few days before. He was the one who had joked about the telegrams. Now, in a day or two, those he loved would receive the dreaded envelope and even before opening it would anticipate its awful contents. While not understanding why, I found myself wishing I had got to know him better. Perhaps I would have learned something of his hopes, his life, his family and friends. Given the chance I could have visited his home next time I was on leave to tell them how he died. I would not say that he had met his end cowering in the bottom of a muddy trench but that he died bravely, facing the enemy. That death was quick and that he never felt a thing. By doing so it would give them some consolation and pride in their grief and perhaps help them, more easily, to come to terms with his death.

"Our Freddie was a hero", they would tell their friends, "One of his soldier friends told us so. There with him when he died. Brave as a lion he was. We always knew when it mattered, young Freddie wouldn't let us down."

What was there to be gained by them knowing he died, grovelling like the rest of us under a hurricane of fire he could do nothing about. Why describe the terror he was experiencing, or that he was probably screaming to God for it to stop when his life was snuffed out like a candle. Much better and kinder for them not to know the real truth. I was lucky; he wasn't. Maybe next time it would be me. The telegram would read, "Killed in action", let them draw their own conclusions. It was best to leave it at that!

Disposing of the dead was a problem. Only minutes before they had been alive and a vital part of the army machinery, now that they were dead they became a nuisance!

Leading off the main trench were several blind trenches and saps, some abandoned others not yet finished. These had been used recently to store ammunition and site the latrines, now they became cemeteries. Each body was bundled roughly into a groundsheet. In some cases all that was left was a gory mess of arms legs and shattered torsos, held together by blood soaked scraps of uniform. It was my first experience of death of any sort let alone violent death at such close quarters and I could hardly stop myself from shaking as I desperately tried to sort out which bit belonged to which body. I was rescued by a veteran of trench warfare with no such illusions, who to my great relief put me out of my misery.

"It doesn't matter whose bit is which young fella, leave them to sort that out in heaven or hell, wherever they're going. As soon as you've got a bundle, tie it up and let's get 'em out of here before Jerry starts shelling again".

I was only too glad to do as I was told and soon all the remains were wrapped in their ground sheet shrouds and out of sight, the dripping blood and oozing guts the only testament to their ghastly contents. We dragged or carried our gruesome bundles into the saps and buried them in shallow graves scratched out of the clay with trenching tools. Now only remains of odd bits of body, too small to identify or bury, littered the trench. These we threw over the parados on our side of the trench to be trampled into the broken ground or eaten by the rats. How could we treat the remains of what, less than a hour ago, had been a man, with such little respect? He had been living and breathing, capable of experiencing all the emotions I was experiencing now. Life had been as sweet and full of hope and expectations for him as it was for me. Now he was nothing more than so much unwanted offal, swept from a butchers slab.

I was to discover later the subsequent horror of disposing of bodies in such a rudimentary fashion. During every bombardment, graves and unclaimed bodies hit by shell fire spewed their rotting remains all over No Man's Land as well as into the lines. It was therefore not uncommon to find bits of putrid and decaying flesh littering the trench or find an arm or leg sticking out from its sides, the contents of a previous grave or perhaps some unfortunate, buried alive by a fall of earth. Sometimes the head and shoulders of such a victim would appear. If this happened it was customary to cover the part sticking out with a bit of sacking or camouflage netting held up with cartridge cases stuck into the dirt. Should the decaying limb be too offensive, it would be unceremoniously hacked off with a bayonet or trenching tool and thrown to the rats. I had heard that on one occasion a section of Pioneers had been detailed to open up a disused trench only to find it filled with the rotting remains of hundreds of French troops who had been killed and buried the previous year. Needless to say, the excavations were abandoned! Bodies, disintegrated by countless hits, were turned into a rotting, stinking, pulp, transforming the ground into a giant carnal house. Like so many rotting summer windfalls, they were left discarded and unwanted on the battlefields of France, crushed beyond recognition by the giant hooves of war. These men had no known resting place but simply disappeared off the face of the earth without trace. After the war their passing would be recorded on the many memorials under the banner "Known Only to God".

While we were tending to the wounded and disposing of the

dead, the sappers had been busy repairing the damage done by the bombardment. Dirt blown in by the explosion had been shovelled out and added to the mound that guarded the firing line. Extra sand bags had been filled and used to repair the sagging sides. Wattle revetments and corrugated iron sheets had been brought up to repair the damage done by the first shell burst. Soon, the only sign of the recent destruction was the ugly red stains where blood had soaked the chalky soil and coloured the mud that lined the trench a dirty pink. In less than a hour these too had gone, obliterated by the trampling boots as the trench once again returned to what could be loosely called normality!

The next night, as I had promised, I volunteered to join the reconnaissance party that was going out to monitor the position and depth of the enemy wire and if possible bring in Corporal Johnstone's body. When Nobby heard I was going, although he was scheduled for a rest period that night he volunteered to come too. As soon as it was dark we gathered at the jumping off point, our faces blacked out with burnt cork and mud. Anything that might reflect the light was either removed or blacked over including our newly issued steel helmets which we daubed with mud, puddled from the result of the numerous nervous pees each of us had. We were to be led by a large Scottish sergeant whose method of communication seemed to consist of a combination of strange grunting sounds, interspersed and punctuated with strings of foul language, the latter being the only bit I could easily recognise.

On his whispered command we slid out of the trench and moved gingerly forward into the darkness. About a mile away to our left a skirmish was taking place in No Man's Land, causing us to dive for cover every time a star shell lit up the scene.

"Some beggars are at it early," whispered Nobby as we crouched together in a convenient shell crater, relieved that it was them not us who had been found in this exposed position. We inched our way forward led by the sergeant who, we had been told, did this sort of thing most nights! Passing through our own defences and taking evasive action several times to avoid detection, we eventually made it to the edge of the enemy wire without being detected. What we found was a massive entanglement of rusty picket stakes and coil upon coil of razor sharp wire leading back into the darkness. It was obvious that if indeed the big push was scheduled to begin from this part of the front, this wire would need to be cut by shell fire before any advancing troops could make contact with the enemy. Every soldier carried wire cutters as part of his kit but it would take many weeks of cutting by hand to have any effect on this forest of wire.

While the rest of us huddled in a shell hole, the Scotsman calmly went about the business of drawing maps of what we'd seen, cursing quietly to himself as he did so. Apart from his steady stream of foul language in which it appeared that at no time did he repeat himself, the whole operation was carried out in silence. The enemy front line was only about fifty yards away and from where we lay we could plainly hear the voices of the occupants and the occasional burst of laughter, probably at some ribald joke. In the darkness a sentry whistled to keep himself awake and a gramophone began to play a popular tune. We lay there for a while and listened, forgetting for a moment the perilous position we were in should we be discovered. Together we crept from crater to crater, covering more than two hundred yards of front, hoping every moment that the sergeant would be satisfied with the information he had recorded. To some men, going out into the night on raiding or fact gathering missions was their worst nightmare. Others revelled in the danger, only coming alive after dark when they would venture out to carry out the hazardous duties of the night raider. I suspect the sergeant was one of the latter.

The first glimmer of dawn was beginning to lighten the sky beyond the ruined landscape before he was satisfied with his nights work and we turned thankfully back towards our lines. In single file we followed him across the broken ground, dreading every moment the crack of a rifle or tac,tac,tac of a machine gun as some alert guard saw us silhouetted against the lightening sky.

As the night wore on we had come to a tacit agreement that any thoughts of searching for, and retrieving Corporal Johnstone's body would be forgotten. There was little chance of finding him, in the dark each crater looked the same, and the desire to reach the safety of our lines was uppermost in our minds. It was agreed therefore that we would keep a cursory look out on the way back and only if we came across him in the process would we do anything about it. Nobby was reluctant to give in, convinced he knew the location, and soon fell behind the rest of us as he dodged from crater to crater searching in vain for the one which contained the body. His actions infuriated the sergeant who was determined to get all his charges back in one piece, blaming himself for staying out so long. Eventually he gathered us together in a large crater with orders to wait while he went back for the reluctant Nobby. He quickly and silently disappeared into the darkness, leaving us peering anxiously after him like so many baby birds huddling together for safety and comfort in a nest, each one of us hoping that at any moment he would loom out of the night with Nobby in tow and lead us back to safety.

All at once there was a whoosh and a bang and a star shell arced into the sky, illuminating the scene with its icy blue light. There, out in the open, we saw the sergeant and just behind him came Nobby. Between them they were carrying what looked like the body of a man. For a moment they stood there, as if frozen in time in the ghostly light. Now a machine gun opened up, its tracer bullets splitting the night as it homed in on the stranded pair. After what seemed like an age they started to run but it was too late. Nobby was the first to go down, the force of the bullets bowling him over and over in the mud like a shot rabbit and I watched in horror as the exploding bullets found their mark. His right arm above the elbow was blown from his body and cart wheeled away in a lazy arc across the ground, coming to rest only twenty yards from where I lay. As if part of some dreadful nightmare, I saw that the hand was still clutching a pair of wire cutters! The sergeant was also hit, but not fatally for I could hear his curses getting louder and more blasphemous by the second from where he lay and licked his wounds in the shelter of a shell hole. Finally and mercifully, the star shell spluttered out and darkness drew a curtain over the whole dreadful scene.

We were still not out of danger. By now both the enemy's and our trench were both stood to and a hail of bullets whistled in both directions above our heads. Soon the German bombers had marked our position and trench mortars began to rain down all around us. Shocked, cursing with anger at the plight I found myself in, yet sick with fear, I lay and listened to the sound of my probable death rushing nearer and nearer.

Mercifully the fire fight soon died down to the level of the usual morning hate. In the absence of the sergeant I realised it was my responsibility to take charge of the situation. Warning the others to keep down, I peered cautiously over the rim of the crater. The first thing I saw was Nobby's body lying in the mud. During the bombardment a mortar had exploded almost alongside him and there was little left to identify what, only a short while ago, had been my friend. I took comfort in knowing that he would have been dead from his original injuries before he hit the ground. Of the sergeant there was no sign, only a steady flow of curses coming from a nearby crater indicated he was still alive.

"Are you alright, Sarge, how badly are you hit?," I called. The curses changed to a series of guttural noises from which I interpreted he thought he was not too badly wounded but was bleeding heavily. Looking back towards our lines, I realised that we were too far away to make a dash for it so made the decision that we would have to sit it out until night fall. This was confirmed some minutes later when Sergeant Hawkins, watching procedures through the safety of a periscope, hailed us and agreed that that was the wise course of action to take.

Slowly the dawn broke on a wonderful summer's day. Soon the sun was shining down from a cloudless sky, burning our skin and parching throats already tinder dry from fear. As the morning passed we soon discovered that the shell hole provided little if any shade, neither did any of us carry any water. Through what seemed like an endless day we lay with parched throats under the burning sun, seeking what shelter we could from covers made from our tunics. The crater was barely deep enough to cover us so that we were in constant fear that at any moment the enemy would spot us and start firing again. The hours crawled by and after what seemed a lifetime the sun finally set below the wooded hills and the safety of darkness fell upon us. Almost as soon as it was dark, a party led by Sgt. Jenkins himself came out and led us back to safety. Medics tended the injured Scotsman where he lay and carried him as carefully as they could back to the lines. They found his wounds, coupled with the days wait for attention, were more severe than at first though and although he died some hours later it was not before he had handed in his maps drawn the night before and given a graphic account of the strength of the enemy wire on the section which we had reconnoitred. Each returning patrol that night was interrogated by the CO and asked to describe what they had seen. Each of them stressed the formidable depth of the enemy wire and the fact that nowhere had it been cut. It is almost certain that all the other patrols along that three mile front must have reported similar conditions but if they did each was ignored making all our efforts and sacrifices a waste of time.

The events of the next few days would show that our urgings of caution, if they ever got back to command headquarters, fell on deaf ears. In later years, when all the facts were put before them, military historians would conclude that a series of military blunders coupled with ill luck, faulty equipment and outdated tactics would result in the almost total annihilation of an entire army. Many years later and with the benefit of hindsight the following lessons would be learned.

The decision by the French commander Marshall Foch to start the summer offensive on the Somme, where the enemy held both the high ground and were dug in in deep, well defended positions, merely as a diversionary tactic aimed at relieving the French, should have been more strongly argued against by the British Commander Sir Douglas Haig . Unfortunately, failing to do so was in keeping with the commander of an army which could boast a tradition firmly based on the longest unbroken series of strategic blunders in military history!

The British commanders at the front had been convinced that the preceding barrage had destroyed the enemy wire when in fact almost half the shrapnel shell employed on this task failed even to explode.

The attacking troops had been heavily burdened with unnecessary kit and had been ordered to walk across No Man's Land, preventing them from reaching their objective before the German defenders had time to leave their deep bunkers to man their weapons.

These and other blunders would lead to the massacre of thousands of men, trapped like rats against the uncut wire, sitting targets for the German machine guns ranged and sighted on the perimeter of their own wire. But now we have the advantage of hindsight. As Mother used to say, "If ifs and ands were pots and pans there would be no need for tinkers." And I'm sure she was right.

The ground where we lay that night as the sergeant drew his maps was soon to be piled high with British dead. Thankfully, by that time I would not be around to witness it.

The night of the 23rd June had been no different from the rest. I had taken my turn on the fire step in the quiet of the night, savouring the cleaner air washed by the thunderstorms of the previous afternoon, while the morning found me sleeping on the duckboards, curled up beneath a canvas sheet in an unfinished sap. It got light late, heavy thunder clouds obscuring the sun promising another wet day. Stand to sounded at first light and I reluctantly rose to man the firing step with the others. Far away to the rear, clear on the morning air, we heard the sound of bugles sounding reveille in our reserve divisions and somebody remarked that this was earlier than usual. The expected hate session was followed by the preparation of breakfast and completion of ablutions. Everything seemed normal. Then, on the stroke of seven, our whole world suddenly turned upside down. All along a front several miles long, the order to fire was given and the greatest number of guns ever to be assembled in one place began to fire in unison on the German lines. Two hundred pound shells started spinning over our heads, each one making the noise of an express train, falling with a mighty explosion on the enemy trenches. We watched for hour after hour as shells of every size rushed and hissed on their way to burst with a crump and a cloud of smoke and flame in endless succession on the enemy positions on the forward slopes or on their reserves to the rear. Some fell short, causing us to dive for cover but for the first and probably last time in my life I was enjoying the spectacle of a drumfire bombardment.

The shelling would go on for another four days and nights before lifting at the start of the ill fated big push.[4]

At mid-day, surprisingly and even with some regret, my section was told to pack our kit as we were being relieved of our duties. That night, with the sound of the guns still roaring behind me, I boarded a train taking me south, back the way I had come, to a quieter billet at the Étaples training camp where I should have first gone, and a reunion with my old mates from the KSLI. Taffy Edwardss came with me.

Chapter 5
The Training Camp at Étaples - June 30th 1916

In Flanders Fields
In Flanders fields the poppies blow,
Between the crosses, row by row
That mark our place; and in the sky
The larks, still bravely singing fly
Scarce heard amid the guns below.
McCrea

The train I would travel in had certainly seen better days! Few of its carriages contained seats since most had started life as cattle wagons before having been commandeered by the military at the outbreak of war and crudely converted to troop carriers. To achieve this the two large sliding doors originally used to accommodate the animals had been removed and reduced to a single entrance and a small window added in the additional space this created. Unfortunately it had not been considered necessary to allow it to be opened! The remainder of the carriage had been left untouched except for the addition of a number of bales of hay to act as seats. Loose straw had been thrown on the floor, presumably both for extra comfort and to hide the large gaps evident between the roughly sawn planks from which it was constructed. It was obvious that the straw had not been renewed for a very long time as it was littered with cigarette stubs, old English news papers, discarded sweet wrappers and every other type of everyday debris discarded by the many hundreds of troops who had travelled in it. Inside, the hot, sticky air smelled of sweat, urine and unwashed bodies and I wondered how many of its previous passengers were still alive today. It was possible that for many of them this could have been their last ride on earth? I imagined them saying goodbye to their families only hours earlier in England before boarding a troopship to cross the Channel, then on by rail to the front. Now, the only evidence of their passing lay in the litter that covered the dirty floor all around us. For me and my fellow travellers things were all together different. Now, thankfully the train we rode in was travelling in the opposite direction, taking us away from the killing and the maiming of the battle fields to a safer place well behind the lines.

It was late afternoon by the time all the carriages were loaded with their cargo of troops and horses together with a large number of damaged artillery pieces destined for repair back in England. Last to arrive, carried in a fleet of ambulances, were a party of severely wounded soldiers accompanied by a number of pretty nurses who fussed and fluttered around their charges like large, anxious white birds, ensuring that each one was safely on board and on their way back to England, for almost all were the recipients of a much coveted "Blighty", a wound not severe enough to be fatal but bad enough to ensure that with a bit of luck for them the war was over.

The thunder storms of the morning had cleared away and by midday a baking sun had turned the interior of the carriage into a stinking oven. Gasping for breath, cursing and swearing at the incompetence of the captain quartermaster supervising the loading of the train, we sweated and fumed in the airless carriage. Finally, after what seemed like hours, the train got under way so that its motion created a cooling breeze which blew through the gaps in the carriage sides and the rattling window frame, helping in some way to alleviate our discomfort.

The journey took us away from the battle zone and soon the broken buildings and ruined landscape to which we had become accustomed gave way to fields of golden corn and picturesque French farms and villages, still as yet untouched by war. Lit by the glow of the setting sun, each surrounded by the now familiar acres of neatly planted orchards and vineyards, it seemed hard to believe that this was the same country whose devastation and destruction we had witnessed less than a short days march away.

I found myself a place in the corner of the carriage and making a bed as best I could from the loose straw and using my pack for a pillow I settled down for the journey. Others around me were doing the same and soon the air was filled with the contented snores of exhausted men. For a while I watched the countryside slipping by but soon the warmth of the carriage and the soporific rhythm of the train dulled my senses and I fell into a deep sleep. Away from the danger and discomfort of the trenches I had so recently left, I dreamed of home and my family and many other things I was missing so much. Sometime later I woke with a start to find the carriage in darkness and the train at a standstill. Ice cold drops of rain were dripping in through the roof, cooling my burning face. Clear in the silence of the night, above the contented snores of my fellow travellers, I could still hear the ceaseless roar of the barrage, still firing along the Somme. Looking back through a crack in the carriage wall, I saw the distant horizon, now many miles away, illuminated by the flickering pink glow of the guns like some giant fireworks display. I shuddered at the thought of the men back there, even though they were our enemy, cowering and dying under the falling shells. No man, friend or foe, should be subjected to that form of hideous torture. The guns had been firing now for nearly twenty-four hours and it was easy to believe what we had been told by our officers, "When the barrage lifts and our boys go over the top, there won't be a single Boche left alive to bar our way to Germany".

For a moment I wished I was there, waiting expectantly somewhere in the line to make that historic dash for victory. Then, remembering the uncut wire and the formidable enemy trenches I had seen only days before, I was not so sure. Snuggling down in the straw, I pulled my greatcoat over my head and once more fell into a deep, untroubled sleep, the first I had enjoyed since the beginning of my stay in the trenches.

A movement disturbed me and I woke with a start, momentarily disorientated and unsure of my surroundings. Bright shafts of sunlight were streaming into the carriage and all around me men were coming awake, stretching and yawning, rubbing sleep from red rimmed eyes or straightening tousled hair and crumpled uniforms. Looking outside I saw that both our carriage and a number of others had been uncoupled from the train and shunted into the sidings of a station. Military policemen and other soldiers who, from their badges and insignia I knew to be members of the Guards regiment, lined the platform, each of the guardsmen wearing a yellow armband to distinguish them from the men now piling off the train. This was my first sight of the infamous drill instructors or "canaries" as they were called by the trainees from the camp from which they came. Their reputation for harsh discipline and ill humour was well known to everyone who had experienced the toughening up process dished out to all new arrivals before going on to the front. The camp was known as Étaples, taking its name from the small town in whose station the train now stood. For a moment I watched the "canaries" stamping up and down the platform urging everybody to disembark from the train. Then, still numb with sleep, I gathered up my kit and, and following the rest of my fellow passengers, stumbled out onto the platform and the bright morning sunlight.

"Get fell in, fall in columns of three, you slovenly bunch of bastards", roared the Canaries, striking about them with their pace sticks at those reluctant or tardy to comply. Indignantly we obeyed their instructions. Surely they realised we were not a bunch of raw recruits just out from England, but bloodied veterans fresh from a stint in the trenches? If they did it counted for nothing and in time we would learn the hard way that everyone under training here were treated just the same, for it was customary for men returning to the front after being wounded to spend some time in Étaples and even these, many with decorations for bravery, were treated more like prisoners in a concentration camp than volunteers willing to fight for their country.

At the order "Quick march", we swung away out of the station and through the outskirts of the town. Following a dusty, cobbled road lined with towering poplar trees, we broke step to cross a small river bridge and marched out into the country. In the distance, far away across the open farmland we caught a glimpse of the rows and rows of white bell tents shimmering in the sun and the scattering of more permanent wooden buildings which made up the camp. As we drew near we could see that its perimeter was guarded with a tall wire fence. As some wit in the ranks observed in a loud voice, it was not obvious if this was to keep the occupants in or the locals out!

Every recruit in the army had heard of Étaples with its iron regime and reputation for breaking even the hardest of men's wills. At the outbreak of war the English army had consisted of only a small number of regular divisions, these being supplemented by either Territorial soldiers or reserves released from service after the African wars. It was these troops, including my two brothers, later described by the Kaiser as a "contemptible little army" who had first landed in France and suffered so many casualties in the opening battles and subsequent retreats at Ypres and Mons. Now, very few of these seasoned troops remained so that the new armies which replaced them were made up of fresh volunteers like me, only basically trained and still untried under fighting conditions. To counter this, several training camps had been set up in France where new arrivals could be put through a rigorous toughening up process before moving up to take their place in the war zones. Étaples soon gained a reputation for being the severest of these camps, it was even said that training here was a worse experience than the real thing, but with hindsight and my own experiences behind me, I think that was an exaggeration.

I knew that this should have been my original destination before I and many others like me had been diverted to the front to assist with the preparations for the coming offensive. Now like the rest of my travelling companions, all new recruits or returning wounded, I was expected to start my training afresh, regardless of my experience gained over the last few weeks. Clearly, this was another case of the army thinking with its backside and not with its brains!

Entering the camp through two large wire gates guarded by a posse of military policemen, we were marched straight to a large mess tent, fell out, and fed a breakfast of porridge and fried bacon, washed down with mugs of hot, sweet tea, the first proper meal I had enjoyed for some days. From here we were taken to the lines and allocated billets in a number of newly pitched tents where I was astute enough to grab a sleeping billet as far away as possible from the tent entrance. My experiences of living under canvas at Oswestry had taught me that as everybody slept in a circle around the tent pole with their feet facing inwards, the man with the billet nearest the door was constantly disturbed throughout the night by others entering or leaving the tent. Once I was settled in I found time to take stock of my new surroundings. Looking around me I found it incredible that this was a camp whose business it was to prepare soldiers for life at the front. Surrounding each tent and marking the perimeter of each road were neat rows of whitewashed stones, while the sides of each tent was rolled back and inside I could see that the kit and bedding of each occupant was laid out as if for kit inspection. Everywhere was neat and in good order with nothing out of place, reminiscent of the camps were I had trained back in England. We had been warned that here nobody was allowed to walk within the confines of the camp and that all movements had to be at the double. Woe betide anybody breaking this or any other of the many apparently pointless rules we would learn about, many the hard way, during our stay. I can't imagine what the authorities thought could be gained from soldiers whitewashing stones or enduring endless kit inspections that would be of any benefit to them under battle conditions. Everybody who had spent any time at the front new that all the rules were instantly forgotten the moment the first whiz-bang landed or the enemy opened up with a well-sited machine gun! Then it was every man for himself and the overpowering desire for self preservation that automatically took control of the mind!

The rest of the day was a "make and mend" with time allowed to tidy up both ourselves and our kit before reporting the next morning to start our training. This was always the rule throughout the war, even for troops just relieved from the trenches. Each man was allowed one day for delousing, getting a wash and shave and cleaning the grime and filth of the trenches from bodies, uniforms and weapons. After that they would be expected to parade ready for inspection, and heaven help anybody who didn't come up to the high standards demanded by their officers. They, of course, even the most junior of them, enjoyed the services of a batman to do their bidding, including the cleaning and pressing of their kit, so most of the time they could be expected to be well turned out.

In the evening, Taffy Edwards and I walked over to the large wooden hut which served as the canteen. I had hardly got in through the door when to my surprise and delight I saw the familiar face of Ernie Pye grinning and waving to me from across the room. Pushing my way through I was greeted by many of the good friends from the

Shropshires who I had last seen at Pembroke Barracks. There was Billy Capper, Arnie Griffiths and the two Hughes brothers. Later on we were joined by Frank Evans and two of the Birmingham lads. It seemed that their company had been held in reserve back in England and had only recently arrived in France to support the latest offensive. Better still, they were part of the 5th Division to whom I would be attached. We spent the rest of the evening drinking bottles of cheap French beer and yarning about our adventures. I soon discovered that I was the only one who had been to the front, let alone seen any action. Feeling slightly superior to the others I lost no time in regaling them with gruesome tales of what I had seen and experienced, graphically describing the bombardment and the terrible injuries I had witnessed, the night raid and the deaths of the Scottish sergeant and my friend Nobby. As the evening wore on and the beer flowed freely, we talked of lighter moments, roaring with laughter at old stories told a dozen times before, of our days in training back in Shropshire and South Wales. Finally, with spinning heads and tongues loosened by the drink, we said our elaborate goodnights.

The others went their separate ways, leaving Taffy and I to find our billets in what, under the influence of the drink, turned out to be very difficult as in the unfamiliar surroundings and the dark, all the rows and rows of tents looked exactly the same. On unsteady legs and with gales of drunken laughter we tried tent after tent, unperturbed by the anger and curses from their sleeping occupants who we disturbed. At last we found the right row and the right tent and had just managed to stagger inside, stumbling over the legs of the sleepers as we did so, before the arrival of a posse of military policemen alerted by the commotion. Two of my mates grabbed me and dragged me unceremoniously to the ground, quickly throwing a blanket over my head to stifle my drunken laughter while two others did the same for Taffy. By the time the MPs shone their lights into the tent all they saw was a circle of contented sleepers, head to toe to the middle post.

I didn't get away Scot free though. As soon as the coast was clear we were duly hauled outside by the other occupants of our tent and doused down with several buckets of freezing cold water.

Our punishment didn't end there. With two troopers sitting on my chest and another on my legs I was obliged to promise that the next night the drinks would be on me, an undertaking gladly given, for even though I would be paying, a night in the canteen with my new mates was far better than the punishment which would surely have been handed out by the MPs had they not come to my assistance. More sober now, we crawled back into the tent, found our billets around the centre pole and settled down for our first night at Étaples.

Chapter 6
The Start of the Battle of the Somme - July 1916

Marching Men
All the hills and vales along,
Earth is bursting into song.
And the singers are the chaps,
Who are going to die perhaps!
Sorley

It seemed as if I had hardly closed my eyes before a terrible commotion outside the tent made me sit bolt upright in my billet and peering sleepily outside, I was able to see where all the noise was coming from. A bugler, standing between the lines of tents, was blowing reveille and beside him were twenty or so Canaries, each armed with an empty ammunition box which they started to bang with a piece of wood the moment the last notes of the bugle had faded away, all the while urging the reluctant sleepers to get out of their beds.

"Wakey, wakey, wakey. Rise and shine, the mornings fine", they yelled. "Hands off your cocks and on with your socks", beating out the rhythm on the boxes with their sticks. Predictably their demands were greeted with muffled curses and insults from the disgruntled occupants of the tents with cries of "Sod off you conchie bastards" and worse hurled at their tormentors. Everyone had heard the rumours, none of them confirmed, that many of the instructors at this and other camps in France were either the younger sons of gentlemen, holding down a safe billet, or conscientious objectors who had refused to fight on moral grounds. Suddenly the mood changed from good humoured banter to ugly threats as the Canaries started opening tents at random, dragging men from their beds and beating them about the head and body with their sticks. In no time at all a full scale fight erupted as the rest of us piled in to their aid. The resulting melee was only brought to order when reinforcements arrived, backed up by large numbers of military policemen, who eventually managed to restore order, but only at the expense of some bruised and battered bodies. Ignoring our remonstrations at the unfairness of the decision, despite loudly protesting their innocence, ten men were selected at random, charged on the spot with failing to obey an order and marched away to be paraded before the CO. Within the hour, all of them would face summary trial, be found guilty, and sentenced to receive four hours number one field punishment. In the scuffle I managed to get in a few good licks but suffered a bruised head for my trouble, already delicate from the previous nights drinking. What an auspicious start to my first full day at Étaples!

The rest of us were given five minutes to roll and display our bedding, lay out our kit for inspection, then fall in in full battle order, wearing gas respirators, shorts and vests and carrying rifles.

"I'll show you mouthy buggers who's a conchie bastard", snarled a Canary, sporting a rapidly closing eye, as he sent us off on a three mile cross country run, he and several of his mates following on their bicycles! This didn't bother me one bit as I still kept myself in trim for boxing. Cross country running was a pleasant diversion as far as I was concerned, even though it was the first time I had tried it in a gasmask! Nobody was excused so it became an unpleasant ordeal for some, particularly those just returned from sick leave. To make matters worse, stragglers were encouraged to keep going by the mounted Canaries armed with canes with which they laid about the backs of those labouring runners who fell behind. Their added threats that the mess hall would shut promptly at six thirty and any latecomers would go without breakfast seemed insignificant at the time although the full implications of this would not be realised until later in the day when it became apparent that this was the only meal we would receive until that evening.

Those of us who made it in time grabbed a hurried breakfast before joining the less fortunate ones now fell in on the parade ground in full battle dress. This time we were carrying rifles and packs filled with stones to make up the sixty pounds in weight each infantry man was expected to carry into battle. Next we were inspected by a fastidious sergeant instructor who found fault in almost everything he saw. In my case, a loose tunic button resulted in fifty press ups on the spot, with the foot of another Canary planted firmly in my back for good measure. Others were less fortunate receiving various lengths of time confined to barracks with extra fatigues. The inspection completed, we set off on a route march to the small town of Touquet-Paris Plage and back, a round trip of about twenty miles. When leaving the camp we were marched past the unfortunate ten men, and several others besides, who had been randomly selected then sentenced to suffer field punishment.

Guarding the gate were several field artillery pieces and now each had a man spread-eagled on its wheels. Unable to escape the attention of the swarms of mosquitoes that gorged themselves on their blood, their faces were already red and swollen from the mass of bites they had received. No matter what their condition, they would not be released from this torment until their allotted number of hours had been completed. The mood of the men was a mixture of anger and guilt as we abandoned them to their torture and marched out into the country, for each of us knew that it was only luck coupled with the whim of the Canaries that we were not suffering with them. Seeing the distress of our comrades yet powerless to intervene, should the opportunity arise, many of us vowed to exact revenge on their tormentors, who, at this moment, although wearing the same uniform as us, seemed more hostile than any enemy we were ever likely to face.

The satisfaction of taking revenge would not be ours, although several months from now it would be inflicted by men not present there that day. When the time came it would be quick, violent and bloody and Étaples and its iron regime, designed to break men's wills so that they would blindly follow orders without question, would never be the same again.

Most of us were young and fit, able to march all day if asked to, so it was with some pleasure that we left the rigid confines of the camp and set off into the open countryside. Our route took us as far as the coast and before starting back we were allowed a few moments on the sea shore. Gazing out over the blue waters of the Channel, the thin line of the White cliffs of Dover shimmering on the horizon in the hot English sunshine might as well have been a thousand miles away.

At midday we were given water to drink but no food. This would be the order of the day throughout my stay at Étaples. Breakfast in the morning if you were lucky, followed by an evening meal at night. During the day we survived on nothing but water and any food begged or stolen along the way. Hungry men ate unripe grapes and oranges stolen from nearby fields and experienced agonising stomach cramps and diarrhoea as a result. Their condition was mockingly called being "staked" and often led to full dysentery, further weakening their condition and on rare occasions, proving fatal. In the afternoon we completed the march, stopping on the way back for our first look at the notorious training ground situated in sand dunes about seven miles from the camp. This infamous place was known to everyone who passed through Étaples as the Bullring. Here men were subjected to the most appalling abuse by the instructors, doing everything at the double and ordered over the severest of assault courses. Tired and hungry, we were expected to fight our way through barbed wire entanglements while live ammunition was fired over our heads. Worst of all was the hill, a man made incline constructed from loose sand. Already exhausted men were forced to fill a sand bag with sand, carry it at the double to the top of the hill, empty its contents, then sprint down the other side. A man could be ordered to do this twenty, or thirty times a day or even more if he fell afoul of the bullying Canaries.[1]

Back at camp we were given a meal and after parading for evening colours our time was our own. Later, as promised, I took the lads from my tent for a few drinks but after such a hectic day we were all almost out on our feet so that long before the bugler sounded "lights out", most of us were wrapped in our blankets and fast asleep.

Not so many miles away that night, men were finding sleeping less easy. Crouched in their bivouacs and makeshift billets and almost deafened by the endless crash and roar of the barrage still passing over their heads, thousands of men all along the front anxiously awaited the dawn. Others spent the night moving silently forward in the darkness to their jumping off points in the forward lines. In the valley of the Somme and all along the line stretching away some thirty or so miles to the north, the hours were ticking down to zero!

The next day was a Saturday and we fell in as usual for the early morning inspection. Even at this distance, the rumble of the barrage along the front created a constant background noise, audible throughout both the day and night. It had been incessant for the last five days. Now as unexpectedly as it started it lifted and for once everything was quiet. All of us knew what this meant. The lifting of the barrage signalled the start of the big push, the break out leading all the way to Germany and the end of the war!

The word spread through the ranks and for a while you could hear a pin drop as each man strained their ears as if, even at this great distance, they would hear the noise of the battle as the men engaged the enemy. I imagined troops obeying their officers whistles and moving confidently out from the shelter of their trenches, glad the waiting was over and at last the time had come to face an enemy already destroyed or disorientated by the ferocity of our artillery. Hadn't our officers assured us that it was going to be a piece of cake and how I wished I could be part of it and not condemned to even one more day's training at this awful place. I wasn't to know just how lucky I was!

The battle that erupted with such ferocity on the morning of 1st July will always be known as the Battle of the Somme. The name is taken from the shallow river which meanders through that pleasant part of Picardy on whose banks the battle was fought. In reality the battle was fought not only there but all along the front which I had so recently left. This divided the two opposing forces and stretched from the fortified village of Fricourt, just to the south of Thiepval, for over thirty miles to the Ypres salient in the north. It was here, already the scene of two major battles, that my brother Jack had been killed the previous year. But it was on what had once been the fertile water meadows of the Somme, long since transformed into a pockmarked moonscape of shell holes and manmade fortifications, that the greatest number of fatalities were recorded that day. It was here that Joffre, the French Commander in Chief, against the advice of the British generals, decided that the major thrust would take place. It was also no coincidence that it was also here that the German defences were at their strongest. With deep, well constructed dugouts and trench systems designed to withstand the severest of bombardments, our enemies waited, confident that they could withstand and survive anything that was thrown at them. So, as we waited in anticipation in the safety of Étaples camp on that sunny Saturday morning in July and wished, almost to a man, that we could be there, the scene was set for what would become the most terrible of a catalogue of military and strategic disasters for which this war and its commanders would be remembered. At seven thirty, when the barrage lifted after five days of incessant shelling, thousands of troops left the shelter of their dugouts and started the steady uphill advance towards the enemy trenches. They had been told to expect little or no opposition and had been ordered by their officers to walk but were unable to run anyway due to the broken nature of the ground and the sixty pounds of equipment each of them carried. This delay provided ample time for the Germans, mostly unharmed by the bombardment, to leave their deep shelters and man the firing lines. From behind a barricade of uncut wire, some of which I had seen and the dying Scottish sergeant had reported, they watched and waited as our men advanced into open ground. When they opened up, dozens of machine guns, firing on fixed lines, cut men down in their hundreds. Some got no farther than the lip of their own trenches, others actually reached the wire only to find it uncut by the bombardment in contradiction to what they had been told by their officers since a great number of the shrapnel shells employed to do this task had failed to explode.[2] Trapped against the wire, they died in their thousands, for even where a gap was found, the bodies were soon piled so high that nobody could get through anyway. Thiepval Wood, through which I had made my hesitant and fearful way to my first experiences in the trenches and from where only weeks ago I had watched my first aerial dog fight, was the scene of ferocious fighting and mass slaughter with casualties counted in their thousands. Many of these were the Ulstermen we had so lately relieved in the trenches. The huge mines, set in saps beneath the German trenches by my miner friend and his tunnelling colleagues were exploded just before zero hour and accounted for hundreds of the enemy dead. At Delville Wood, just a few pockmarked acres of shell holes and broken, splintered trees hardly worth fighting for, the South Africans died almost to a man. Some of these I counted as my friends as they had trained with me at Pembroke and later at the machine gun school. In the end they all died for nothing. At the end of the first day, a roll call showed that twenty thousand British troops had died and nearly forty thousand were either wounded or missing. As night fell and the men began to trickle back behind the lines, they came not in companies or even sections or platoons. They came in ones and twos, many of them wounded and supported by their friends. These were all that was left of what that morning, had been fighting divisions. Each one told the same story of uncut wire and enemy forces still able to defend their lines to the bitter end. Of territorial gains there were none. As night pulled a welcome veil of darkness over this horrific scene, both opposing forces were in the same positions that they had been that morning. The slaughter however, was not over. That would continue along the whole length of the front throughout the summer until, almost mercifully, the November snows and a sea of mud would bring a halt to the carnage. By that time I would be back in England.[3]

To those of us who eagerly awaited confirmation of its success, with the full extent of the failure of the attack not yet known, it seemed as if the long, hot day would never end. Each and every one of us was preoccupied with the thought of the battle raging little more than fifty miles away, with many of us experiencing mixed feelings both of guilt at not being there and envy for those who were. Even the instructors seemed to lose some of their enthusiasm for discipline, never pushing us to the usual extremes. Perhaps they realised that with the anticipated success of the summer offensive, their training posts could soon become redundant and they would be expected to return to the ranks and duties of ordinary soldiers. Should that be the case, there were hundreds of men out there with painful memories of the brutalities they had suffered at their hands who would, should the opportunity arise, be waiting to settle a few old scores, and without the protection of the yellow armband they could be in for a very rough time. With that in mind, it now seemed a good time to mend a few fences and make a few friends!

If this was the case it certainly made things much easier for us. Although we did the usual forced march to the Bullring after breakfast, this time there was no one chivvying and bullying the straggles at the rear while training consisted of gentle bayonet practice and trench work in the morning, followed by bomb drills in the afternoon. According to those veterans of the camp nearing the end of their training, this was the first day that they could remember when nobody had been sent over the hill as punishment. Unusually, early in the afternoon the order was given to stand down from our duties and soon two long columns of men marched gladly back to camp, happy to have got away with what had been an easy day. Such was the feeling of good will in the ranks that we broke into song as we marched along, singing all the old favourites from our training days; to our surprise, many of the instructors joined in! Back at camp the feeling of euphoria had affected everyone. For the first time there were no men doing field punishment at the gate while in the mess hall extra helpings were freely given. That night the canteen was full to overflowing with happy men, drinking each other's health, convinced that the war was surely over and soon they would be going home. How wrong they would be proved to be!

The next day was Sunday with the inevitable church parade at which we gave thanks and said prayers for the success of the offensive whose incessant rumbling we could once again hear in the distance. One astute listener, perhaps a little brighter than the rest of us, questioned the need for shelling an enemy apparently already beaten and in retreat. As this was before the rolling barrage had been perfected, he was quite right in posing the question, "Don't they usually only fire barrages from fixed positions at entrenched or static targets?"

His concern was brushed aside by the rest of us with howls of derision, and he was branded a pessimist for his lack of belief in the system. We were quick to remind him of what our officers had told us.

"When the big push comes, you lucky lads will march all the way to Germany without firing a shot in anger, for there won't be a Hun left alive to oppose you."

They were officers and gentlemen weren't they, in the know about the commanders every move and privy to his plans? As honourable people their word was their bond so it was not possible that the information they had told us could be untrue! Knowing this, we explained to the doubter that what certainly sounded like howitzers firing from fixed positions must, in reality, be field artillery well forward of the line, pursuing and firing on a retreating enemy. After some argument he begrudgingly accepted this explanation although I don't think he was entirely convinced.

After lunch, passes were issued and we were allowed leave until the midnight curfew, so Eddie, Taffy, and I walked the short distance into the small town of Étaples. Although it was still early afternoon, every bar was packed with soldiers drinking and dancing with the women and girls who stood at every street corner. The whole town was buzzing with excitement and laughter and everyone seemed determined to enjoy themselves and to drink as much as they could in as little time possible. As if by magic, Union flags had appeared at many windows, and flowers and streamers hung from the branches of every tree. Money was no problem. At pay parades we were paid five francs per man so with wine costing as little as half a franc a litre, most men had more than enough and some left over to drink themselves into oblivion! Some of the lads, fortified with the Dutch courage which comes in a litre or two of wine, took advantage of the coaxing of a formidable Madame who went from table to table describing in lurid detail the various exotic and sometimes unbelievable services her girls had to offer. Her girls, if that was an accurate description of what to me looked more like middle-aged hags, were a sorry, jaded lot, servicing the queue of soldiers waiting impatiently and expectantly at the door of each bedroom without any apparent show of emotion, their blank, weary expressions as they welcomed the next customer graphically illustrated what each experience meant to them! Five minutes per customer at two francs a time seemed a lot of money for very little satisfaction, even to an inexperienced country lad like me. Not as I had any choice in the matter. Most of my pay had gone in the canteen, buying my mates drinks in way of payment for keeping me out of trouble the night before. Still only seventeen, even if I'd had the money I was too shy and embarrassed to indulge in the services, I offered so made myself useful by holding the hats and minding the drinks of those who did!

We had been in the town about an hour when the first rumours began to circulate that things at the front were not going as planned. As the afternoon wore on, these began to grow and take on more credence as men coming into town from camp told of seeing trains heading for the coast filled to overflowing with wounded men. Some had seen open carriers usually used to transport guns being used to transport casualties, the wounded men lying in rows on stretchers exposed to the elements. The camp, they said, was buzzing with rumour and counter rumour, each one gaining more credibility by the way the instructors were acting.

"Them buggers know more than they're cracking on", muttered a disgruntled late arrival, gulping down the contents of a bottle of wine as if his life depended on it.

"Best get your drinking done in a hurry lads, it could be the last chance you'll be getting for some time!"

As if on cue the door burst open and the bar was full of military policemen.

"All leave is cancelled", they yelled, "Leave the bar immediately and return to camp."

As might be expected, this order was not received with any enthusiasm at all so that calls of "Bugger off" and worse came from every corner of the bar. While some men drank up and made to leave, others, mainly a large squad of Australians fortified with good wine and spoiling for a fight, were prepared to make an issue of it, some even seeing the chance to settle a few scores with the MPs. Trapped by the crush of people at the back of the bar, my mates and I had no option, nor anywhere to escape. Not that I wanted to! I'd had a few drinks and had always enjoyed a good scrap so when somebody shouted charge, in we went, fists flying. The MPs, realising that they were vastly outnumbered, retreated back into the street with the angry mob, howling for blood, hot on their heels. In other bars, men originally intending to return to camp saw what was happening and turned back to join in the fight so that suddenly the street was filled with brawling soldiers. Peace and good order was not restored until a young officer, popular with the men, persuaded the two warring factions to stand off while he explained the reason for our leave being cancelled. He told us the news of the failed assault and dreadful casualties of the previous day. He explained how the Germans had not been wiped out by the prolonged barrage but instead had been able to man their guns and mow down our lads as they crossed No Man's Land. He described how they had died in their thousands, trapped against uncut wire so that most of those men who only yesterday we had envied, were now dead.

In the failing light and now thoroughly subdued, we fell in and marched back to camp in silence with all thoughts of revenge against the hated MPs temporarily forgotten. Now we had a real enemy to fight, an enemy only two days march away who was very much alive and confidently manning the firing steps of his deep shelters. He had no doubt suffered massive casualties in first the bombardment and then the attack, now he would be licking his wounds, waiting for the next onslaught. When that happened we would gladly be there. Yesterday we thought the war was over, for most of us it was just beginning.

Chapter 7

La Boiselle and the Long Straight Road
August 1916

Base Details

If I were fierce and bald and short of breath,
I'd live with scarlet majors in the base
And speed glum heroes up the line to death.
You'd see me with my puffy, petulant face,
Guzzling and gulping in the best hotel
Reading the roll of honour, "Poor young chap"
I'd say, "I used to know his father well,
Yes, we lost heavily in that scrap"
And when the war was done and youth stone dead,
I'd toddle safely home and die – in bed!

Sassoon

On arriving in camp we were ordered to fall in on the improvised, stone painted, parade ground, stood at ease and left to wait while the MPs and Canaries rounded up other stragglers still coming in from the town. Some, too drunk to walk, were either supported or, in the worst cases, carried back on makeshift stretchers by their more sober but indignant mates and any man incapable of standing unsupported when called on parade was carted off to the cells to be dealt with by the commanding officer the following day. Being drunk and unable to carry arms was a capital offence on active service and men had been tried by courts martial and shot for less. On this occasion it might be argued that there were mitigating circumstances for the men's condition, for was it not true that while they had gone into town on their Sunday break to celebrate what they thought was a certain victory, this now seemed to have turned into a very costly defeat? Even so, drunkenness was not tolerated under any circumstances in the army and although this would be taken into account in their defence, each could expect to be sentenced to a minimum of several hours on the wheel in the morning. Of course, in military logic there was always an exception to every rule! In the front line it was not uncommon for men going over the top to be given ample measures of tea laced with rum to bolster their courage so that it had been known in isolated cases for some troops with unofficial access to the rum ration, to be staggering drunk when they faced the enemy.

Either through drink, pure bloody mindedness or both, back in town a few men objected more than others to being ordered back to camp. These were given short shrift by the MPs, who beat them senseless with truncheons or rifle butts before piling them in a commandeered farm cart for the journey back to camp.

Some had been on picket duty that day and had already been on parade for several hours before we arrived and the sight of their more fortunate comrades, still merry from their visit to town, did nothing to improve their tempers.

When as many as could be mustered were on parade, we were addressed by the camp Commandant who repeated the same disturbing news in much greater detail than what we had already heard. Now we learned that the casualty figures which previously had been only speculation had now been confirmed, making things sound even worse than seemed possible. Many of us had clung to the hope that the original news had been exaggerated but now that we knew the awful truth it had a shattering effect on everyone's morale. Few of us present that day had ever seen twenty thousand men gathered together in one place, so that the news that so many had been killed or maimed in only one morning was beyond our comprehension.

The CO informed us that he had been ordered to strengthen the line using whatever means were at his disposal and it was therefore his intention to provide fresh troops without delay, regardless of their readiness or experience of active service. To achieve this, all trainees who had been at the camp for more than three weeks, including any previously wounded men returning to their units via Étaples would terminate their training immediately and be drafted to their own or new regiments. Once identified, these men were fallen out and hurried away to pack their kit before receiving orders ready to move off at first light the following morning. Among those leaving were most of my friends from the Shropshires. Two of these were friends I'd grown up with but would never see again. One was killed within days of leaving Étaples, fighting with his regiment at Delville Wood. The other, the youngest of three brothers, none of whom would survive the war, would die of his wounds only weeks later.

The remainder of us would stay at Étaples for the time being, but training would be intensified and shortened to three weeks. After witnessing the devastating effect produced by the large number of enemy machine guns in the recent battle, the CO had been ordered by the top brass to expand and develop the existing machine gun school already sited at the Bullring, and to this end all machine gunners would report there for additional and intensive training.

This was not surprising. The invention of the machine gun had already effectively spelled the demise of mounted cavalry, now it would change the rules of trench warfare forever. Previously, when foot soldiers were attacked by mounted lancers, the method of defence was to form squares and fire volleys into the advancing horsemen. Even this had only limited success due to the time it took to reload each individual weapon. Now here was a weapon that was capable of repelling mass attacks practically single handed. At a single stroke the concept of both mounted and trench warfare changed almost overnight. Originally, in the British army there had been only two machine gun teams allotted to each battalion, but as their capabilities were realised, more and more were trained so that soon, whole units were armed with these fast firing weapons. Military tacticians realised that a well placed machine gun crew or two could hold a complete army at bay or bring down an entire battalion as it advanced over open ground. The Germans, recognising the significance of this long before we did, rewrote the military text books, concentrating their defences around dug in machine gun positions, only using infantrymen to protect these gun positions from attack by bombers. These same machine guns, manned by highly trained crews, had been responsible for the huge casualties already sustained by our forces since the beginning of the war. Always averse to change, it was not until the catastrophic failures against defended positions, first at Ypres and then the Somme, that the emphasis was switched in the British army from the infantryman to the machine gunner.

There was not much sleep for any of us that night. Groups of men gathered between the rows of tents smoking their pipes and gloomily discussing the implications of what they had just heard and as the light faded and evening turned to night, the warm summer darkness was filled with the murmur of subdued and, occasionally, angry voices. From inside tents the glow and sweet smell of smoke from more comforting pipes testified to the difficulty men were finding sleeping so that long after first light when the dawn chorus heralded another fine day, men could still be found huddled in groups outside their tents, either talking passionately or simply lost in thought, many unwilling to sleep, perhaps fearful of the horrors that their dreams might bring.

In the morning, many of us were already dressed and fell in long before the bugler blew reveille, anxious to get on with a war we felt we had just inherited. Suddenly there was a fresh resolve in everything we did, not evident since those first euphoric days in training. Now there was urgency, a burning desire to take up the quarrel so recently joined by our fallen friends, so that we went about our duties with renewed vigour. Those of us left behind had both the same weaknesses and the same strengths as other men, now we had that added ingredient that sets such men apart, a burning desire to right a terrible wrong so recently inflicted on our friends and comrades in arms.

It soon became evident that the temporary good will displayed by the instructors in the last two days was a thing of the past once it was established that they were not going anywhere. With the threat of returning to normal duties now greatly diminished and a new mandate to lick men into shape at whatever cost and in a greatly reduced time, they set about their task with all the ill will and barbarism they had displayed before. Now, when we marched out of the camp on route to the Bullring, the guns at the main gate once again supported prisoners doing the odious field punishment. When these were all accommodated, anything, even trees, being pressed into service instead of the traditional wheel, an even more painful experience because the roots, forming a wedge at the base, meant that after a short while the prisoner's feet would slip away, leaving him supporting his weight solely on his arms. As the blood drained away from captive limbs, the agony of the cramps that developed plus the attention of the ever present mosquitoes made this form of punishment a thing to be dreaded by those who had experienced it, even more than the prospect of time spent in the front line. During the next three weeks we toiled away at the Bullring sharpening our skills on the Vickers and Lewis guns, both of which required a different technique to fire. At least here the instructors were all Corps members who had experienced life at the front so were more sympathetic to our feelings than the hated Canaries. Misdemeanours were not punished on the hill, although we started each morning there as a prelude to the days training. As before there was no food from the time we left the camp to the time we returned but by now even the worst of the stragglers were fit enough to complete each mornings cross country run in time to eat some breakfast. For those who never made it, we devised a method of smuggling food out to them which they ate surreptitiously as we marched along.

Days were filled with bayonet drill, company drill and live firing. Most days were fine but when it rained, training was suspended and company fatigues took its place. Now I knew who painted the white stones that had taken my eye on the day I first arrived! While I was at the camp I took the opportunity to write some letters home and received some in return. Both Mother and my sisters wrote regularly, sending news of the village and how the community was coping without its young men. They wrote of mundane, everyday things, hiding their fears, wishing I could be there to share them, hardly ever mentioning the war. But in the local papers the trickle of names on the casualty lists had grown to a flood. Now, whole pages were devoted to them where before there had been only single paragraphs. Reading these, sometimes seeing names they recognised but unable to do anything about it must have been hell for those left behind. Before the war was over they, especially Mother, would spend many sleepless nights praying for myself and my brother's welfare.

The town had been put out of bounds so the only place to go in the evening if not on fatigues was the tin roofed canteen with its crude trestle bar and watery beer. Sometimes the torrential summer rain striking the roof could be deafening, making conversation impossible. Even this had its compensations for at least for a short while it masked the distant thunder of the barrages still rumbling constantly along the front. Most nights though I was too exhausted to bother with the canteen, climbing gratefully into my billet as soon as my duties was over. There I would lie in the darkness, toe to toe with my mates, listening to the sound of the guns forming a constant reminder of what lay in store for me.

After three weeks additional training it came almost as a relief when it was time to leave the camp and join my division on active service. My original orders had been to join the Twentieth who were on active service in the line near Caterpillar Valley and Guillemont and, surprised to find that this had not changed, accompanied by the rest of my section I once again boarded the down train to Amiens. From there we made our way either on foot or by motor transport to the Divisional Headquarters situated in a small village on the banks of the Willow stream called Fricourt and from here a guide took us the rest of the way to where our company was holding. The division was made up of three Brigades, the 59th, 60th and 61st which consisted of companies from the Kings Royal Rifle Corps, the Rifle Brigade, the Oxford and Bucks Light Infantry, Somerset Light Infantry, the Kings Own Yorkshire Light Infantry, the Duke of Cornwalls Light Infantry and of course the sixth KSLI. Each had sections of the newly formed Machine Gun Corps attached to them in support.

On the way up we met stretcher parties bringing wounded men back to the clearing station at Corbie. Once, we had to get quickly off the road when we were overtaken by a mounted artillery company drawn by wild eyed horses galloping at great speed, the drivers hanging over their necks, the gun limbers bouncing and bumping erratically over the broken ground while on another occasion we came across one of the latest developments in warfare, the rusting remains of an armoured tank lying disabled on the side of the road.

As was often the case in their early days, this one was broken down and had been abandoned by its crew. None of us had seen one before so the guide allowed us time to have a look at what Kitchener had referred to as "a pretty mechanical toy but of limited military use". Had he been alive and at Cambrai a year later he may have been asked to eat his words! This one was a "male" tank carrying two six-pounder guns and four Hotchkiss machine guns, and we marvelled at the strength of its armour and the apparent invincibility of the whole device. Tanks were of particular interest to me. Before the tank regiments were formed the earlier ones were manned by members of the Heavy Machine Gun Corps and it was with some regret that I never got to serve in one.

We followed our guide onto the long straight road that leads from Albert to Poziers, the scene of fierce fighting in the first few days of the assault. It was here that the 34th Division, particularly battalions of the Northumberland Fusiliers, had lost more than half their strength in casualties less than two hours after leaving their trenches on Tara hill. This was my first introduction to a regiment which would play an important role later on in my career. Passing through the Glory Hole, an area of overlapping shell holes where the opposing trenches had been only fifty yards apart, we skirted the gaping crater left by one of the huge mines which had been detonated just before zero hour. From here it was only a short distance through the aptly named Mash Valley into the ruins of what had once been La Boiselle. My section would become attached to and support the eleventh Kings Royal Rifle Corps who had just been withdrawn for a rest period to this once fortified but now ruined village, the scene of fierce fighting only weeks before. It was with some relief that I learned that they would be held in reserve for the time being, awaiting developments at the front. This was a welcome diversion for it gave me time to get to know my new mates, especially the NCOs and officers.

We were held for the next two weeks, bivouacked on the embankment of what had once been a railway line. The village itself was a tangle of broken buildings, crumpled masonry and rubble, now inhabited only by rats. These grew fat on the stinking bloated corpses, both military and civilian, still entombed in the cellars of the collapsed houses. In the heat of the day the smell was appalling but like everything else in this war, we soon became accustomed to it. Occasionally French civilians could be seen wandering aimlessly in the ruins. Whether they were looking for lost possessions or missing relatives I do not know but they made no effort while I was there to either recover or bury their dead.

The road to the front was busy day and night with traffic travelling in both directions. On most nights convoys of motor transport would attempt the tortuous journey carrying bombs, artillery shells and rifle rounds by the thousand to replenish stocks at the forward positions. There would be horse drawn supply limbers loaded with food, rum and water, bales of empty sandbags and of course the mail, that tenuous link between the fighting men and their families. In the other direction came men going on relief after days on the firing line who passed through our camp in the moonlight, white faced, unshaven, tired. They seldom spoke, only to answer in monosyllables any questions asked specifically about conditions at the front. They would appear like a column of ghosts out of the gloom and disappeared just as quickly when night with its dark blanket, swallowed them up. Sometimes there were casualties being escorted back to the clearing stations. Worst of these were those who had been gassed. I saw lines of coughing, vomiting and blinded men; each one guided by the man in front, their eyes covered with bandages, their skin, where it had been exposed to the mustard gas, hanging off in shreds.

During the hours of darkness it had become the custom for the enemy to shell the road, firing blind in the hope of catching anything on the move and occasionally rounds landed too close for comfort, forcing us to abandon our tents for the odorous but safer ruins of the village.

As a company held in reserve we were pressed into service as stretcher bearers or assisting with the ferrying of supplies up to the support trenches. From there they would be manhandled by working parties through the dark maze of muddy trenches leading to the front line. On some nights, if there had been a particularly severe bombardment the previous day, we would go up to the front itself carrying corrugated iron, sandbags and all the other paraphernalia required to repair the damage. This was the first visit to the forward trenches for many of the section, but to me with my previous experience it came as less of a shock to see the crude conditions in which our troops were fighting.

On the 22nd August we relieved the 24th Division and took up positions in ZZ trench leading to the village of Guillemont. This was the first time I had been in the line on what was considered to be active service. Before leaving the support trenches we were required to complete a field post card to our next of kin, erasing everything but the message, "I am quite well", before signing it. With the chances considered slim of surviving for more than a few weeks in all but the quietest of front lines, it was hard to understand what this achieved. We put the postcards in our packs which were left with the quartermaster in the reserve trenches to be picked up when and if we returned. Such was the carnage at that time that platoons of men were employed solely with the task of sorting the packs of the dead and wounded for personal effects which could be sent back to their families. Presumably the field postcard with its message, "I am quite well", was not included!

After only two days in the line we were the target of a heavy bombardment from enemy trench mortars and howitzers. Tons of steel and high explosive rained down on our forward positions and once again I crouched for cover in the inadequate trenches, deafened and dazed by the detonations. Such was the ferocity of the attack that the very air we breathed seemed to vibrate with shock waves and black clouds of dust danced in the smoke, lit scarlet by the fires which raged up and down the line. After about twenty minutes the shelling stopped and those who were still able stood too anticipating the attack which was bound to follow. We hadn't long to wait. Out of the fog, grey coated figures could be seen, running straight at our positions cheering as they came. Unlike our attacking troops, these carried their rifles slung across their backs leaving their hands free to throw the wooden handled mills bombs and grenades which they carried. Although the fog masked the movements and intentions of the charging storm troopers, it also blinded their machine gunners providing them with covering fire so unable to see our lines they were unable to provide the attackers with any support, leaving them practically at our mercy. Now it was our turn to play the butchers role. I cocked the cranking handle on the Vickers, aimed into the advancing figures and pulled the trigger. Prone on my right my number two was screaming encouragement and feeding belt after belt into the hammering gun. Firing over an open sight, for the attackers were now less than a hundred yards away, I saw men going down by the dozen, flung backwards by the unseen force hitting them. To my left and right riflemen were selecting their targets with equal success and farther down the trench another machine gun team were wreaking their own kind of havoc with a smoking Lewis gun. Even for men especially selected and trained as storm troopers this concentration of fire was too much to take. In a matter of minutes, though at the time it seemed like hours, first the attack hesitated and then broke down. Those Germans still able to stand, turned and fled back the way they had come, quickly swallowed up in the smoke and mist from the earlier barrage. All up and down our lines men were cheering, slapping each other on the back, boasting of the part they had played in repelling the attack. For our part we had received only a few casualties, none of them fatal, for only a few of the attackers had managed to get close enough to reach us with their bombs. For a while, intoxicated by the adrenalin created by success we failed to noticed the screams and groans from the wounded and dying men lying in front of us. Perhaps it was better that we didn't understand their pleas for help as their lives slowly ebbed away out there in the mud. Some of the less seriously wounded tried to drag themselves back to their lines, only to be shot the minute they broke cover. Others crawled towards us, hands held high in surrender, but attitudes had changed since that first hellish day on the Somme and hearts had hardened so that many of them suffered the same fate in this new war were no quarter was asked or given. On that warm summer's day in France, this was the first time that I realised that all the ideals of British honour and decency which I had been taught and expected to live by, had been lost forever. Had he been there, I wonder what my old headmaster, that staunch defender of propriety and good sportsmanship, would have made of it!

It seemed as if even in war everything settled into a set routine. Time spent in the line, rest, reserve, support, then back in the line again, but now there was a greater urgency about everything we did. Aided by the warm sunny weather we were enjoying, the conditions in the reserve and support trenches were not too bad so that it became a pleasant diversion from the constant fear and hardships of the front line and we made the most of it. A roster would be agreed in each platoon so that each of us took turns to cook breakfast over the little fires fuelled by charcoal brought up from the rear, which we lit in the bottom of the trenches. It was pleasant sitting around the fire using improvised ammunition boxes for seats, the sweet smell of frying bacon stirring different memories in all of us. Almost inevitably somebody would produce photographs of his wife or family and soon the conversation would turn to that one subject never far from our thoughts, home. Before long we all knew each other's business as though we had been acquainted all our lives, so that on mail calls we eagerly awaited news of each other's family almost as much as our own. Enquiries would be made almost before the recipient had finished reading his letter, even though the news was often several weeks old.

"How's your Elsy's leg then Fred, did she go and see the quack like I said? My Murial had the same problem and it damn near crippled her. Hope she took my advice, didn't sound too good to me", this from a man who had never met Elsie in his life but had formed an affinity with her solely through seeing her photograph and long hours spent talking to her husband!

Slowly the Germans were falling back under the pressure of the summer offensive, still going ahead despite the setbacks of the first few days. Gains were measured in feet rather than miles and each foot gained was paid for with the lives of many men. Soon after I arrived in the trenches I learned that less than a mile and supporting our left flank, the 14th Division, including sections of the fifth KSLI, had been given the task of clearing the infamous Delville Wood, still partly held by the Germans. This of course had once been Jack's regiment and now my brother Tom was serving in it. Tom had been here almost from the start, part of the original Expeditionary Force, and so far had managed to come through unscathed. Unfortunately for Tom his good luck was about to run out. This was the first time our paths had crossed since I had enlisted and I hoped that there might be a chance for us to meet. Regrettably, before I could manage a visit, he was caught in the open in one of the frequent gas attacks now used by both sides and badly gassed. Hovering on the brink of death for many months, he was eventually evacuated back to England, never to recover completely from his injuries.

On 3rd September, we supported 59th Brigade in an attack on the small town of Guillemont, with the attack being preceded by a barrage from some of our bigger guns and field artillery enabling some of us to creep forward under the fall of shot to be in a position to surprise the German defenders when it lifted. Zero hour was at noon and it was strange in the silence just after the battery had lifted to hear a clock striking the hour from somewhere in what appeared to be the ruined town.

As soon as the whistle blew giving us the signal to charge, I scrambled to my feet and started to run forward, clutching the heavy machine gun tripod in both hands, but had only taken a few paces when a mortar bomb exploded directly in front of me, the blast lifting me off my feet and flinging me to the ground. One minute I was on my feet and running, the next I was somersaulting through the air, landing with a bone shattering crunch in a roadside ditch. Totally disorientated and blinded by the dirt that caked my face, it took me a few minutes to recover my senses and when I did my immediate reaction was to feel gingerly about my body for signs of injury. Incredibly, apart from being half blind and totally deaf from the explosion, my only injury seemed to be a jagged gash in my right thigh from which blood was already oozing. Once I had regained my bearings it became imperative that I find the tripod which I'd been carrying, without which it would be impossible to fire the gun. Also my steel helmet which must have been blown off by the explosion was missing. I franticly searched the immediate area, crawling around on my hands and knees, leaving a trail of blood as I went. It was with some relief that I discovered the tripod and my helmet, battered but intact, lying half buried in a nearby shell hole.

Farther down the ditch I could see others who had been caught in the blast, some already picking themselves up, others too badly wounded to take any further part. Nearest to me, lying in a crumpled blood soaked heap was my number two who had been slightly in front and to the right of me as we ran and had caught the full force of the explosion full in the face. The ground around his head was stained grey with shattered skull and brains and it was obvious that he was close to death so that all I could do was cradle him in my arms until he died.

Other members of my team had fared better and like myself had only suffered superficial wounds. Slowly we pulled ourselves together, first bandaging each other's wounds with field dressings, then retrieving the gun and tripod from where they had fallen.

While we were sorting ourselves out the attack had pushed forward at such a pace that on entering the ruined outskirts of the town we could see no sign of either friend or foe but sounds of rifle and machine gun fire coming from around a bend in what had once been a tree-lined avenue, plus the bodies of several dead Germans lying in the grotesque positions in which they had fallen, indicated the direction we should take. Using the ruined houses and shops as cover, working our way cautiously forward, we eventually came across a party of Kings Royal Rifles, pinned down in what had once been a grand hotel. Now its windows and roof had gone and the marble steps and studded oak door which had once graced its entrance lay in ruins across the street. Directed by a sergeant, we set up the gun in one of the upstairs windows giving us a commanding view of the street and the cobbled square it ran into. Enemy snipers were holed up in the shops surrounding the square and for the next few hours held up our advance by shooting at anything that moved. We replied with the Lewis gun, letting go bursts every time a puff of smoke appeared from a window. Although it seemed unlikely that we hit anybody, after a while it had the desired affect and the enemy withdrew, melting away into the maze of streets and alleys leading from the town. By mid-afternoon, the last few pockets of resistance had been mopped up and the town was secured.

Later that day the enemy mounted a counter attack in strength but by then we were dug in in good firing positions and had been joined by the rest of the section so they were easily repelled by our massed Lewis-gunfire.

The next day, after some early morning skirmishes on the Ginchy road, we were relieved by 49th Brigade and withdrew back once again to La Boiselle and some much needed rest.

Chapter 8

The Clearing Station at Corbie - September 1916

Clearing Station

Straw rustling everywhere,
The candle stumps stand there, staring solemnly.
Across the nocturnal vault of the church,
Moans go drifting and choking words.
There's a stench of blood, piss, shit and sweat,
Bandages ooze away beneath torn uniforms,
Clammy, trembling hands and wasted faces.
Bodies stay propped up as their dying heads slump down

Bridgwater

Sometime in the night I awoke in agony from the wound in my leg. Assuming that it was just a delayed reaction from the mortar blast, I was determined to get through until the morning but by then the pain had become almost unbearable. Also, despite the chill of the morning air, I found that both my body and my bedding were soaked with sweat. I also had a throbbing headache. My groans of pain awakened the chap sleeping next to me.

"What's up mate," he enquired crawling over to where I lay, "By the horrible noises you're making it sounds as if you haven't got long for this world?"

Almost as soon as I'd returned from the line I'd reported sick, when one of the medics had bathed and dressed my wound with fresh bandages, assuring me that it was only a flesh wound and that everything seemed to be OK. Now, on inspection, it was clear that this was anything but the case.

During the night the whole of my leg had turned a dark blue colour and become swollen to such a size that when I tried to get my trousers on I found this was not possible without splitting the leg. To add to my problems I saw that, yellow, stinking puss, was oozing from beneath the blood stained bandages.

"Jesus Christ ", exclaimed my new friend, sniffing the air with the air of a man who had seen it all before while poking at my leg with a not too clean finger, "Looks and smells as if you got gas gang there old lad. You've got a Blighty one there if ever I saw one, that's if you don't keel over first!"

Gangrene! Just the mention of the word sent a shudder of apprehension down my spine, making any thought of my wound being severe enough to get me back to England the last thing on my mind. Everybody knew that gangrene was a serious condition, nearly always fatal, and a constant threat when wounds became infected by the filthy conditions in which we lived.

Sadly shaking his head, my mate hurried away to find a medic, leaving me praying to God his diagnosis was not correct![1]

When the medic arrived, having taken one look at my wound and not able or willing to confirm or deny my mates diagnosis of gangrene, I was immediately dispatched by field ambulance for treatment at the forward clearing station at Corbie.

Hours later, after a nightmare journey where every bump and hollow in a road pockmarked with shell craters sent waves of agony coursing through my body, I was relieved to arrive at Corbie which had once been a picturesque French village, nestling in the valley formed where the river Somme and its smaller tributary the Ancre met. Now it was in ruins. For hundreds of years the village had been overlooked and guarded by a large château and it was here in its grounds and outbuildings that the clearing station had been set up. With the makeshift, overcrowded conditions, it was obvious that the medical staff stood no chance at all of coping with the huge influx of casualties that arrived here almost daily. With all the rooms in the main building full to overflowing with the more seriously wounded, additional shelters had been constructed by hanging sheets of canvas over lines suspended on posts driven into what had once been immaculate lawns and gardens . Wounded men lay everywhere, some in makeshift beds and others still on the stretchers they had arrived on, while some of the less severely wounded could not be accommodated at all. These slept where they could find cover, using their ground sheets as beds and their greatcoats as blankets.

I would soon learn that due to the poor sanitary conditions, gangrene and dysentery were endemic here so that as many men seemed to die from these as from their original wounds.

I was found a billet in what appeared to be a partly ruined coach house where, for the next day and night I lay in agony; my pain only briefly relieved by an occasional but very welcome injection of morphine administered with a blunt needle by an extremely harassed and overworked medic.

It was therefore with mixed feelings of both relief and fear that on the second day I was taken into the makeshift operating theatre to have my wound treated. This had been set up in a big marquee in the centre of which an ordinary trestle table being used to carry out life saving operations, many of which were amputations of limbs shattered beyond repair. I knew that with the primitive conditions in which they were carried out that many men died from shock while still anaesthetised or from infection of their wounds afterwards, so when my turn came it was with some apprehension that I clambered gingerly up onto the table. Carried out without anaesthetic, the pain was almost unbearable but it was to my great relief, perhaps tinged with some disappointment that I learned that I had suffered no lasting damage and, given time, would make a full recovery. Based on my mate from the line's assessment, I had secretly hoped that this might be a Blighty wound, but no such luck! The actual cause of my injury was even more surprising, for instead of finding shrapnel from the mortar round embedded in my leg, what the surgeon dugout was a four inch piece of barbed wire, complete with razor spikes, which must have been lying on the ground and then blown into my leg when the mortar exploded so close to me. This was not as unusual as it might seem. Later in the war, as the Germans grew short of steel they resorted to using all sorts of scrap metal to pack into shrapnel shells and I heard of one case where the main cog of a grandfather clock was dugout of a relieved but indignant patient's bottom! Definitely a case of "having the time on him"!

The conditions in the clearing station were appalling and although the doctors and nurses did their best, every day men died and were taken for burial in the fields beyond the château. Already hundreds of graves marked with basic wooden crosses bearing the occupants name and official number, ran in rows beneath the branches of the huge stands of beech trees which had somehow avoided destruction. Like many other burial grounds originally attached to clearing stations, this would one day become the site of one of the beautifully kept military cemeteries sited all across France today.

A few days later and by now well on the way to recovery, I was wandering through the tented wards looking for anyone I might know, when I heard a voice call out "Walter", and looking round, was at first unable to identify where it came from.

"Walter, over here, don't you recognise me?"

To my horror I realised that the voice came from a skeletal figure lying on a makeshift bed I now recognised as a man I had met during initial training. Such was his condition that I'm sure I wouldn't have recognised him if he hadn't identified himself. Suffering from dysentery, it was obvious that he was in a very poor condition. We sat and talked, reminiscing about the good times we both remembered, of mutual friends and the things we had got up to during our stay in Shrewsbury. He knew that he would never be going home and I was glad to be there to comfort him in his final hours. By a strange coincidence, the same ward contained another Shropshire man who was also severely wounded and throughout the afternoon the three of us whiled away the time in idle talk. When it was time for me to go, I promised that I would be back the next day to visit them but this was not possible and it was another three days before I was able to return. When I did, I found new patients lying where my two friends had lain, while under the trees two fresh graves, marked with simple wooden crosses, joined the swelling ranks of the fallen dead.

I stayed at Corbie for two weeks and it was almost inevitable that like almost everybody else I too suffered from dysentery but fortunately was strong enough to fight the infection that was killing others all around me. By now the disease had taken on such epidemic proportions that a decision was made to evacuate all those strong enough to travel to a hospital in Rouen. We went by train, accompanied by a posse of pretty nurses who made a great fuss of us, keeping us comfortable on the journey. It was the first real contact I had had with British girls since leaving England so I made the best of the experience. They all looked so attractive in their starched white uniforms that we fell in love with them to the last man, even though there was no chance of romance. For their part, although each kept their distance I'm sure they secretly welcomed our attention and particularly the chance of being away, even for a short while, from the horrors of Corbie .

When the train pulled into the station at Rouen they handed us over to fresh nurses before waving us goodbye and returning to the death and infection that was Corbie, each one knowing that in going back they were possibly signing their own death warrant. In spite of this, at no time did they allow those fears to interfere with their resolve to make us comfortable

The hospital at Rouen was a more suitable building with well equipped wards, excellent care and most important, plenty of good food, so that I enjoyed every day of the two weeks I spent there. With dedicated nursing both my wound and the dysentery improved a little each day and soon I was able to walk in the grounds without the help of crutches.

Much to my regret the day came when the doctor decided that I was fit enough to return to duty and to my surprise I received orders to report back to the machine gun school at the Bullring. Before the disaster on the Somme this had been standard practice, with men who had been wounded undergoing a toughening up process before returning to the front.

By now it was November and the weather had turned very cold with most days seeing flurries of snow and night temperatures dropping well below freezing. Once again Étaples was packed with new recruits fresh out from England, supplemented by wounded men like myself who were there for retraining, so that now tents which previously had accommodated sixteen men were expected to sleep as many as twenty-six.

It was obvious that conditions were just as harsh with the gun-carriage wheels occupied on most days by victims of field punishment and about once a week it had become customary to parade the whole camp so that the verdicts of courts marshal could be read out to the men. This was done ostensibly to comply with kings regulations but was also to ensure that none of us would be under any illusions as to our fate, should we not come up to scratch when the moment came. Occasionally there would be a case where the sentence of the courts martial had been death by firing squad when on some occasions the citation would end "and the sentence of the court was duly carried out."

On one occasion we were fell in on parade so that a letter handed in by the censor could be read out by the commanding officer, the contents of which were considered to be defeatist. It was just an ordinary letter, written home by a young man in which he mentioned the futility of war, questioning the reason for his being here. This however was considered to be defeatist by the officer censoring the letter who had the man arrested. The CO reminded us that by writing this the man was undermining the resolve to support the war by the people at home and should be subject to court marshal. However, because of the age of the writer, it was decided that he would be paraded before the company while his letter was read out before receiving five hours field punishment on the wheel. The young man, flanked by two military policemen and near to tears, was paraded up and down the ranks before being taken away to begin his punishment. Sadly, on completing his punishment he went to his billet, loaded his rifle and shot himself. Another young life needlessly taken, not by the enemy, but by the unsympathetic hand of the bureaucracy that commanded him.

One day I was told to report to the orderly room where myself and a corporal were detailed to escort a man with what had been established to be self inflicted wounds, up to the village of Beaulincourt where his regiment where holding in reserve. Here the intention was that he and several others facing various charges would be tried by courts martial.

The days when everyone was a volunteer had long gone. Earlier in the year Parliament had amended the Bill governing conscription and now married men as well as others who had previously been excused due to their occupation were required to enlist. This seemed only fair to myself and many others who had volunteered and were already in the thick of things, for surely it couldn't be fair that regular soldiers, some of them middle-aged, as well as wounded men, were being returned to the front line time and time again while strong young men stayed safely at home simply because they were married, for it was a well known fact that many had undergone hastily arranged marriages, just to avoid the draft. Because of this new situation, the ranks were now filled with men who had been conscripted into the services, most if not all of them much against their will, so that much of the old esprit de corps of the earlier years was no longer in evidence. As a consequence, the resolve and team spirit displayed by men who had been volunteers was now missing, reflected in the increasing numbers of men who were either deserting or simply laying down their arms and refusing to fight. A serious situation in any military force and one that the top brass wanted stamping out immediately if any level of moral was to be maintained. A similar sense of this kind of disillusionment with the cause would later lead to a mass mutiny by the French army.

For our part, the authorities went about tackling the problem with a will, staging show trials and dishing out punishments whenever and wherever a battalion was in reserve. The trials were by courts martial and the verdict in almost every case was guilty. The sentence was carried out swiftly and on the spot, witnessed by as many members as possible from the victim's regiment for it was felt that this would leave none of us in any doubt as to the consequences of our actions should we consider insubordination in any way.

Although a self inflicted wound was not considered to be a capital offence, it was taken very seriously by the authorities with the perpetrator being treated both as a coward and a criminal. Even in hospital anyone desperate enough to take such drastic action, a self administered shot through a hand or foot was the favoured practice, could be expected to be ostracised by the other patients and given only basic attention by the medical staff. Some field hospitals even had special wards set aside for men who were suspected of causing their own wounds.

In spite of this our prisoner was cheerful enough as we boarded the train south. As he pointed out, "Even five years hard labour but being alive was better than one more day in the trenches and being dead" and I suppose in a way he had a point, for in reality he was perhaps far braver than many of us who felt the same but did not have the guts to do it!

On reaching Beaulincourt we reported to the local police station which had been taken over by the military police. In spite of the verbal abuse and rough handling received by the prisoner when we handed him over, he went cheerfully into his cell, giving us a broad wink and a thumbs up as the door was slammed behind him.

By now the short autumn day was coming to an end and there was no possibility of our making the return trip to Étaples before morning so we were directed to the main camp where we would stay the night. Here, after a meal reluctantly put together by a sleepy cook, we drew blankets and mattresses and settled down for the night in the cellar of one of the ruined houses. Once again it was almost too cold to sleep, even though we did not remove our service greatcoats and goatskin jerkins.

Although our orders had been to return to Étaples as soon as we had delivered our prisoner, the authorities at Beaulincourt had other ideas. After breakfast the next morning I heard to my horror that today a man would be executed by firing squad and all those present would be paraded to witness the sentence being carried out. Although we tried desperately to explain to the provost sergeant that we were only visitors and our orders said we should return immediately to Étaples, he would have none of it. His orders were that all those in camp that day should be called on to witness the execution and as far as he was concerned we were no different from the rest.

So just before eight o'clock we paraded with the rest of the regiment in a field next to the camp were each section was formed into a hollow square, the post to which the man would be strapped occupying the empty side. On the stroke of eight, even before the pale light of a cold, new day was dawning, the condemned man, a lad only in his twenties flanked by two military policemen was marched up followed by a party of mounted officers and another two MPs carrying a stretcher. By now it was snowing gently. Surprisingly, the condemned man showed no signs of fear, fixing the officer who read out the charge, that he had deserted in the face of the enemy, with a look of cold contempt. The preliminaries over, after first being paraded before his regiment, he stood calmly while he was strapped to the post by his chest and legs and a blindfold placed over his eyes. Like many others, I found it impossible to watch, looking steadfastly at the ground even though we were stood to attention. A Captain, wearing the insignia of a doctor, dismounted and using a stethoscope located the exact position of the man's heart which he marked by pinning a piece of white cloth to his tunic. It seemed obscene that at this very moment in field hospitals all over France, overworked medical staff were fighting a losing battle with the growing numbers of casualties, while here a doctor could be found who was willing to take part in this ghastly charade. Next it was the duty of the senior officer to carry out the execution but now he seemed reluctant to proceed for perhaps, like us, he was hoping and expecting a last minute reprieve from the Colonel of the regiment, the only one who had the authority to offer clemency to the condemned man. Surely the point had been made, time to release the prisoner and return to the job we were all here to do which was to defeat the Huns. But no messenger hurried forward carrying the news and it eventually became plain that there was going to be no last minute reprieve.

After what seemed like an age he could wait no longer. Looking pale and shaken, in a trembling voice he gave the order.

"Carry on Sergeant Major."

The sergeant major raised his arm.

"Firing squad, aim."

Eight rifles came up in unison, each marksman taking careful aim at the white cloth. There was no need for care, from this range they couldn't miss, wouldn't miss, even though their nervous tension showed in the trembling of their rifle barrels.

"Fire",

The crash of the rifles, firing in unison, rang out as a single shot echoing back and force around the surrounding hills. At the post the man gasped and his head flew back as the bullets hit home. For a few seconds his body jerked spasmodically, before slumping forward, saved from falling by the restraining straps at his chest and legs. By the time the last echoes from the shots had faded, he was dead.

Now only the nervous fretting of the horses and the creaking of their harness broke the silence as the doctor went forward to ensure that the man was dead. On his nod the party of officers wheeled their horses and rode away, their part in the gruesome business over.

All that was left was the steadying voice and quiet authority of the sergeant major to restore some normality to this sordid event.

"Parade will march off in single file, front rank leading. From the right, by the right, quick march".

One by one the single files of men marched away, past the limp body of the executed man, still hanging at the post. By the time I passed by, the military policemen had released his body and were lowering it gently onto the stretcher. The earlier wintry flurries had thickened and now it was snowing hard, covering the head and face of the man with a white veil. Where the bullets had hit, the snow on his chest was stained scarlet like gaudy medal ribbons.[2]

We marched the short distance back to camp in silence, even our marching feet muffled by the snow on the frozen ground. Only when they had fallen out were men able to express the anger and outrage at what they had been forced to witness. Some swore and cursed at the injustice of it all. Others relieved their anger and frustration by striking out at inanimate objects, wishing it could be their senior officers they were hitting. Others simply knelt in prayer. What was universally agreed, was that if this was supposed to set an example giving us greater resolve to carry out our duty, then it had been a failure. At that moment many of us saw the enemy not as the Germans but as our own officers to the point where even with the passing of time we would never have the same respect for them again. For my part I would retain this feeling of disrespect for the rest of my life.

It was with some relief that the corporal and I climbed aboard the train that afternoon for the journey back to Étaples. I don't think we noticed that the carriage we travelled in was a draughty cattle wagon and the day was once more freezing. Suddenly it didn't seem such a bad place to be after all.

Chapter 9

Sent Home to England - November 1916

Futility

Move him into the sun –
Gently its touch awoke him once,
At home, whispering of fields unsown,
Always it woke him, even in France,
Until this morning and this snow.
If anything will rouse him now,
The kind old sun will know.

Owen

Although I had no idea what had been taking place at home, while I had been serving in France wheels had been turning which would eventually bring me back to England. After my brother Jack was killed, my Mother had sought and received comfort from the church, particularly from the curate of Weston-Under-Redcastle, a pretty little village of half timbered houses a few miles from where we lived. His name was the Rev William Walkerdine and although our house at Daneswell only bordered on his parish, he took it upon himself to visit my parents and express his condolences at the death of their son. His intervention and compassion would probably save my life.

He began calling regularly after this visit; striking up a friendship with my family even though they still worshiped every Sunday at their local chapel in Paradise. Mother, who would never recover from Jack's death, now carried the added burden of my brother Tom, suffering from the effects of gas and still in a critical condition hospitalised somewhere in France. At that time the prognosis was not good and our family has accepted that even if he lived it was unlikely that he would ever recover from the damage the gas had done to his lungs.

During a conversation with Mr Walkerdine in which she poured out all her fears and anxieties for the safety of her boys, Mother let slip the fact that I had enlisted while under age, expressing the guilt she now felt for not preventing me from doing so. For his part he was determined that something must be done about it and without telling Mother, and thus avoid raising false hopes, had resolved to investigate how he might go about remedying the situation. Having initially sought guidance from the higher authority of the Church, he then petitioned Sir Beville Stanier, our local MP, who was already aware of the scandal brewing in Parliament regarding the recruiting of underage volunteers. Encouraged by the support he also received from the local Squire and his wife, Sir Beville put in motion a train of events that would eventually lead to me and many others like me, being brought back home.[1]

Winter had arrived early in France and conditions at Étaples were worsening. Here the intense cold and crowded tents made sleeping almost impossible for those undergoing training, while the instructors, billeted in the few permanent huts, enjoyed all the comforts of home. Soon the repetitive and often painful training regime become a trial of mind over matter with each day taken as it came, so it was with some relief that I heard that I was to report to the orderly room without delay. With a bit of luck it would be another trip as an escort or even better, as a messenger into town. If that was the case it might offer an opportunity to relax for a while and enjoy a few drinks in one of the many bars which, although open, were still out of bounds to all but the instructors. Anything that would break the monotony and hardship of training would be a welcome change. Having reported, somewhat to my alarm and without any explanation or reason for my summons, I was marched in by the orderly sergeant to see no less a worthy than the commanding officer. Sitting in silence for a few moments while he looked me up and down, he finally spoke.

"I believe you've been telling us lies Williams?."

This was a new one on me. We all told a few porkys from time to time but nothing important enough to interest such an exalted presence as the camp CO. Whatever could he mean?

Seeing my bewildered expression and perhaps even enjoying the moment, he continued,

"It's my understanding that you've been lying about your age and I'm now told that you are not as old as you told the recruiting sergeant you were, before you swore the loyal oath. Is that true?"

So that was it, they had finally found me out. I'd never been quite sure how I stood on this, whether what I'd done was a punishable offence, as most things seemed to be in the army.[2] Pausing to think for a moment I decided that now the game was up I might as well come clean and take whatever punishment he awarded me.

"Yes sir, I'm afraid that's true. You see, I already had two brothers serving in France and wanted desperately to do my bit. I admit that what I did appears to be a bit stupid now, but I suppose it seemed to be a good idea at the time!"

I thought of adding that, knowing what I know now, if I was given the chance to do it over again he wouldn't see me for dust!

His stern face creased into a smile.

"Well Williams, what you did might sound very commendable but was also very silly. I've been looking at your service records and believe that you have the makings of a good soldier. It is therefore fortunate that in a couple of years time if the need arises there will be a place in this conflict for someone like yourself who is prepared to do his bit. In the meantime, what seems to me to be a good idea is that we get you back to England as quickly as we can."

I couldn't believe what I was hearing. Could it really be true that I was going home? In a daze I received my orders from the orderly sergeant and rushed back to the lines to pack my kit. Many of my friends were still at the Bullring so there was no time or chance to say goodbye to anyone other than those left behind on fatigues. These were amazed to hear what I had to tell them, wishing me all the best after telling me what a lucky so and so I was. By mid-afternoon I was once again aboard the now familiar up train to Calais and on my way to Blighty.

As soon as it docked at Dover the ship was met by an army of volunteers from the Red Cross and women's organisations determined to give us a hero's welcome, showered each of us who disembarked with gifts. Scores of ambulances, each with a team of nurses in attendance, were waiting to whisk away the wounded while the rest of us were treated to as much free tea and "wads" as we could manage. Although it was wonderful to be back and seeing the smiling caring faces all around me, one of the greatest pleasures was to hear English spoken again instead of the French or at best the halting English that I'd become accustomed to.

Once my papers were cleared I boarded the troop train up to London, staying that night in transit accommodation in Woolwich Barracks. My orders were to eventually report to the machine gun school at Grantham but first I had been granted five days leave so couldn't wait to get started for home. Up with the larks the next morning, I got a lift to Euston station from a cabby who refused to accept any form of payment and caught the first train going north. The journey seemed to take an age as the train wound its way north, stopping at almost every station to discharge and take on its passengers. Beyond Birmingham I looked expectantly ahead until I saw the Wrekin, filling the horizon with its familiar bulk and only then did I accept that I was home. On leaving the train at Wellington it seemed as if nothing had changed since the day, not so long ago, when I had changed here for Shrewsbury on my way to enlist. The platforms were still crowded with ordinary passengers going about their normal lives but as before there were little groups of men, many of whom had been called up under the new conscription bill. Some were saying tearful goodbyes to their families while others were accompanied by women who might have been their wives. The time had gone forever when all enlisting men would be both single and volunteers. There were other men in uniform like myself, burdened with kit, either going on or returning from leave. These often stood apart from the crowd, perhaps feeling uncomfortable at this public show of emotion. I found myself remembering the day when I had joined and first met and then made friends with those honest, eager young men, many of whom would not be coming back. I stood for a moment looking down the line, imagining once more the Birmingham train steaming in with all those laughing, smiling faces at the windows. I couldn't bear to think that some of them must be dead or so badly maimed that they would never be the same again.

"Give her a kiss for me old son. If you can't take a joke you shouldn't have joined", the ghostly carefree voices came echoing back.

Some joke! Old Brum had been right, we shouldn't have joined. One thing was for sure, if he hadn't he might have been alive today instead of another rotting corpse buried in some forgotten foreign field!

I hitched a lift to Peplow before walking the rest of the way into Hodnet. Life seemed to have stood still; the usual collection of housewives and old men standing gossiping at their gates or talking with neighbours across the street. When they saw me coming many of them stopped what they were doing and ran to shake my hand, asking a hundred questions all at once. The news that I might be coming home had circulated around the village and most wanted to know what the army intended to do with me now that I was back. Some asked about Tom, had I managed to visit him in France, while others, especially the men, wanted graphic details of the war or news of friends and relations I might have seen on my travels. I answered as best I could, not wishing to be rude but anxious to be on my way. Saying my goodbyes and thanks for their good wishes, I climbed the hill leading from the village, and hurried through Paradise, seeing for the first time for more than a year it's neglected, silted up pools and overgrown hedges. Just as I was about to start up the hill for Kenstone, a voice hailed me from behind.

"Walter, Walter, wait for me."

Turning round I saw the familiar figure of my Father running up the road towards me. I ran to meet him and to my surprise he threw his arms around me in an embrace that nearly took my breath away, slapping me on the back until my head spun. He breathlessly explained that he had just finished work at the Hall when a lad from the village had brought word that I was back and on the road for home. Leaving everything, he ran to catch me up, and laughing and talking ten to the dozen, we walked arm in arm for the rest of the way, joined as we went, by a small gaggle of neighbours and their children, anxious not to miss my mother's face when she heard that I was home. Even before we reached the gate leading off the road, some had run ahead, eager to be the first to tell her the news.

"Better get the cider out Mrs Williams", they cried, "Your Walter's home and half the parish is with him wanting to drink his health".

Dropping what she was doing she ran outside and threw herself into my arms. There we stood, the three of us, Mother, Father and myself, laughing and hugging, while all around us our good friends and neighbours nodded and whooped their approval.

Once the initial excitement was over it was time to get down to some serious celebrating. Father went to the pantry and brought out several stone flagons of cider he had been maturing for Christmas. By the time the girls started coming in from work, adding their shrieks to the babble of excited conversation, a small crowd had gathered. Many hurried home and brought back more to eat and drink so that soon an impromptu party was in full swing. Mother left the drinking to the men and busying herself in the kitchen helped by several of her neighbours, soon produced an array of hot scones, pies and other good things to eat to which everybody tucked in with a will.

The celebrations went on late into the night and never could the greatest of heroes have been given such a welcome home. Finally, when the last drop of damson wine had been shaken from the bottle and the final flagon of golden cider passed around the happy crowd, we said our drunken, merry goodnights. Standing with my family in the little porch at Crin Cottage, lit by the flickering light of a stable lamp held high by my Father, I watched our neighbours weave their uncertain ways home, listening to their happy laughter fading into the night. My head was spinning from too much drink and the intoxication of my welcome but I would sleep that night in my own bed and for the first time in many months, know that I was safe.

Chapter 10

Home on Leave - November 1916

My Autumn Walk

On woodlands ruddy with Autumn,
The amber sunshine lies
I look on the beauty around me,
And tears come into my eyes.
For the wind that sweeps from the meadows,
Blow out of the far Southwest,
Where our gallant lads are fighting,
And the gallant dead are at rest.

Bryant

Home! A few days ago just the thought of it would have been enough, but in reality, after the excitement and trauma of the last few months, I found it hard to settle. During my stay in France there had been many long sleepless nights filled with fear and discomfort when I longed for my cosy bed with its feather mattress, tucked safely beneath the sloping roof of my bedroom. Now, after so many nights spent in the open, I found it so claustrophobic that sleep proved almost impossible, making me long for the canvas canopy of a sun bleached tent or a starry sky above my head, the snores and groans of my companions, not the hooting of the resident owls, providing the comfort I longed for in the night. To make matters worse, Mother and the girls fussed and flapped over me for every minute of the day, never allowing me to lift a finger to help, even though in the short time I had been away I had become independent and used to fending for myself. There were even times when I found their constant attention irritating, so after only a couple of days I walked into Hodnet, only to find that most of my friends had gone, leaving only the old men and their women folk to take their place. In the Bear Hotel I became the centre of attraction. It was now the regulars making a fuss of me, some offering me drinks in return for graphic descriptions of conditions at the front, when all I wanted to do was forget for a while what I had seen. In the end I stayed at home or walked the woods with Floss, the only one who seemed happy to share my company while demanding nothing in return.

On the Sunday, after he had taken the morning service and knowing that I was home so anxious to make my acquaintance, Mr Walkerdine rode over from Weston. I was still finding it hard to settle and to while away the time had set myself the task of clearing the old dead flowers and plants from Mother's garden before preparing the beds for next year's crops. I was busy there when she came rushing from the house to tell me the curate was at the gate.

"Quickly Walter", she cried, "leave what you are doing and come inside; it would not be seemly for the parson to see you working on a Sunday!"

I couldn't believe my ears. Sunday was no different from any other day in the trenches and at this very moment men might be being bombed, gassed, shot or maimed or, if they were really unlucky, all four, without even knowing it was the Sabbath. Could it really be true that those secure at home were still afraid to be seen working on a Sunday in case it angered the clergy! Not wishing to offend Mother with her strong Christian beliefs and blinkered upbringing, keeping my thoughts to myself I did as she asked and went to meet the man who had been such an influence in bringing me home.

Riding towards me on a sturdy Welsh cob I saw a short, well built young man, dressed all in black with a fine moustache and mutton chop whiskers. I went to meet him, shaking his outstretched hand as he dismounted and we walked together the short distance to the house. He had an open, honest face and I found I liked him from the start. I told him of Mother's concerns about working on the Sabbath and was not surprised by his laughter.

"I've just eaten a fine lunch at Mrs Peppers which needs shaking down", he said, "Show me where you're working and we'll dig it together, row for row."

So it was, when Mother came bustling out to announce that the kettle was boiled and a pot of tea was on the table, she found the parson, his sleeves rolled up and his braces flying, half way through his row. We worked and talked, each taking our turn while the other rested, until the afternoon light faded and we could no longer see to do more. While we worked he explained that although he would like to stay longer, he had to take the evening service at Hodnet and on an impulse I decided that I would like to hear him preach. While I got changed, Mother made fresh tea and cut us each a piece of her cake, wrapping what was left with paper and string for him to take with him. Then, together we set off for Hodnet, him astride his horse while I walked beside him, talking as we went.

He was curious to hear about life in the army, asking many questions then listening intently to my replies. It soon became obvious that he was acutely embarrassed about not having already joined himself and was particularly interested in the role of the army padres at the front so I couldn't help describing, tongue in cheek, an experience I had shared with one such God Botherer, as army padres were universally known, while I was there.

I explained that I had been sitting on a board acting as a latrine cut into a sap off the main trench, when as if from nowhere a padre appeared, took down his trousers and sat down next to me. We sat there for a while, saying nothing, both deep in our own thoughts when, perhaps to break the silence, he turned to me and enquired, "Considering all that's going on, do you believe in God young man?" Wondering if this was the time or place to join in such a conversation, I was considering my reply when there was an almighty crash followed by an enormous explosion as a stray whiz-bang hit the galvanised roof right above our heads, sending clouds of smoke and red hot pieces of shrapnel flying in all directions. By some miracle neither of us was hurt but a piece of jagged metal the size of a dinner plate struck the board right between where we were sitting. This was too much for the poor old padre. Letting out a terrified yell and not even stopping to pull up his pants, he shot off down the sap like a frightened rabbit, his shirt tails and braces flying in the wind.

No sooner had I made myself decent when a second whiz-bang landed only a matter of yards from the first one making me quick to follow him to the comparative safety of a dugout in the main trench. By the time I got there he was gone, never to be seen again. For his part he would never know or I suspect care, whether or not

I believed in God. On the evidence of our lucky escape, had he stayed long enough to listen, he would have been pleased to know that on that day at least the answer would have been very much in the affirmative!

So the days passed quickly and soon it was time to leave. On the day before I was due to go, I walked over to the rectory and said goodbye to the parson, for by now we were firm friends. When the time came for me to go, things were much easier than before, with my parents safe in the knowledge that at least for the time being I would be staying in England. Added to that was the prospect of more leave to come at Christmas time.

I reported to Grantham were I stayed until after Christmas, working in the Church of England canteen serving tea to the troops! There had been a fuss in Parliament about the number of young men who had been allowed to enlist while underage, many of whom were still in France, so that the authorities were doing what they could to get them home.

In early March I was on the move again, joining a group of about sixty of these, boarding a train which would take us to Skegness and a spell in the oddly named Army Cyclists Corps. This was a Territorial regiment which had spent the war manning the East Coast Defences, patrolling the coastal roads on their bicycles watching out for enemy invasions!

When our train pulled into the station we were surprised to see a brass band and a party of civic dignitaries waiting to greet us. At a signal from the mayor, the sergeant major, a part time soldier and a local councillor, fell us in before calling us to attention.

"Recruits, 'shun", he yelled, fully aware of the importance of the occasion and the part he was playing in it. In the ranks nobody moved, remaining solidly at ease. Recruits, he must be joking! All of us, without exception, had seen action at the front and so considered ourselves very much veteran soldiers. To make matters worse, some of those amongst us were wearing the distinctive ribbons of the Military Medal and at least one the DSM. For a moment only the suppressed laughter of the band and welcoming committee broke the silence,

Realising too late his mistake but still angry at our response, the sergeant major tried again.

"Platoon, 'shun".

This time, to a man we snapped to attention, just like the old days in training camp, and on his next command, marched smartly away accompanied by a rousing military tune from a band who could hardly play for laughing.

I stayed with the Cyclists for two of the happiest months of my army career, taking my turn on the coast road or at the lookout stations along the way. Lazy days were spent lying in the heather that lined the coastal tracks, scanning the miles of open sea for any sign of invasion. Dressed up warm against the chill, I spent sweet scented hours under the stars with only the elusive, scurrying creatures of the night to keep me company. History has shown that no invasion came.

Needless to say, this state of bliss could not go on forever.

With the winter months over and the big push once more under way, back on the Western Front men were once more dying in their thousands. But this time it was not only the weapons of war that were responsible for the many casualties, but the appalling conditions in which the men were fighting. Now men and machines were bogged down in a sea of mud, so deep that many drowned merely by stepping off the wooden duckboards that took the place of roads. In a battle ground that had become a waterlogged morass, churned up by the British barrage so that even simple movement was almost impossible, conditions were worse than any soldier could ever have been expected to endure. Officially this action would be recorded by military historians as the Third Battle of Ypres. To the men who fought in it, it would take its name from a small village at the centre of the action.

The village's name was Passchendaele.

So, with still two months to go before my nineteenth birthday, still the minimum age when men were allowed to serve at the front, I was on my way back to France, this time as an infantryman with the Eighth Battalion Northumberland Fusiliers!

Chapter 11
The Royal Northumberland Fusiliers
September 1917

The General

"Good morning, good morning" the General said,
When we met him last week on our way to the line.
Now the soldiers he smiled at are most of them dead,
And we're cursing his staff as incompetent swine.
"He's a cheery old card" grunted Harry to Jack
As they slogged up to Arras with rifle and pack.
But he did for them both with his plan of attack!

Sassoon

It might seem strange that a Shropshire lad who had never in his life been farther north than Yorkshire should find himself joining a Geordie regiment. By using army logic the explanation was simple. The Royal Northumberland Fusiliers and Tyneside Scottish, for that was their official title, had entered divisions into the war right from the start. At that time every serving man of the regiment was a volunteer and a regular so it was almost inevitable that they should become part of Kitchener's original Expeditionary Force fighting the Germans. They had seen action in most of the earlier theatres of the war and in doing so had gained a reputation for being first class fighting men, always ready and willing to lead from the front. As a regiment recruited entirely from the cities and towns of the Clyde, they had a campaign history and list of battle honours second to none and it had been said that they did not care who they fought or where they fought, just that they be allowed to get on with it and finish the job. With such a reputation as tenacious fighters, it was inevitable that a succession of battle commanders had readily pitched them into the forefront of the line from Ypres south to the Somme and anywhere else where a bit of guts and raw courage might come in handy. In doing so they had suffered a great number of casualties and the loss of almost the entire male population of some northern towns. Although it was already too late, by the summer of 1916 a decision had been made in Parliament that never again would these aptly named Pals regiments be recruited from small catchment areas alone but would contain troops drawn from right across the country. By doing so this would ensure that regional losses, where the men of whole towns or villages could be wiped out in a single battle, might be avoided.

Thus it was, with the summer offensive once more under way against an enemy now in full retreat and the added demand for fresh troops at the front even greater, I found myself travelling north to meet my new comrades.

On the way I would be joined by many other comb outs, as we were collectively referred to, returned wounded, unhorsed cavalry, unsaddled cyclists like myself, men from non-combatant regiments and even Territorials, would supplement those already recruited from the northern counties.

I soon found that the Geordies were everything I had been told they would be. Solid, dependable, down to earth chaps, they could be relied upon to stick together through thick and thin, backing one another in a scrap with no questions asked or explanations given. I must confess that at first I found it difficult to understand the local dialect which, to the unaccustomed ear, seemed to consist mainly of a series of incomprehensible grunts and other odd noises.

In no time at all I was accepted into this close knit team where I found the extreme loyalty and concern they showed for each other's welfare something I'd not experienced anywhere else since joining up. Before long I would take it for granted.

For a couple of weeks I underwent a rigorous training programme with my new mates, getting shaken down prior to embarking for France.

On the day we left, marching through the city on the way to the station there were no cheering, patriotic crowds, no enthusiastic applause and good wishes from the small groups of workers and bystanders who hardly paused from their labours to watch us pass by. Even the few people who bothered to turn out to see us off were muted in their applause and there were more tears than cheers to speed us on our way. They had just cause, for here was a city that had known sorrow on a grand scale. Identified by the black ribbons and armbands that nearly every person seemed to be wearing, almost everyone had lost someone to the war. Even the train that we boarded, the midday express to London, had become known as the Train of Tears by the locals, a reference to the loved ones who had left on it, never to return.

I was glad when we pulled away from this grim city, steaming out into the sunshine and the fresh green English countryside when I could settle down for a journey which would take me to whatever fate awaited me on the other side of the Channel.

In France there had been a drastic change since my first visit little more than a year before. The urgent need for men to replace the heavy losses sustained in the summer offensive had forced a change in military strategy so now most would go straight to the front and not to the training camps as they had before. Besides, there was a rumour going around that the harsh instructors at Étaples, the camp where I had witnessed and experienced so much needless brutality, had finally got what many felt they fully deserved. It was said that a rebellion, mainly involving Scottish troops but aided by both Australians and New Zealanders, had taken place against the hated MPs and Canaries, when, in a spontaneous gesture of defiance, hundreds of men sat down in the Bullring, that notorious training ground in the dunes with its manmade hill, and refused to move or obey orders. The instructors had been furious, inflaming the situation by threatening the men with violence and various punishments if they did not get up. But nothing would make then return to training and it wasn't until an officer promised that nobody would be punished that they agreed to march back to camp. Once there and flushed with their new power, the men tried to break out of camp to visit the town which was still out of bounds to all but the instructors. Unfortunately, at about the same time a rumour started that during an argument over a girl in the Women's Auxiliary Corps, a military policeman had shot dead a Scottish soldier and when the Scots heard this they went berserk, surrounding the MPs quarters in search of the alleged killer. In a frenzy of bloodthirsty revenge, by now completely out of control, they pursued both MPs and Canaries through the camp, throwing some over a bridge to their deaths. It was said that they hunted them down through the dunes, shooting many with weapons looted from the armoury, while others made their way into the town, smashing their way into the many bars already hastily closed as news of the trouble spread. Once in a bar they would refuse to leave before drinking the place dry, all the time harassing and terrifying the inhabitants. Once a group of officers tried to restore order, only for one to be dragged from his horse and his throat cut with a bayonet. Mutineers went to the Brigadiers office and piled wood against it, threatening to burn it down with him and his officers inside unless their grievances were heard. Fearing for his life but afraid to tell his superiors that he had lost control, the Brigadier had given way and training was cancelled indefinitely with each man given ten days wages to spend in the town.

The drinking and revelling went on for days, only stopping when the exhausted men had finally had enough and returned to camp. But their absence had bought enough time for extra military police to be drafted in and these were able to restore order. The rebellion had been quelled just in time for the battle of Passchendaele where many of the men involved would fight alongside me in the muddy battlefields with which that theatre of war became synonymous. It can only be assumed that in the next few weeks, hundreds of the rioters must have been killed or injured for as far as I know no one was ever charged with mutiny nor was its happening made known to the people at home. On the contrary, in private, many who had suffered at the hands of the instructors at Étaples, doing their hours of torture on the wheel for trivial or none existent offences, would say that each of the mutineers deserved a medal!

We travelled north, through the blasted vineyards of Flanders to the Ypres salient to disembark in this once fine city, now reduced to a crumbling, smoking, stinking ruin. Actions had been fought here on and off since 1914 and there were few buildings still left untouched by the destructive hand of war. Part of the city was still burning as we marched away in single file, past the cathedral and the shattered Menin Gate where a lone military policeman directed us on our way. Whole streets were nothing more than rubble while complete rows of houses had only their fronts torn away, exposing what once had been cosy homes with shreds of colourful wallpaper and even pictures still on the walls. A double bed, its once white sheets now grey with dust, hung crazily from one gutted house, shreds of tattered curtain blowing from its gaping windows.

Dead, putrefying horses, still harnessed to their splintered limbers, lay amongst the rubble, dragged to the side by their living counterparts in order to clear a way through what had once been a pleasant, tree-lined street. This was the centre of the infamous Ypres salient, a great bulge protruding into the German line covered by enemy artillery on three sides that had been held for many months at the cost of thousands of lives for no strategic advantage, other than a misguided sense of accomplishment. Now the shell scarred track on which we marched, winding its way through collapsed buildings and splintered trees, had assumed an importance even greater than it had in its prewar days. This was the Menin Road, gateway to the city and now the artery of the offensive and the only remaining route which enabled Allied transport carrying all the essential supplies of war to reach the front. Drivers would run the gauntlet on this road every night, pounded from three sides by enemy artillery ranged in on every yard and bottle neck of the way. Not until these guns could be silenced and the heights they commanded taken by our troops could any sign of normality return to this ruined city. The gentle rolling hills which concealed the guns, allowing their gunners the luxury of firing on targets bereft of cover on the plain below, were named after a village which nestled in their folds. The name of the village was Passchendaele, the hills formed the Passchendaele Ridge.

Out in the suburbs we saw our first bodies since we had landed, first one, then two, lying like grey rag dolls half buried in the piles of rubble which lined the road, their white waxy faces shining in the falling rain. Now the shattered remains of a young woman still clutching the broken body of her child, lying beside a dead French soldier, his one arm blown away, the other flung protectively across her shoulder as if, even in death, he was shielding her from danger. I wondered if they had died together or had they only been united after death, two strangers thrown into each other's arms on the hazard of a shell?

Rounding a corner we came across a small square, just off the road. Where there had once been pleasant pavement cafés, set beneath the shading trees, now there were only corpses piled up three and four deep, presumably taken there for burial before the city had been abandoned. Now they filled the square with a rotting tangle of bones and putrefying flesh held together with shreds of what had once been clothing but was now nothing more than grey, rain-soaked rags. This was too much for many of the lads, many of whom were witnessing such scenes for the first time. Even to those like me, considered to be a veteran despite my tender years, what I saw was enough to turn my stomach into jelly.

"Steady boys, steady now bonny lads, nothing to get yourselves worked up about, only a few dead bodies."

That was the calming voice of Sergeant Sims, veteran of first Ypres and back again in spite of what he thought was a sure fire Blighty wound. Steady as ever, now he was doing his best to shield his younger charges from this gruesome sight. Farther up the line somebody was being sick, another was crying uncontrollably. Poor devil, if a few dead French civilians upset him so much, how would he cope in action when his mates started going down around him, not in their ten's but in their hundreds? He'd probably cut and run, unless a bullet got him first and rescued him from his misery.

A young officer, his face ashen, rode back along the column, urging the men forward out of the bottle neck they were forming.

"Eyes front, look to your front, keep moving," he cried and it was obvious from the sound of his voice that he was near to cracking up himself. His horse, a remount as green as its rider, smelled the scent of death, rolling and chaffing at its bridle, nostrils flaring and eyes bulging as he shied away from the square and its awful contents.

"That buggers going to be useful in a fight", muttered the man next to me," first time a whiz-bang lands near him some poor sod will be expected to empty his trousers"

The nervous laughter caused by his remark went some way to relieve the tension, even though it was probably not true. Often straight out of public school, many of these young officers would be the first over the top, with their life expectancy at the front measured in days rather than weeks. At least they would die like soldiers in the line with their men, not like their superiors, safely in their beds after many years of relating tales of valour and human sacrifice which they had only heard about, being too far behind the line to actually witness any.

Slowly the suburbs then the city itself fell behind us as we marched doggedly on out into the countryside and now it was possible to breath fresh, unpolluted air, free from the stench of death and decay from what had once been a lovely city. Even though the land we now toiled through was a morass of stagnant water filled holes and shattered trees, anything was better than the smoking, stinking, corpse riddled ruin that we had gladly left behind.

It was almost dark when we left the road and guided by the shaded lamp of a military policeman, made our way to what had once been the village of St Julian which now contained our regimental headquarters. Only a few broken walls and shattered buildings standing in a sea of muddy water and reached by a duckboard path that led away through the swamp, marked the place where there once stood a tiny village. By the time we arrived it was almost dark. There was barely time to make up bivouacs from our capes in any dry place we could find and bed down for the night as best we could on the waterlogged ground, soaked and weary from our extended march. In no time at all I fell into an exhausted sleep, lulled by the patter of rain on the waxed surface of my cape. In the background, the flare and noise of the guns, firing their nightly salvo at the road we had so recently travelled, left me in no doubt that I was back in France.

Chapter 12

Mud, Mud, Glorious Mud (Passchendaele)
November 1917

Prelude: The Troops

Dim gradual thinning of the shapeless gloom,
Shudders to drizzling daybreak that reveals,
Disconsolate men who stamp with sodden boots,
And turn dulled sunken faces to the sky.
Haggard and hopeless, they who have beaten down
The stale despair of night, must now renew
Their desolation in the truce of dawn
Murdering the livid hours that grope for peace.

Sassoon

The lasting memory of all those who fought and survived at Passchendaele [1] would be the mud. Mud was everywhere so that we spent every moment of every day and night either standing in it, lying in it or even wading up to our waists in it. At best it was ankle deep, filling our boots with its black slime until after a while we hardly noticed it, not, that is, until the agony of trench foot reminded us of its presence. Mostly it was knee deep, making movement over even a short distance as exhausting and arduous a task as doing a full day's work under normal conditions. Worst of all, it was often waist deep in the water filled craters and ditches that passed as trenches, spelling certain death from drowning for any wounded man or exhausted animal unfortunate enough to fall into its black, repulsive clutches. There was mud in our hair, in our eyes, even in the food we ate. Often it blinded us, to be washed away by the almost continuous rain, only to be replaced by the mud covered debris of the next explosion. In time we came to regard it as a greater threat than the enemy, who must have been suffering just as badly as we were despite the fact that they held the higher and therefore drier ground. It was not some accident of nature that this once fertile plain had been transformed into an inhospitable landscape of blasted trees and mile upon mile of water filled craters, for the devastation in which we found ourselves was entirely man made. Once a vast marsh, this land had been reclaimed over many years by building an elaborate drainage system of dykes and canals, and in doing so, turning it into some of the most fertile agricultural land in northern France. In the winter months when the drains could no longer cope with the annual torrential rainfall, it once again became untenable but by then nobody cared as, with the crops having been harvested, the land could be abandoned and allowed to rest until the following spring. So predictable was the arrival of the winter rains that the locals knew that the summer crops had to be in before mid-August or they would not be harvested at all, so when the Germans first attacked Belgium, local farmers destroyed the dykes to the north and flooded the river Yser in a last ditch attempt to hold back the invaders. After that, a nonstop barrage of shells fired by both sides, accompanied by almost continuous rain which, for the first time in living memory had started in July, combined to destroy what remained of the delicate balance of the drainage system. It was into this muddy, flooded hell that first Gough, then later, old White Whiskers himself, General Plumer, sent troops to fight, not knowing or perhaps caring about the conditions they would find there. In an action originally calculated by Gough to be completed in two days but which would drag on for nearly two months, almost as many men would die here for just as little gains or justification as there did on the Somme.

I awoke stiff and cold to this featureless desolation on a bleak, misty morning, to find the inevitable rain still falling in a steady downpour. After a quick swill in a comparatively clean puddle, I followed my nose to where the battalion cooks were using a field kitchen to prepare breakfast. Life became much more bearable after a plate of sweet tasting fried bacon and a hot mug of tea so that when my section was ordered to fall in I was well prepared for whatever challenge the new day might bring. That was where I made my first mistake. Being new arrivals I knew from experience that we would not go into action straight away but would most likely be put on fatigues or other unpalatable duties. With this in mind, when the sergeant asked for any volunteers who could ride a bike, I was one of several who eagerly stepped forward to offer my services.

Never volunteer had been Jack's advice, echoed by my father on the day I left home and I would soon live to regret not heeding either of them.

"I want you volunteers to form up into groups of four" said the sergeant with a wry smile, "then peddle along to the quartermaster, draw a stretcher apiece and stand by to assist the stretcher bearers up the line. This bloody mud is killing more of our lads than Jerry is and to make matters worse it's almost impossible to get the wounded back because all the medics are out on their feet. A few fresh legs will help the cause no end and be very much appreciated".

So much for riding a bike! Still, it was a good cause and I had been full of admiration for the medics during my short stay on the Somme. I was young and fit and was prepared to give it a go, not that I had much choice in the matter anyway! Even so, I made a mental note that the next time anybody called for volunteers I would be extremely backward in coming forward, as Mother used to say when she was looking for someone to take on an unpleasant chore. It's worth noting that when the time came to volunteer some months later, I forgot all of their good advice and stepped forward once again. Fortunately on that occasion it would be to my advantage.

Later that afternoon, transported part of the way by commandeered French buses, the twenty or so volunteers supplemented by as many more pressed men it needed to make up the numbers were moved up nearer to the front line. Movement after that was very difficult, almost impossible in the places where the wooden duckboards which acted as roads had been damaged by shellfire or had simply sunk beneath the mud. Because of the shallow water table, deep trenches were out of the question, filling with water and mud almost as soon as they were dug. Instead, the forward defences consisted of large, inevitably flooded shell holes, joined together by shallow scrapes just deep enough for a man to crawl through without offering a target to enemy snipers. The Germans had long since abandoned the conventional trench system in favour of semi portable concrete pillboxes armed with machine guns, set at strategic positions along the front. This meant that what little movement was possible through the open ground would come under remorseless raking fire from one of these positions. Unfortunately for our enemies, so unstable was the condition of the ground that some of the heavy pillboxes had been known to sink into the mud, making it impossible for the occupants to open the heavy metal door. Caught like rats in a trap, unable to escape, they faced a lingering death by either suffocation or drowning as the concrete bunker sank slowly into the mud.

Late in the afternoon we made contact with the Eighth Battalion bivouacked beside the Ypres-Roulers railway track in what had until recently been the German front line. The next day they would be supporting the Australians in an attack on the Gheluvelt Plateau, high ground from which the enemy artillery held such a commanding position that no further advances were considered possible until they had been eliminated. Although we still carried our rifles to defend ourselves should we be attacked, as stretcher bearers we would be in a supporting role to evacuate the wounded and assist the medics in any way we could. Because of this we were not allowed to wear red cross arm bands as the medics did and were not protected by the convention which prevented any form of hindrance to medical teams. To put things mildly, while we were out there in the open we were on a very sticky wicket!

The evening before the assault we were briefed by a senior medical officer about the role we would play and to where we should attempt to evacuate the wounded. I was surprised to hear him refer in his plans to familiar names like Clapham Junction, Stirling Castle and the beer woods Bass and Stout. Paradoxical of all was the name given to the huge wood that flanked the lower slopes of Passchendaele Ridge which had been named 'Shrewsbury Forest'. It would be ironic indeed if I had travelled all this way only to be killed, fighting in a place named after my own county town.

As soon as it was dark we moved off to our assembly areas closes to the front. In the inky darkness we struggled through mud often waist deep, each section calling out to each other at frequent intervals in order to keep together. We had only about two or three miles to go but even so dawn was breaking on another wet and miserable day long before we reached our destination. The plan was that the Aussies would go in first, supported by the Queens and Bedfords on their left and right, but as zero hour approached there was no sign of the latter who had apparently fallen behind in the mud so would not reach the jumping off point until after the attack was due to get under way. This was bad news for without them we would be totally exposed on our right flank to any counter attack by the enemy. The word was that we wouldn't be going without them, so it was with some dismay accompanied by some very choice words regarding our senior officer's parentage that at exactly seven o'clock the barrage started up, the whistles blew, and we were on our way. The art of firing an artillery barrage had come on a pace since my earlier experiences the previous year. Now with the ammunition more reliable, the gunners were confident enough to employ the rolling barrage, essential against an enemy in scattered positions. The principle of this was simple. First the guns ranged on a specific target and fired for a set time, before increasing their range by about fifty yards and firing again. When this happened the infantry would dash forward under the cover of the guns, wipe out any enemy still alive, before moving on again the next time the barrage lifted. This sounds simple in principle but is not so simple in practice. The main problem was that the infantry, being encouraged to follow as closely behind the fall of shot as possible, experienced almost the same terror as the targets at which it was directed. The choking curtain of dirt, mud and smoke, combined with the ear splitting noise, urged every nerve in the men's bodies to take cover or, especially the inexperienced, to turn back rather than follow its slow advance. Added to this was the danger of "shorts", defective shells that fell on friendly forces, making the whole experience something not to be relished.

So it was with some trepidation that I slipped and slithered my way forward across the muddy wilderness of the lower slopes of the Gheluvelt plateau, following both the barrage and our own attacking forces. In order to cover every eventuality it had been agreed that we would be grouped into parties of four, each group carrying two stretchers, and for every four stretcher parties there would be one trained medic.[2]

After only a short distance we came across our first casualties, three Australians hit by a short. Two were already dead but the third was still alive and receiving attention from a medic. As soon as his wounds were dressed, as agreed, myself and my opposite number, a lad from Leeds I only knew as Yorkie, piled him aboard our stretcher and headed back the way we had come.

The going was tough especially with the heavy stretcher and several times we made wide diversions around particularly difficult ground so that it was not before long that the familiar landmarks that we had been using to guide us had disappeared from view. Another hundred yards of slipping and sliding in this blasted landscape and we were forced to admit that we were lost. We had only just paused to gain our breath and take stock of our surroundings when a sudden movement over to our left sent us diving for cover in a nearby shell hole.

"Tommy, Tommy," called a voice in guttural English, "Surrender, please surrender".

"It's the bloody Bosh", whispered my mate, "the beggars must have us surrounded and are offering us surrender. I reckon we've not got much choice in the matter Walter, it looks like this is the end of the war for us old lad".

Weighing up the odds he was probably right. There were only two of us plus the casualty who was barely alive, against goodness knows how many of them. This was not very good odds at the best of times but with a wounded man to consider, not really worth the gamble. Best save our skins and throw in the towel. Gingerly I raised my head above the rim of the hole and looked around me. Across a clearing from where we lay I could see the bowl of a huge uprooted fir tree from which somebody concealed in its roots was waving a white piece of cloth tied to a stick! It suddenly dawned on me that the Germans didn't want us to surrender, they wanted to surrender themselves! Realising the situation, I un-slung my rifle and sprinted across the clearing, followed shortly by my mate Yorkie. Cowering in the hole we found four thoroughly wet and dejected Germans who greeted us more as their saviours rather than their enemy.

After a quick council of war it was decided what we would do

.On the toss of a coin, whoever won would take both the casualty and the prisoners back, while the loser would retrace his steps back up the hill and rejoin our unit. You've guessed it, the lad from Leeds won the toss so it was me who stood and watched this unlikely procession picking their way cautiously over the broken ground until they were finally lost from sight. In the lead was the stretcher carrying the wounded Australian, a grey coated German bearer at each corner. Behind them, a jubilant Yorkie urged them on their way, four German rifles slung around his shoulders and another loaded rifle clasped in his hand.

There is a final twist to this remarkable story. When several hours later he made it back to the clearing station at Beer Wood, Yorkie was greeted as a hero and as a result of his dedication to duty in not only getting the casualty back but taking four prisoners as well was later promoted to corporal. There but for the grace of God and the toss of a coin went I; it's a funny old world isn't it?

Chapter 13

A Charge through the Forest - November 1917

Name Not Known

They ask me where I've been,
And what I've done and seen.
But what can I reply
Who knows it wasn't I,
But someone just like me,
Who went across the sea
And with my head and hands
Killed men in foreign lands...
'Though I must bear the blame,
Because he bore my name!

Gibson

As soon as the stretcher party were out of sight I scouted around for a route which would lead me back the way I'd come. Now that I was left to my own devices, in the eerie silence of the forest I suddenly felt very vulnerable and alone. By now the barrage had stopped and only the occasional distant burst of rifle and machine gun fire, punctuated by the louder crump of a bomb, interrupted the sighing of the wind in the broken trees. Looking around me I saw that most of these seemed to be spruce and larch and because they had grown so tightly together any thought of movement in a straight line was practically impossible. To make matters worse, a lot of them had been hit by shell fire and in many places heavy boughs blown from the trunks littered the ground, or had become tangled together to form a thick, impenetrable curtain overhead. Despite the bindings of my puttees, dead and splintered branches jabbed like spikes into my already bleeding legs, making walking very painful and difficult to make any significant headway.

Eventually I stumbled upon a rough track made by either men or animals and for a while I made good progress. Slowly the fir trees gave way to stands of beech and oak and it became possible to catch an occasional glimpse of the leaden sky overhead. It was still raining. Eventually, in an attempt to get my bearings I rested my rifle and pack up against the base of a large oak tree which I then climbed as high as I could . From its higher branches, far off to the left and still more than a mile away I could just make out the lingering smoke and dust marking the path the barrage had taken, while some way ahead of where it finished, the occasional flash and puff of smoke indicated the present location of the attack and where I might find my unit. It also came as a shock to realise that even though it was more than an hour since I had left the stretcher party I had travelled less than a mile from my starting point. I had been well up the ridge at that time but now it was obvious that by following the track I had been angling across and back down the hill. To return to the battle zone I must abandon the easy option of the track and once more plunge into the uninviting tangle of the forest.

As I sat at the base of the tree cursing my position, the sudden crack of a breaking twig told me that I was no longer alone. Peering cautiously around the bole of the tree I saw to my horror that a German soldier was standing a little way further up the track, his eyes fixed on the ground as if he was looking for something. I knew that as soon as he looked up he was bound to see my rifle and pack still where I had left them resting against the tree. My only chance was surprise and I had no time to lose. Diving from cover and grabbing the rifle at the same time, I aimed and fired all in one movement. Alerted by the sudden movement, the German looked up, a startled expression on his face. From that range I couldn't miss, the bullet hit him squarely in the chest, the force of the blow flinging him backwards off the track where he hung suspended in the tangle of brush. For a moment I lay there, expecting his comrades, alerted by the shot, to come running to his aid. Seconds turned into minutes and nothing happened. Could I be that lucky, if so, what was he doing here alone in the woods so far behind our lines?

I waited for a full half hour but all was quiet; only the savage thumping of my heart filling my ears. Eventually, throwing caution to the wind, I broke cover and warily approached the place where he lay. He was obviously dead, the red stain on his chest where the bullet had struck home already congealing and turning black as it dried. It was a shock to see how old he was, with grizzled hair sticking out from beneath his helmet and his moustache and stubbled chin flecked with grey. On seeing this it was with horror that I realised the enormity of what I had done and was filled with remorse imagining how this could be someone's father lying dead at my feet. It was with some regrets that I untangled his body from the thicket and laid him gently down to rest, covering his body with a blanket of dead leaves. Finally, I stuck his rifle in the ground, placing his helmet on top both to mark his grave and to ensure his body might someday be found and returned to his family.[1]

With one last backward glance I went on my way, striking off the track and plunging once more into the tangle of trees that barred my route back up the hill.

It was more than two hours later when I finally rejoined my comrades to find that the advance was going well. The Australians, hard as nails and many of them fresh from Étaples and the reported mutiny, were spoiling for a fight and had taken everything before them in the early stages of the attack. Now back with my unit but still unable to locate any of the medical sections, I joined up with them, giving up any thoughts for the moment of resuming my duties as a stretcher bearer. I still had my rifle and once I'd acquired an extra issue of ammunition I was raring to go.

In mid-afternoon our artillery opened up again and we were away following a barrage which almost without exception should have killed or wounded any German defenders caught in its path. Many had taken refuge in the pillboxes scattered along the hillside, seeking what shelter they could from the welter of high explosives falling on them. These we either bombed or mowed down the occupants the minute they emerged into the open. It was perhaps regrettable that even some waving handkerchiefs or bandages in surrender suffered the same fate, for having tasted blood the Aussies were rampant now and completely out of control. Their enthusiasm for a fight spread like wild fire through our ranks so that I found myself caught up in the exhilaration and excitement of it all, and screaming encouragement, plunged headlong through the clouds of brown cordite smoke and debris left by another barrage. As we ran, ghostly, grey-clad figures sprang up before us only to be brought down by bullet or bayonet as we passed. High on a cocktail of adrenalin and excitement, I slashed and stabbed or clubbed at those who blocked my way so that when my bayonet became wedged between the ribs of one screaming victim I remembered the procedure taught us by Sgt Bishton and practised on the Race Course at Shrewsbury "If your bayonet gets stuck, pull the trigger and blow the bugger off!"

It was almost as if he was there beside me. The kick of the rifle and the impact of the round hurled the shattered body away from me like a broken doll. On and on we charged, a seemingly unstoppable force bound for certain victory.

But all this was too good to be true. Suddenly our way was blocked by deep belts of uncut wire strung in an impassable tangle between the stumps of shattered trees. Behind this, well-sited machine guns opened up the minute our forward sections came into view, taking a terrible toll on those troops leading the attack. Exposed in the cleared ground and blocked by the wire, men went down like ninepins, caught in full stride by this raking fire. Now it was our turn to go to ground. Diving for cover in a still smoking crater, I dug in as best I could, using my bloodied bayonet and whatever came to hand to deepen and improve my refuge. Men all around me were doing the same. Now our exposed right flank, not yet supported by the absent Bedfords came under attack from parties of infiltrators skirting around and behind us. Worse still, these were soon strengthened by more Germans who emerged unscathed from dugouts and positions behind us, incorrectly assumed to have been wiped out and overrun in our initial advance. Fired on and bombed from both directions, our situation became more and more untenable by the hour. With night drawing in and most of us low on ammunition there was nothing else to do but withdraw or face capture by the ever increasing numbers of Germans opposing us. Reluctantly the word was passed from man to man to effect an orderly retreat as soon as it got dark, when it would be every man for himself.

Fighting our way back the way we had so recently and triumphantly come proved to be a nightmare of hellish proportions. In the gathering darkness every broken tree trunk seemed to conceal a sniper, every crater a machine gun, as the enemy launched a spirited counter attack. Only the blackness of the night and its cover of darkness saved many of us from capture or certain death. Others, not so lucky, were left where they fell on that muddy hillside where only hours before they had carried all before them with such enthusiasm.

Day break found us back behind our starting lines with only the timely intervention of another artillery barrage preventing the Germans pressing their attack even further.

Much later that day I was able to rejoin my section still held in reserve at St Julian. They listened enthralled as I and those other stretcher bearers who had survived, described our exploits. Many had hairy tales to tell, describing their experiences evacuating the wounded out through the mud. Others, like me, had been forced through accident or design, to abandon their stretchers and fight for their lives with rifle and bayonet. That, after all, was what we were here for! Some, like Yorkie had returned to safety with their casualties and had then tried but failed to rejoin the action. Just as many had stayed on and had either survived or died in the fighting.

We stayed at St Julian for another three weeks in which time other assaults, just as bloody and just as futile as the first were made on the ridge. In all that time the German guns kept up their nightly battering of the Menin Road and the heroic transport drivers using it. It would be October before they were silenced, once again by a daring attack led by the Australians. By then the rain had turned to snow, churning the already waterlogged ground into an impassable soup of mud and ice. Finally common sense prevailed and the Ypres campaign was abandoned until the drier months of spring. Before then I was on the move again when my Battalion moved farther north, relieving the 24th Division on the Vimy Ridge. They would take part in the first great tank battle at Cambrai. But more about that later.

Chapter 14
My First Visit to Vimy Ridge - December 1917

Attack

At dawn the ridge emerges massed and dun,
In wild purple of the glow'ring sun.
Smouldering through spouts of drifting smoke that shroud,
The menacing scarred slope; and, one by one,
Tanks creep and topple forward to the wire.
The barrage roars then lifts. Then clumsily bowed,
With bombs and guns and shovels and battle gear,
Men jostle and climb to meet the bristling fire.
Lines of grey, muttering faces, going over the top.
While time ticks blank and busy on their wrists
And hope, with furtive eyes and grappling fists,
Flounders in mud. O Jesus, make it stop!

Sassoon

The only relief from the flat featureless coalfields which form much of the border between France and Belgium, is the lowering bulk of the Vimy Ridge, rising abruptly some two hundred feet above the plain. At first sight it seemed hard to believe that its steep wooded face and broken summit towering above our heads could have been wrested from the hands of any defending force determined to hold it. How on earth could such an imposing position ever have been taken by infantrymen fighting their way foot by bloody foot up its slopes, against well trained German troops resolutely defending positions dug in less than two miles below its summit? But it had been taken, needless to say with the inevitable huge cost in lives, in a series of attacks first by the French and then more recently by the Canadians. Now the Germans had gone and the elaborate trench and tunnel system they had created was in our hands.

Remarkably, during my stay there the sector was unusually quiet with only a few token attacks and sporadic bombardments to let us know the enemy were still about. After suffering several crushing defeats, the German command had issued the order for a strategic withdrawal back to the Hindenburg line, at the same time concentrating their troops in and around the fortified town of Cambrai, some miles due east from our present position. This was recognised as the weak link in their otherwise impregnable defence and they knew that should a breakthrough be attempted anywhere, this was the most likely place for it to happen.

With time on my hands I took the opportunity to write some letters home, at the same time receiving some myself. Mail drops were sometimes weeks overdue with the division almost constantly on the move so that when one came I would often receive several letters all at once. The ritual of sorting them into order before reading them added much to the pleasure of receiving them, tracking the events as they unfolded, each one described in Mother's hesitant hand. Ever since I had returned to France she had written at least once a week, describing all the things that were happening at home, including any news she had heard regarding the welfare of my friends from the village. Written in pencil, each letter consisted of several pages filled on both sides with local gossip and events that had taken place that week. She only wrote of ordinary things, never mentioning the war and the growing lists of casualty figures which by now were appearing on a daily basis in the newspapers. It was both obvious and understandable that by ignoring these reported horrors she might excise them from her mind, blocking, even for a few moments, her fears for the safety of my brother which must have been on her mind for every minute of the day.

In one letter she described how our dog Bess had given birth to five puppies, writing tongue in cheek that while Bess was not particular who she mated with, it was suspected that on this occasion Ted's dog had somehow found enough time off from his habitual search for hedgehogs to father the litter. Unfortunately, she wrote, the puppies were unwanted so Father would have the unpleasant task of destroying them as soon as he could bring himself to doing it. Fortunately, by three letters later everything had been resolved, each of the puppies having been found a new home and the unrepentant Bess welcomed back into the bosom of the family. It became a sort of ritual that Mother would end each of her letters in the same way.

"Hope you're keeping warm and getting plenty to eat" she would write, and having read about the horrors of trench foot in the local papers, "remember to change your socks whenever you can and always wear your steel helmet at all times!". This latter advice was a result of the latest government propaganda assuring the people back home that casualties from head injuries had almost halved since the previous year since the issue of steel helmets to all front line troops. The fact that at that time the most likely cause of death for men in the line was from artillery fire, against which even the strongest of helmets were useless, seems to have escaped their notice!

I knew that my letters home were always censored so it was not possible to say where I was, let alone what I was doing, so each usually contained nothing more than trivia and snippets of information that I hoped would get past the censor. In each one I ended by telling my parents not to worry, that I would be OK, that I loved them and would soon be home. I only wish I could have believed the latter part myself!

While Mother had written the earlier letters in late summer, here in France winter was setting in with a vengeance so that on most mornings the harsh contours of the hills were softened by a thick blanket of snow, only broken by the deeply scarred lines of trenches. Night watches were particularly arduous with the temperature falling well below zero, and the frequent flurries of sleet or snow obscuring their vision making the most alert lookout's task almost impossible. Occasionally we rebuffed sporadic attacks seen as token gestures by an enemy, who like ourselves, had little heart for a fight in such harsh conditions. As an added deterrent, to our front any decent cover had long since been destroyed, leaving only the uncertain fog to obscure the presence of any would-be attackers. Always unpredictable, this would suddenly sweep up from the frozen ground before lifting as inexplicably as it had come, exposing any enemy seeking shelter in its cover to the mercy of our guns.

The routine was always the same, seven days in the line followed by eight days on relief. When not in the line we were billeted in the cellars of a ruined village where at least it was possible to get out of the biting winds which blew constantly on the exposed flanks of the ridge. It was an uncomfortable fact that the fleas that infested our clothes seemed to survive even in these sub zero temperatures so that the first day of relief was always spent "chatting" or "reading your shirt", as the term for ridding our clothes of this constant irritant was called. This was done either with a lighted cigarette or candle which we used to incinerate both them and their eggs where they sheltered in the folds of our uniforms.

Eventually this would lead to shirts and vests having little or no material under the armpits or the crotch, both having been burnt away in a number of over enthusiastic chatting sessions. After the first day's 'make and mend', the remainder of the relief was spent on the inevitable training exercises or fatigues, a routine rigorously followed throughout the war regardless of circumstances or conditions.

Having just been relieved, one day in early November we were about to make our way back through the three miles or so of communication trenches leading to the reserve lines when an enemy shell exploded in the open space between our two platoons. As we dived for cover, a great column of earth and cobbles was flung into the air before raining back down on us, but by some miracle nobody was hurt except for some minor injuries caused by falling stones. As I picked myself up, first another and then another shell fell close to where we stood and, recognising the pattern of a creeping barrage concentrated on the staging areas behind our lines, the young officer in charge decided that it should be every man for himself.

"Fall out and make your way back to the billets under your own steam", he yelled, setting off at full gallop down the road. We didn't need telling twice. As more and more shells began to fall astride the road, we ran for our lives, eventually picking our way through the ruins of what had once been a small village. Soon I found myself in an overgrown churchyard filled with many ornate headstones and as I ran a shell exploded away to my right almost blowing me off my feet. Regaining my balance I dived for the nearest shelter I could find, a flight of stone steps leading down into a vaulted crypt. In the crypt I was joined by another soldier from my section and we looked around, taking stock of our surroundings while above our heads the barrage rumbled on. There were coffins everywhere, many broken open by a previous explosion, spilling their grisly contents onto the floor. Several skulls were stacked on shelves around the room and in the dim light I could just make out the outline of a small alter covered with a faded velvet cloth. Picking my way gingerly through the debris of bones and broken coffins, I discovered little alcoves carved out of the rock walls, each containing faded pictures of those who perhaps had been the occupants of the coffins. Standing at either end of the alter were two crucifixes, despite a thick covering of dust still gleaming silver in the gloom.

"Fancy a souvenir", enquired my colleague, stuffing one of the crucifixes into his tunic pocket while offering me the other.

"Not on your life," I replied, remembering from my youth a sermon describing the awful punishment imposed on those caught stealing from the church and the dreadful fate for those who stood accused of robbing the dead.

"I wouldn't nick one of them for all the tea in China. You're pushing your luck if you pinch them", I warned, "Better leave them where they are mate, I'm having nothing to do with stealing from graves."

"Please yourself," he laughed, "I'll have 'em both myself then. I don't give a damn for that superstitious nonsense, I reckon if your number's up there's now't you can do about it anyway. I bet these two are worth a bob or two and will look fine on my mantlepiece back at home anyway."

Soon the shelling stopped and we left the crypt and made it safely back to our billet so that I thought no more about it until several days later after we had returned to the line. Probably merely in order to check the serviceability of one of their guns, the enemy fired a ranging shot at our position which happened to hit the parapet on the bay farther down the line from mine. These were trenches constructed by the Germans, deep and safe and almost impervious to anything short of a full barrage so it was a surprise when I heard that somebody had been hit and curiosity made me go over to see if there was anything I could do. Imagine my surprise when I found that the unlucky victim of this speculative shot was none other than the man with whom I'd shared the crypt. A stray shrapnel splinter had struck him in the head, killing him instantly. So much for robbing the dead. Was it pure coincidence or was its God's judgement for his needless act of vandalism. I will never know the answer but at the time it certainly strengthened both my faith and fear in God; a belief that I kept and often called upon until long after the war.

In the middle of November we heard the news of the sudden and dramatic victory which had taken place some miles to the east at Cambrai. For the first time in the history of warfare, tanks had been used to batter a hole five miles deep into the enemy defences, smashing all before them as they went. Once again our hopes were raised that this new and terrible weapon which terrified all who faced it, must surely spell the end of the war.

Christmas came and went and the routine never changed as once more hope changed to disappointment as the enemy staged a counter attack, regaining most of the ground taken by the tanks. In early spring at last we were relieved from Vimy and the division moved to be based at a small town called Vermelles, a few miles to the west of the larger town of Bethune. For once we were able to visit both towns during our days on relief and I spent many enjoyable evenings in the bars and cafés which still remained open despite the close proximity of the fighting.

It was during one of these periods on relief that I experienced a bit of good fortune which would see me right for the next few weeks. We had just completed the usual routine of morning prayers followed by inspection by the duty officer when, instead of marching off parade, we were stood at ease to be read a directive he had received that morning.

He explained that the enemy submarine blockade of shipping transporting supplies into Britain was beginning to take effect. Food had been rationed for some time but now people had to tighten their belts even more as the most basic of commodities began to run out. To make matters worse, with most of the farm workers conscripted into the forces there were few left to work the land. Those that remained were doing their best to produce what crops they could to supplement any supplies which escaped the blockade but with most farm horses gone to the war they were fighting a losing battle using the old and decrepit stock which remained. Now, with spring just around the corner and many fields still lying fallow, the government had been forced to take drastic steps to ease the situation. To do this it was decided that any soldier on active service who had the necessary skills and was due for some leave could earn extra days by volunteering to work on the land.

The CO concluded by calling for any previous agricultural workers who were entitled to some leave, especially ploughmen, to step forward. This was too good a chance to miss. Even better, I was due to go on leave in the next few days so had all the necessary qualifications to volunteer. Forgetting all about my previous vows, I was one of the first to step forward, followed quickly by another five volunteers. This time it was not a trick. Sure enough we would be given a full months leave as long as we spent the time working on the land.

The next morning saw me once again aboard the train for the short trip to Calais and then home. The ship was crowded with returning servicemen and there was laughter and good humour everywhere. I stayed on deck, watching the coast of France grow smaller while ahead the dim grey line that marked the horizon gradually took shape and became the familiar white cliffs of Dover. I had been so excited at the prospect of going home that I had hardly slept the night before but soon the hum of the engines and the gentle rocking of the ship in the calm sea lulled me to sleep. It was late and almost dark when we reached the harbour where I was roused from my sleep by the rattle of the anchor going over the side. All around me the lights of the town were coming on, for these were the days before the blackout. Gathering up my kit I was almost crushed as I joined the rush to get ashore. As usual the ladies were there to greet us with mugs of hot tea and food for those who wanted any so once again I found myself surrounded by laughter, love and good wishes. It was spring time, I was back in England and I had the prospect of a whole months leave stretching before me. What more could a young man ask for?

Chapter 15

Home on Agricultural Leave - February 1918

A Shropshire Lad

Into my heart an air that kills
From yon far country blows.
What are those blue remembered hills,
What spires, what farms are those?
This is the land of lost content,
I see it shining plain.
The happy highways where I went,
And cannot go again.

Housman

As usual London was a frenzy of activity and noise which never seemed to decrease in volume either by day or by night. Victoria station was particularly busy with hundreds of troops milling around in great confusion, many not quite sure what to do next or where to go. Lots of kindly ladies, many from religious organisations, pressed them with tea and sandwiches and, with some reluctance, tobacco to those who wanted it, all of this only adding to the general disorder. Red-capped, self-important military policemen, shouting orders mostly unheard above the babble of voices and the noise of arriving and departing trains, did their utmost to restore some order. They were at best ignored, at worst jostled and mocked by soldiers both safe in the anonymity of the crowd and high on the euphoria of being home.

Carried along by the crush, I noticed a sign directing me to a building bearing the legend "Transport Officer" in large letters over its door. Deciding that it would be wise to report my presence to somebody in authority, I joined the long queue which had formed outside and settled down to wait my turn to be dealt with.

Inside the building a number of harassed and quarrelling clerks manning a long wooden desk divided into two sections by a barricade, sweated and sworn over an ever increasing mountain of paperwork.

The barrier separated men coming into the country from those going back to France and it didn't need much to identify which were which. There was no mistaking the drawn, pale faces of those fresh from the front, or their crumpled "gorblimey" service caps and puttees still caked with the pale grey mud of France.[1] You could even sense the desperation in their eyes which never left the large clock hanging on the office wall as it ticked away the hours and minutes of their leave, for every precious moment wasted here was one less to be enjoyed with family and friends. On the other side of the divide were those whose leave was over, many of them returning to the front for a third or fourth time. Among them were many new recruits going for the first time, unmistakable by their show of false bravado, their shining buttons and polished boots contrasting starkly with those of their more dishevelled comrades whose gaunt eyes stared from faces ravaged with exhaustion.

At last my turn came and I attempted to explain to an already overburdened clerk that I was on extended leave as an agricultural worker. He looked at me as if I was some sort of mad man.

"Look mate", he said, "you can be on leave as a bus driver or a pox doctors assistant or what the hell you like, it makes no odds to me, but what makes you think that being an agricultural worker entitles you to extended leave?"

This would be the first time that my extraordinary reason for extended leave would be questioned, the next time it would have a serious affect on my liberty. By now there were impatient shouts from the men queuing behind me to "Get on with it!" so to avoid a riot, the clerk decided that the best thing to do was for me to wait until his superior came back from lunch, a time which apparently varied from day to day dependent on the company he was keeping ! Knowing that further protests were useless and resigned to a long wait, I found a vacant chair in a far corner of the room, curled up in a ball, and fell fast asleep.

Sometime in the afternoon I awoke with a start as I was shaken rudely from my slumbers. Standing over me was an ancient Territorial army Captain, smelling strongly of drink and decidedly unsteady on his feet.

"On your feet, Private, when there's an officer present", he bellowed, "and pay the necessary compliments and respect to my rank!"

I scrambled sleepily to my feet, throwing up a token salute as I did so. Better humour the silly old bugger, it's not the man you salute it's the uniform I thought, and in this case bugger the uniform as well! Satisfied that I had complied with army tradition and perhaps realising how close to exhaustion I was, his attitude softened.

"What's this about you wanting to be a farm worker, young fellah? I daresay we'd all like to be farm workers but there's a wretched war on, don't you know", he barked, fixing me with a watery gaze.

Once more I patiently explained what I was supposed to be doing, telling him about the order sent to all units in France and how I had qualified to take advantage of it. I tried in vain to convince him that I was genuine, even producing my pay book which clearly showed my occupation prior to enlisting as "farm worker" as well as my leave pass, stating the reason for my being there. But all to no avail. Who could blame him? That a situation had developed where farm workers were being withdrawn from the front, just at a time when our fortunes had taken a turn for the better, must have seemed as improbable to him as it had to me when I had first heard the order. Even I had to accept that even by the army's often incomprehensible standards, this one was hard to believe. In true military fashion, as might have been expected he had received no brief to expect or cope with such a situation, neither was he aware of the order permitting it. Unable to find anybody in his present staff who had heard of such a thing before, there was only one course of action he could take. He did what generations of military commanders had done before and passed the problem up the line. Until somebody could be found to sort things out and at the same time relieve him of any responsibility for such a decision, he decided that the safest thing to do was to post me to the Barracks at East Croydon for the night while he sought guidance from his superiors.

So it was, with the better part of my first day's leave already wasted I reluctantly climbed aboard a lorry crowded with other troops and their equipment that would carry us through the city to the south London borough of Croydon.

On our way through Brixton, I saw the first evidence of damage caused by the recent bombing raids. So rapid had been the development of aircraft that already this part of the city was well within range of the German bombers so that the daylight Gotha raids were adding further misery and hardship to the women and children who joined the daily queues for the meagre supplies still to be found in the few shops that were not already closed.

As our lorry lurched and rumbled its way through the dingy, cobbled streets, desperate women and children ran from their houses, begging for pennies or any spare food we had to give. While I only had francs in my pockets which I had not bothered to exchange before leaving France, others had packed meals or sweets and cakes given to them by the ladies welcoming them from the train. All of this we tossed to the grateful people who fought and squabbled with each other over every morsel. Who would have thought that I would be witnessing such scenes in an English city? We had been told that some items of food were becoming scarce, that was the reason for my being here. In one of her letters, Mother had written about the rationing of many things like sugar and bread but I had not realised things were as bad as this! This was poverty on a grand scale. Paradoxically, in the front line food had always been plentiful, if a little predictable, with often more than enough to go around. Now it was plain that in order to provide it, the women and children we had left behind had to go without and were starving as a consequence. I suppose those of us who had already enlisted should have been grateful. Like pigs fattened for the slaughter, at least we were being well fed before being butchered!

The damage to the city from the bombing raids and the poverty of its inhabitants came as a shock to all of us who saw it for the first time that day. I had always assumed our people back at home were so remote and safe from the dangers and hardships we were facing that their welfare had never caused me any concern. What I saw now made me realise how vulnerable these people were and the sacrifices they had to make, sometimes with their lives, to do their bit for King and Country.

At the barracks we were greeted by a cheery cockney sergeant who issued us with bedding and allocated billets before marching us off to the cook house for a piping hot meal. This was a Territorial barracks and most of the other men who arrived with me were either reserve troops just posted in or those returning off leave. I was the odd man out.

The next morning I was first in the orderly room to find out if there was any decision about my posting. Once again I was dealt with by the cheerful sergeant who to his credit appeared to accept my reason for being there which, although on the face of it seemed most unlikely, was bizarre enough to have some element of truth in it.

As he happily put it, "There's probably something in it my son, as the monkey said when he put his hand in the piss pot."

Unfortunately, like the Captain the previous evening, although he had tried he could find out nothing more about the situation and it would be another three days before my posting was at last confirmed and I received orders to report to Copthorne Barracks at Shrewsbury.

During those three days I wasn't required to stay in barracks and so was able to spend some time exploring the city. With some trepidation I rode the new electric trolley buses which had recently replaced the horse drawn trams and on one occasion travelled for a short distance on an underground train, passing below the muddy waters of the Thames rather than the more conventional ferry or bridge over it. It came as a surprise to realise that both the driver of the bus and the conductor were women, as was the constable from whom I sought directions back to the barracks later that evening. With all the men gone to war, women had rolled up their sleeves and taken on the jobs their brothers, husbands and fathers had vacated, keeping the transport systems going and the factories producing all those essential commodities needed so desperately to support and sustain the defence of their country. Never again would women be considered unequal to men, the new role thrust on them by the war would see to that. The demands for their emancipation, gathering support and strength with every day, would ensure that, even after the war, their position in both society and industry would never be questioned again.

The poverty and depredation I had seen on my first evening was evident everywhere I went. It was not just the lack of provisions that had dampened the natural good humour and expectations of these cockney people. By now there was hardly a family in the land who had not lost someone in the fighting and although I never ever heard anybody express their doubt that we would eventually win, those at home were becoming increasingly bitter at the terrible cost of doing so. Even so, they were still prepared to spend their last shilling on the "boys from the front" so wherever I went I found it almost impossible to persuade anybody to accept anything in the form of payment. Knowing the hardships many of them were experiencing, I felt vaguely ashamed of myself for allowing this to happen but as I hadn't been paid since leaving France and my only form of currency was francs, just for the moment I was as broke as they were!

Although I never witnessed it myself, a mate of mine on leave in London told me how he had been challenged by one of the fashionable young ladies who, in the early years of the war, toured the city handing out white feathers, a sign of cowardice, to those who had not yet enlisted. Because he was in civilian dress, she had singled him out for her attention, thrusting a white feather into his reluctant hand. He described with relish the embarrassment she had suffered when he showed her his pay book and she realised her mistake. Not prepared to leave it there, he had taken a great delight in questioning her motives. Angrily, he had demanded to know why she was not at the front like so many of her peers, doing their bit as nurses or even at work helping the war effort here at home? Soon a crowd gathered, taking up the interrogation of the young lady and her escort, accusing them of the very cowardice which they had sought to brand others. Tiring of his sport, my friend had been able to slip away unnoticed in the confusion, much pleased with his exposure of what at best he saw as an unnecessary pastime.

It was Thursday morning before I caught the train for home, in my pocket a twenty-four hour leave pass to be enjoyed before reporting to Copthorne Barracks.

Out in the country things did not look quite as bad as they had in the city, although it was obvious from the many acres of land lying fallow that the problems experienced on the farms were not improving.

As I disembarked at Hodnet station, a family of some substance were saying their goodbyes to a young Welsh Guards second lieutenant making his way back off leave. The head of the family looked familiar and when the station's only porter explained that they were the Stanier family from Peplow Hall and the officer was their son Alexander, I realised where I had seen him before.

His father Beville Stanier was the sitting member of Parliament for North Shropshire and Newport and in that capacity he had been instrumental in the early years of the war in the recruitment of volunteers from that part of the county. I remembered seeing him at Wem on my successful attempt to enlist, urging young men to join the colours from a makeshift stage erected outside the town hall. During another recruiting campaign I had seen him at Hodnet, passing among the inquisitive crowd gathered outside the Bear Hotel, imploring young men to do their bit for King and Country by enlisting. Inevitably, this patriotic fervour had subsequently led to many of their deaths. Now it would seem he was making the same sacrifice that thousands of fathers had done before him, sending his own son where so many others had gone before.

Alexander was about the same age as me and by a number of coincidences and despite our different social positions our paths would cross on numerous occasions throughout our lives. The following year we would be fighting almost side by side on the Canal du Nord near Cambrai where for me the war would come to a painful and abrupt end. Back at home his family were still living at Peplow Hall. Now his father Beville had changed his parliamentary constituency to Ludlow in the south of the county and that year Lloyd-George had awarded him a baronetcy for his work in the sugar beet industry! Some years later, domestic circumstances meant the family had to leave Peplow and move to the Citadel, that dower house castle near Weston-Under-Redcastle which, as a boy, on seeing its distinctive shape shimmering in the distance from the heights of Hawkstone's terraces had mistaken for Camelot. On the death of his father and after a life time in the army, Sir Alexander Stanier,

Brigadier Welsh Guards, would inherit the Citadel and take on the mantel of baron and landowner of much of the community in which I had made my home.

But all that was still in the future. Walking home through Paradise I was surprised to see that without the foresters and keepers to tend them how quickly the woodlands had reverted back to nature. The immaculate lawns that had once swept down to the edges of the pools were gone, overgrown with a tangle of briars and nettles, and the open rides spanning the terraces were blocked with fallen brush and bracken. Already the pools were silted and stagnant and the once clear surface across which we had skimmed our "ducks and drakes" as children, were choked with a tangle of lily leaves and bulrushes. Never again would feeding trout cast rings of bright water at their margins, for these too had gone, gasping their lives away in the weed choked and brackish water or as victims of the poachers nets.

At home things were better than I had expected. Of course they suffered from the same deficiencies as the people living in the city, but Father's well stocked vegetable garden, eggs from the hens, bacon from the pigs and daily milk from the cow, ensured that nobody went hungry. Besides, with all the keepers gone to the war there was nobody left to police the estate, nobody that is, with strong legs and sound of wind to catch those members of the community who saw the well stocked woods and pools as a God sent gift for their survival, for now the keepers who remained, those ancient custodians of the estates, much preferred to stay indoors on moonlit nights. They had no stomach for a confrontation with a young adversary attempting to provide his family with a meal, especially when it had been rumoured that the Squire himself wished them to turn a blind eye to such misdemeanours. As a result, many country families lived better than they had before the war on a diet of rabbit, whose numbers had increased to epidemic proportions since the keepers had gone, and the occasional pheasant or hare, should one come their way.

Although I didn't realise it, I was witnessing the end of a feudal system in which the working classes had relied on their master's indulgence for their very existence. Now children were growing up without the disciplinary restraints or guidance of their fathers, the final generation of this decaying system. In the villages, young people were beginning to question their position and status in life. Could it be right that they were expected to support a system in which woods could be teaming with game while people living in their shadow starved? The result was a gradual breakdown in law and order and a decline in the old, archaic values that people like my father had accepted and set such store by. All this by virtue of a war that had robbed this country of a generation of its young men, fighting for a cause and in a quarrel that was not even their own. In doing so it condemned to the history books a way of life accepted and admired by many, but of benefit to only a few.

At the Hall, things would never be the same again. Father and those older workers who remained did their best to keep things going, but with limited success. Many of his horses had been taken for the war, greatly reducing the acres of land under the plough. Even when against the odds crops were grown, he had to rely on the services of those local women not already working in the factories or the old men of the community to harvest them. As well as the women from the surrounding area, there were those who came from the towns, many of whom were from a middle class background. Perhaps unpatriotically they chose life in the country over the hardships of the munitions factories and, as Father put it, "didn't know a cow's udder from a horses arse"! As a result he was often able to entertain us after supper with the calamities he witnessed each day, puffing furiously on his pipe and chuckling impishly to himself as he described in vivid detail, each disaster as it had happened.

Fox-hunting had been suspended for the duration of the war and although their owners had done their best to prevent it, many of the better horses had been commandeered for the cavalry. Besides, it had been decided by the masters that it would appear unseemly for the gentry to be seen besporting themselves across the country while their workers were dying by their thousands in France!

In the village, its oldest inhabitant, a man known to all as Uncle Tom and a great supporter of Fox-hunting, had taken this news badly, disappearing indoors vowing he would not emerge until the ban was lifted. Whether this was true or if he carried out his threat I don't know but by the end of the war when those sporting gentlemen with both the inclination and the requisite number of limbs to do so once more donned their scarlet coats and polished boots, Uncle Tom had long since gone to the big foxhunt in the sky.

His death marked the passing of one of the many larger-than-life characters who prospered during my childhood, fabled odd-balls and eccentrics the like of which we may never see again.

The weekend went quickly but with a further four weeks in England and the prospect of spending at least part of that time at home, there was none of the tension I had experienced on previous leaves. My brother Tom had been brought back from France, still severely incapacitated by the gas but now expected to pull through. This was heartening news for the family, especially Mother who had always been particularly close to Tom. She and Father had been able to visit him in hospital at Oswestry, thanks to the generosity of the Squire who had arranged and paid for their transport, being driven in one of the new motor cars which were already replacing the horse drawn transport of prewar days. I think this was probably the first time either my parents or anybody else in our rustic community had ridden in such a modern device so they were the envy of all who came to hear them describe their experience. What they found at the hospital, white as the crumpled sheets and blood flecked pillow on which he lay, was a shadow of the fine young man they had sent so unwillingly off to war. He was not well enough even to sit up in bed and could only speak a few words at a time and then only in a whisper. On their first visit Mother had spent the afternoon sitting by his side, holding his hand, hardly daring to speak in case her voice betrayed the fear uppermost in both her and Father's mind. Could anybody so badly injured both physically and mentally, survive, let alone make a full recovery? When the time came to leave they did so with heavy hearts; Mother telling me later that she was convinced she would not see him alive again. Some weeks had passed before I was able to visit him and by then he was on the way to recovery. Even so, I too was shocked with what I saw. Once more I relived the horror of the shambling columns of grey faced, blinded men passing through our camp at La Boiselle, their faces and uniforms spattered with the froth of blood stained saliva. That Tom had survived such injuries was a credit to his nurses, coupled with his determination to get out alive. Even so, he would never be the same again. After many months in hospital he would eventually recover sufficiently to be allowed home where, in Mother's loving care, he would slowly be nursed back to a degree of health where he could live what seemed on the surface to be a normal life. But even during the hottest summers his deathly pale complexion and whispering voice bore testament to the damage the gas had done when it blistered and burnt his throat and lungs. That it was irreparable he understood and stoically accepted that he would live in constant pain for the remainder of his life.

On the Sunday evening I reported to Shrewsbury Barracks where, to my utter astonishment, I was told that I should report to the newly opened RFC air field at Shawbury were I would be employed ploughing between the huts and any other spare land not associated with the flying program! Once again military logic had overtaken plain common sense! Due to the shortage of both horses and ploughmen causing hundreds of acres across the county to lie fallow, it seemed that I was to be employed ploughing up an airfield!

Until the foundation of the Royal Air Force in April 1918, all military aircraft were flown by what was then the Royal Flying Corps and were piloted by either army or navy personnel. For this reason Shawbury was still technically an army base and my being a soldier probably accounted for my being sent there.

The next morning I was told to report to the Unicorn, a public house situated at the bottom of Wyle Cop which in its day had been livery stables for teams of horses drawing the regular coaches which ran from Shrewsbury to London. Now the premises had been taken over by the military to stable horses commandeered from farms or shipped in from abroad, as well as the mounts of officers serving in the two Shrewsbury Barracks. Having been given two Canadian remounts, both spirited, half broken animals and the most unlikely candidates ever to pull a plough, I set off for Shawbury riding one and with my kitbag strapped on the other. It was wartime and the civilian population must have become accustomed to witnessing some odd spectacles passing through their villages, but the sight of a lone soldier complete with backpack and rifle mounted on one horse and leading another carrying his kit, caused many a raised eyebrow and enquiries of what on earth I was up to. Prudently I avoided the real explanation, muttering vaguely about being part of a training exercise. I'm sure that if I had told them the real reason for my being there, that I had been brought back from France to plough the air field at Shawbury, they would never have believed me and would have surely called the police!

Chapter 16

Adventures on Leave - February 1918

Commandeered

Last year he drew the harvest home
Along the winding upland lane;
The children twisted marigolds
And clover flowers in his mane.
Last year he drew the harvest home!

Today with puzzled, patient face,
With ears a-droop and weary feet,
He marches to the sound of drums,
And draws the gun along the street.
Today he draws the guns of war!

L Moberly

Crossing the Severn by the English Bridge I followed the road that ran beside the ruined columns of Shrewsbury Abbey and out into the open countryside. The village of Shawbury is set in the heart of rural Shropshire about seven miles to the north-east of the county town and I was in no hurry to get there, enjoying again the sweet smell of country air and the freedom from fear and uncertainty that had governed my life for so many months. It was midday before I arrived at the airfield, only recently developed to accommodate the rapidly expanding Royal Flying Corps. New squadrons were being formed almost on a daily basis and new pilots had to be trained to fly them.

About half a mile outside the village the flat acres of farmland had proved ideal for conversion into runways so only the year before large numbers of Irish navvies and German prisoners of war had been employed in an operation controlled by McAlpines. Together they had cleared the hedges and fences and filled in the many ditches that criss-crossed the land before laying two grass landing strips running in opposite directions to each other. I was surprised to see how permanent the new establishment already looked, with the seven huge wooden hangers already built and in use as well as other buildings housing stores, messes and all the other offices that go to form an efficient military establishment.

I would soon discover that the base was the home of No 29 [Training] Wing, a unit once within the Australian Flying Corps but now integrated into the RFC. Although they shared the facilities at Shawbury, the Australians, supplemented by some Americans, Canadians and New Zealanders, trained their own men, all of whom would eventually join the AFC, flying squadrons in France.

Accompanied by my two four legged charges I reported to the guardroom and was relieved to find that this time we were expected. Although a billet had been arranged for me, I explained that as I lived only a few miles away I hoped to travel home each evening after work as this was a condition of the original agreement, in that, although I was technically here on duty, I was also entitled to my original ten days leave.

After a good lunch in the airmen's mess I received my orders from the orderly officer who explained what was expected of me. I learned that somebody in authority had decided that by cultivating the unused land on the airfield, until recently productive agricultural land itself, the camp might grow and harvest enough crops to make itself self sufficient. To this end my job was to plough the spaces between the huts and any other spare land not being used in the training process which would then be sown with potatoes and other vegetables, the produce consumed within the service messes. Once more Military logic had overtaken common sense! Surrounding the airfield at that time were hundreds of acres of good agricultural land lying fallow entirely due to a lack of manpower and horses available to cultivate them!

After a brief struggle I managed to harness the two horses to an ancient plough borrowed from a nearby farm and prepared to set to work but it soon became apparent that this was not going to be easy. For a start, although both horses had been born and bred in Canada, the agricultural centre of the world, I was soon to learn that neither had seen, let alone been harnessed to anything resembling a plough before. To make matters worse, the sky now seemed to be full of extremely noisy aircraft with instructors both on board and on the ground screaming instructions through megaphones or waving brightly coloured semaphore flags at the trainee pilots in the air! This was too much for my two remounts, both more accustomed to the serenity and wide open spaces of the New Territories, who threw back their heads and bolted, dragging me, still hanging on to the handles of the plough for grim death, unceremoniously behind them. Both the day and my wounded pride was only saved when a quick thinking airman, one of a small crowd who had gathered, curious to know what was going on, risked life and limb by grabbing the bridle of one of the horses and reining them to a standstill. Red faced with embarrassment, climbing shakily to my feet I dusted myself down, the peals of laughter and good humoured banter from the onlookers ringing in my ears. It was with some relief that I saw that the only damage done, apart from a big dent in my ego, was a deep, jagged furrow zigzagging for some distance across the newly laid turf!

With both horses so terrified by the noise from the aircraft and the restrictions of their harness, I came to the conclusion that neither was completely broken in let alone ready for the plough, so that when the wing commander walked over to see how the work was progressing I was quick to tell him of my suspicions. After some discussion it was decided that rather than abandon the project all together I would try again, this time with two airmen each leading a horse.

This proved a workable solution and after an erratic start things began to improve in that whenever either or both horses attempted to bolt they were hauled to a standstill by their mentors, by the end of the day quite a bit of ground had been turned over.

In mid-afternoon I was summoned by a messenger to report to the cookhouse were I was given a warm meal before being directed to the Station Commander's office. There, to my surprise and delight I found a bicycle had been provided for me with instructions that it was mine for the duration of my stay. This was one of many acts of kindness I would experience during my stay at Shawbury and while I was there I would get to know both the Commanding Officer and the Wing Commander well. The former was Major A. W. Tedder, later to become Marshall of the Royal Air Force, the latter, Major H. A. Petre, was Australia's first military airman. Amazingly, he told me he had been engaged by his government in 1912 having replied to an advertisement in the Commonwealth Gazette seeking "two competent mechanics and aviators". He arrived at Shawbury via Point Cooke, Mesopotamia and Egypt, becoming the CO of No 29 Training Squadron on its formation in 1917!

I found the attitude of the Flying Corps different to anything I'd experienced anywhere else in my army career. Gone was the stuffy "them and us" principles demanded and expected by both officers and senior NCOs in Infantry battalions. The men I got to know were a new breed of fighter, respecting a man for what he was, not the number of crowns or stripes he wore on his sleeve. Charismatic and daring, their philosophy on life seemed to be "live life to the full today, for tomorrow you might die", a philosophy they followed to the letter. Playing hard and fighting hard, they thumbed their noses at authority and all the petty restrictions that it incurred. These were the same breed of young men who had scorned the use of parachutes in case carrying one suggested fear, opting instead to stay and fight or die if fate decreed, falling to the ground in their flimsy, burning craft. When the Germans fitted armour plating beneath their pilot's feet as protection against ground fire, they declined, opting for the greater speed and manoeuvrability afforded by the reduction in weight.

I soon found that everybody, both officers and airmen, treated me as their equal, accepting and respecting me for what I was, although only a private soldier, a veteran of the trenches and a fellow adventurer joined against a common foe. Many of them pressed me for first hand information about the role of the Flying Corps in the front line. Had I experienced attacks from the air? How good were the enemy aircraft and their pilots? I explained that anything I could tell them would be of little use, admitting I knew little or nothing about the various types of aircraft I had seen in the skies over France. They could not understand that to the foot soldier life in the trenches was a daily struggle for survival, nothing more or less. He had no time for plane spotting, taking cover in the handiest hole at the first sign of any attack from the air, and not emerging until well after the threat had gone!

Luckily for my new friends, the single combat dogfights of the early months of the war, greatly romanticised by the press, were over. Then, it took an average of seventeen solo hours to train a pilot for combat and more significantly, only an average of thirteen hours before he was killed! Now aircraft flew in formations often numbering as many as fifty and were employed to attack enemy infantry and artillery as well as supply bases and road and rail links to the enemy's rear. Even so, because we now had almost complete supremacy of the skies, it did not mean that the day of the legendary fighter aces was entirely over. The Germans still had Baron Manfred Von Richtofen in the skies, known universally as the Red Baron due to the distinctive red Fokker Dr-1 Triplane he flew, but he would be dead by the middle of the year. British fighter ace Albert Ball was dead, having destroyed a personal tally of forty three enemy aircraft and winning himself a VC in doing so. Eddie Richenbacker was still scoring successes in his S.E.5a, but by and large the days of the solo ace were over, in most cases quite literally!

Although I got on with everybody, I found the Americans more controversial than the rest. Perhaps, recognising kindred spirits, I admired and got on particularly well with them even though they were viewed with some suspicion, particularly by the locals. Many of them had been "barnstormers" before the war, members of the daredevil flying circuses so popular at that time in the USA and at the outbreak of war had crossed the Atlantic in search of the ultimate flying thrill, to pit their wits and skills in a duel to the death against an enemy sworn to the same philosophy on life as them. They were even more colourful than the most flamboyant of the English and Australian pilots, seeing discipline and military convention as something to be avoided at all costs. It was an open secret that pilots would often land at a prearranged spot in the surrounding fields, pick up their girlfriends, and take them for a flight, contrary to regulations of course! There were even rumours that one of these daredevils, a member of the famous McCudden family of fliers, had flown his aircraft below the arches of the Severn bridges at Shrewsbury, but perhaps that should be taken with a pinch of salt!

During my stay at Shawbury I enjoyed both good and bad days but not one of them was without incident, either entertaining, amusing, downright dangerous or sometimes tragic. Flying accidents were common with inexperienced instructors pushing their pupils through a very short course as quickly as possible and before I arrived the station had already suffered its first fatality. Crashes, both major and minor, occurred almost every day, especially during takeoffs and landings so that I had to be constantly on my guard for near misses. Exposed as I was in the open part of the airfield, on more than one occasion I was forced to abandon my plough and horses to their fate and run for my life at the threat of an out-of-control aircraft hurtling towards me. I'm not sure how both myself and the horses survived but survive we did even to the point where we became quite blasé about the whole thing. In retrospect, I suppose it would have been somewhat ironic if, after what I had already been through, I had met my end, killed by a friendly aircraft on an airfield only a matter of miles from my home!

A common cause of accidents was the undercarriage collapsing while landing, followed by the inevitable destruction of the rest of the aircraft, leaving the erstwhile pilot strapped in his seat, often still clutching the joystick and surrounded by the smoking wreckage of what had once been an aircraft. The trainees saw this as all part of a day's work, disentangling themselves from the wreckage if they were able, accepting with good humour both their instructors rebukes and the banter of their fellow students, they got on with the job.

After a while I was able to recognise the various types of aircraft and grew to know the advantages and shortcomings of each of them as if I were a pilot. That being so, although offered rides on many occasions I always declined, preferring to keep my feet firmly on the ground rather than risk my life in the air! There were Bristol Scouts, Avro 504 Monos, the lumbering but reliable Sopwith Camels for advanced training and even a few Sopwith Dolphins in which many of the pilots would become operational. Each type had a character of its own and has earned a place in aviation history.

February passed into early March and as at the end of each short winter's day I cycled the few miles home through the gathering darkness, I found a peace that I had not known for many months. Tea would be on the table and having finished at the Hall, Father would be sitting in his favourite chair beside a roaring fire, enjoying a leisurely pipe, awaiting my arrival. Tom was out of hospital and on the mend but was still very weak, only managing a few steps before having to rest. He had got into the routine of spending the morning in bed, only getting up after lunch if the weather was fine. On better days Mother would carry a chair into the yard where he would sit, swaddled in blankets, enjoying the fresh air until the afternoon became too chilly for comfort. Although there was no cure for the damage the gas had done to his lungs, the pure country air did much to improve his breathing. After many months of this routine and Mother's careful nursing he would eventually improve to the point where he could lead an almost normal existence.

As soon as I got home we would gather round the table to enjoy a meal prepared by Mother from what resources she had available. Butcher's meat, always a luxury, was a thing of the past. Instead there might be a joint of bacon carved thick from the flitch hanging in the pantry, or a rabbit stewed or roasted with fragrant stuffing made from the wild thyme that grew on the hill. There were always plenty of vegetables grown in the garden and eggs from the hens, so compared with others suffering from the shortage of provisions, we considered ourselves well off. After our meal, with the room lit by the warm glow of the oil lamp, we would gather around the blazing fire to talk often until bed time. Mother would get her sewing out and Father light his pipe, while my younger brothers Joe and Alec played on the mat with the few toys they possessed. Sometimes, if Tom was feeling well enough, they would beg him to read a story from some well thumbed book left behind by one of my sisters. Then Mother would "shush" us to be quiet and we too would listen as the story unfolded, related in his whispering, damaged voice.

Father had seemed to mellow and become more tolerant while I had been away or perhaps it was because I had grown older. Certainly the death of Jack and the injuries suffered by Tom and myself had affected both our parents. Father in particular now seemed to value every moment we spent together, to appreciate my company, so that for the first time in my life I found myself getting to know him for the man he really was.

On the first weekend I was home, Mother drove the three of us into Hodnet in the trap and leaving us at the door of the Bear public house, went off to call on a friend while we went inside. Although I was nineteen this would be the first time I had been there accompanied by Father and it was a new experience to order a drink for him and Tom at the bar. The occasion wasn't lost on the other drinkers who took the opportunity to have some fun at Father's expense. He took it all in good part, laughing with the rest of them, probably secretly proud to be seen out with two of his soldier sons. When an hour or two later we received a message that Mother was waiting in the yard, we climbed aboard the trap, red faced and on legs unsteady with drink, producing an icy stare and a cluck of disapproval from our driver. But seeing us all so happy together for the first time in many months was too good an opportunity to miss. She soon thawed out and together we took the road back home, setting the bare limbed trees of Paradise echoing with our peals of laughter.

All good things must come to an end and all too soon it was the last week before I must return to France. However, without telling me, Major Petre had written to my regiment asking for an extension of my stay at Shawbury, citing as his reason the need for additional cultivation. You can imagine my surprise and delight when on the Saturday of my last weekend, I received a letter giving me a further two weeks leave. My joy however was short-lived when, once again in line with military logic, only two days later I received further orders recalling me immediately to my regiment!

Back in France the Germans had started their final push, an action that would lead to a break out along the whole length of the Hindenburg line. Once more we were on the defensive and all men on leave were recalled immediately to their regiments.

Accordingly, the next day, after saying goodbye to my family and my new friends at Shawbury I boarded a train for Newcastle and my eventual return to the front.

Chapter 17
Return to France - March 1918

Leaving for the front

Before I die I just must find this rhyme,
Be quiet my friends, and do not waste my time,
I only wish my girl would hold her breath,
There's nothing wrong with me, I'm glad to leave.
Now mothers crying too, there's no reprieve,
And now look how the sun begins to set!
A nice mass grave is all that I will get.
Once more the good old sunsets glowing red,
In thirteen days I'll probably be dead.
Lichtenstein

Imagine my surprise when having reported for duty at the Regimental Barracks in Newcastle, I was paraded in front of the orderly officer, charged with being absent without leave, and thrown into a cell containing several other soldiers accused of the same offence! Despite numerous attempts on my part, no amount of explaining could convince the Provost marshal that I had been on approved extended leave as, yet again, my "agricultural duties" pass was treated with the same suspicion and disbelief as it had when I first arrived. Although I pleaded with him to call the station commander at Shawbury who would of course have been able to validate my claims, he was having none of it. I should have known better. Most of the regiment were already at the front so in the absence of anybody more suitable he had been left to his own devices to deal with an unfamiliar task where his priorities lay in getting as many men as possible back to France, no matter how and from what source they came. Unfortunately this decision was failing on two counts. Firstly, as a Territorial, the ability to coordinate such a task was far beyond his limited experience, if any, of troop movements. Secondly, he was one of the old school of military policemen so typical of the provost departments at that time where any deviation from the everyday, run-of-the-mill situation, not dealt with "by the book" was far beyond his comprehension and limited intelligence. He was not unique! It had always been maintained by ordinary foot soldiers that the only qualification to join the military police was "to read or write, not necessarily both!" which of course accounted for why they always went around in pairs!

"I've never heard such a cock and bull story in all my life," he bellowed as he slammed the cell door shut behind him, "I suggest you tell it to your company commander when you get back to France. If you're lucky he might believe in fairies. If he doesn't, then you're in for the high jump!"

In hindsight, this acute need for every fighting man to be made available in France may have saved my bacon for in a less critical situation I could have found myself left behind in England to explain my case, and who knows what the outcome of that might have been had the enquiry been conducted by this individual and his staff!

There was a threefold reason for this sudden demand and urgency for additional troops.

Firstly, the Germans, who over recent months had been hard pressed even to hold their own against determined Allied advances, had now been strengthened by additional troops transferred in from the Eastern front. The previous year the Peoples Revolution and the birth of Communism had resulted in the overthrow and eventual murder of the Tsar and his family, and a cessation of hostilities between the new Russian government and Germany. Lenin, previously in exile in Finland but now the peoples champion, had struck a deal with the Germans allowing him to return home, travelling in a closed train across Germany lest there be any suggestion of collusion with his country's erstwhile enemies. Now he was in control, an uneasy peace had been maintained throughout the winter, enabling seasoned German troops to be transferred to the front in France and Belgium to bolster overstretched divisions fighting there.

Speed was essential if a break out was to succeed, for it was common knowledge that soon the Americans would enter the war and this might be the last opportunity to achieve a German victory.

The third and most fundamental reason for additional Allied

troops lay in the latest German battle strategy which reasoned that the French had grown tired of the fight and without our support would soon capitulate. It was therefore decided that all future attacks would be on sections of the line held by the British. In theory, if they could break the British they could win the war!

On 22nd March the Germans attacked in such strength against already exhausted British troops that within four days they had regained territory twenty miles behind our lines. Now every man available was drafted into the breach, cooks and clerks and even men awaiting court martial or already serving sentences were issued arms and sent to the front. All leave was cancelled and at home, towns and villages were scoured for men absent from duty or overstaying their leave. Those caught were returned to their regiments in closed trains under armed escort.

It was to this atmosphere of anxiety and confusion that I returned to Newcastle, my papers showing that I had been in the country for over a month but with a leave pass permitting only ten days. Who could blame those in authority if it all looked a bit suspicious and worthy of further investigation?

Throughout the day more prisoners were brought in so that once our numbers had swollen to the point where the cells could no longer accommodate us, we were moved under escort to a wooden hut in another part of the camp. Once there we were locked in for the night with a guard posted at the door.

I was fortunate to grab a top billet in one of the rows of bunks that filled the hut and having spent the previous night travelling in the discomfort of a crowded carriage on route to Newcastle, was soon fast asleep.

The next morning I was shaken roughly awake by a very agitated MP who, before I was fully awake, dragged me down from my bunk to fall crashing to the floor in a melee of indignant arms and legs! Or rather, I landed where the floor should have been! Right below my bunk the wooden boards had been torn away leaving a gaping hole, open to the outside world. The hut was constructed on stone pillars, raising it about three feet off the ground and to my surprise and secret delight, I learned that in the night several of my fellow inmates had made a bid for freedom through the hole in the floor! Soon the room was crowded with furious MPs led by a very indignant provost marshal, each demanding to know what part I had played in the escape. Because of my bunk's close proximity to the hole I was obviously the chief suspect and was therefore singled out for individual attention. Although I assured him that I had slept through the night and had heard nothing, neither was I involved in the escape, the provost was not to be convinced. Wasn't I the cocky young bugger he had interviewed only the night before with the highly unlikely story regarding agricultural leave? Did I think he was born yesterday? Not on your Nelly! How could even the heaviest of sleepers remain asleep while the boards beneath his bunk were ripped bodily from the floor! To make matters worse the chap on the lower bunk was one of those missing. This heightened his suspicions, convincing him that even if I had not been part of the escape I must have been aware of it taking place but had not raised the alarm. In the eyes of the law that made me as guilty as the escapers. Paying no attention to our protestations of innocence, me and those men in the bunks nearest the hole were bundled out of the hut and doubled back to the orderly room. Here we were placed two to a cell where we could be further "interrogated" by more military policemen who by now had arrived in some numbers. Once the cell door was shut they set about us with a will, knocking us to the ground, taking turns to kick and punch us until we were soon black and blue.

"Too many pigs and not enough teets, mate", muttered my fellow prisoner through lips already swollen and bleeding, only resulting in an even more determined attack by his tormentors. Of course in their eyes we were already despicable characters who were prepared to go absent at the expense of others more willing to fight our war for us. Not for the first time in the last twenty-four hours I found myself regretting ever hearing about, let alone participating in, the much maligned and apparently little publicised, agricultural leave policy!

The interrogation continued for some time with both of us steadfastly refusing to admit any knowledge of the escape. From the other cells, the grunts of pain, thumps and curses, bore testament that others were doing the same. Certainly, for my part I was telling the truth having somehow managed to sleep through the whole incident. Presumably so had the sentry posted at the door, but I heard no mention made of that!

Had I have known anything I wouldn't have confessed it anyway. With memories of Étaples and beyond still fresh in my mind, in my book aiding and abetting the Provosts in any way whatsoever ranked alongside helping the enemy!

Just when it seemed that the inquisition would never stop, a messenger arrived with the news that one of the escapers had been recaptured and leaving us to lick our wounds, all the MPs hurried away to join in his interrogation. Poor fellow! If he knew what he had coming to him I think he might have preferred to take his chances at the front!

We remained locked up until midday and from snippets of conversation heard outside our cell it became obvious that none of the escapers had got very far and soon all were back in custody. With their recapture any useful information we might have provided was of no further interest to the MPs so when the men remaining in the hut were fell in and marched under armed guard to the station, we were allowed to go with them. This time there were no cheering crowds or waving flags to speed us on our way! Those who saw us coming often turned their backs while others shouted insults and spat at us as we passed. Who could blame them? To them we were cowards and deserters, safe here at home while many of their loved ones had already lost their lives fighting at the front. This was a situation I found particularly hard to accept, considering my complete innocence of all charges!

At the station we were bundled aboard the train, the doors locked and the blinds pulled down. Peeping through a chink, I could see that the platform was crowded with people, both civilian and military. MPs were urging men to board the train, ignoring the insults and blows flung at them by wives and sweethearts stealing one last precious moment with their men folk before saying a final, tearful goodbye.

For the second time of leaving Newcastle it was a relief when all were finally aboard and the train steamed out into the open countryside. Spring had come early that year so that when our guards permitted the blinds to be rolled up it was pleasant to watch the newly awakening landscape rolling by.

The train rumbled on through the afternoon, stopping occasionally at small towns and halts to pick up more troops. At every stop women and families were there to see their loved ones off and once again there was the same hostility that we had witnessed in Newcastle. Gone were the happy crowds of well wishers who had so enthusiastically cheered their men folk on their way only a few years before to fight in a war "that would be over by Christmas". The harsh reality of a conflict that had already robbed so many families of their men folk had taken its toll so that now each tearful farewell was treated more like bereavement rather than an occasion for optimism.

Once, the train stopped in a small town where the black mounds of spoil and the winding gear and powerhouses of several coal mines dominated the landscape.

While we waited, one of the winding wheels hoisted a cage to the surface and disgorged a crowd of miners who emerged blinking into the sunlight, their faces black with coal dust. I watched as they started up the road, still walking bent backed from their recent shift, rubbing eyes still unaccustomed to the light with grimy hands. On seeing our train was packed with soldiers they ran towards us, doffing their helmets and raising a ragged cheer in a spontaneous greeting. I had travelled with one of these on my way to Newcastle the day before and had been surprised to learn that to his disgust he had been conscripted to work in the mine just as so many others had been to the military. He described the frustration and even shame that he now experienced at not being selected to "do his bit", and the envy he felt for those he saw playing the more "glamorous" role as soldiers! Little did he know! Had I been given the choice, knowing what I did now I would have drawn pick and shovel and been hacking away at that coal face faster than you could say Jack Robinson! I suppose it was another case of, "if you haven't been, you haven't seen", as the old sweats never tired of telling us when we were in training. Perhaps if he had, he would have been less reluctant to work in an environment which, although arduous to the extreme, could at least guarantee that with a modicum of luck he would still be alive at the end of each working day!

Just as dusk was falling the train slowed to a crawl on a stretch of the line where the houses ran close alongside the track. Directly opposite my carriage my attention was drawn to a lighted room where I could see a family about to begin their evening meal. There was a man and two small children and as I watched a pretty young woman crossed the room and made to draw the curtains. Knowing that she had seen me and embarrassed at my intrusion, I was about to turn away when she paused for a moment, giving me a smile and a little wave before we were gone, shutting out for ever that vision of safe, comfortable family life that every passenger on the train would have given his eye teeth to be part of. Gazing into the cosy, lamp lit room, sharing for a moment the comfort and security of that little family reflected in the happiness of the woman's smile, brought memories of home flooding back. I wondered, was the man a soldier perhaps on leave from France? If he was, then every moment spent with his family would be more precious to him than life itself with the close proximity of the trains and the relentless ticking clock a constant reminder that all good things could not last forever. Perhaps, in a few days time he too would be on a train, looking across the track to the window hoping for one last sight of his tearful family waiting there. Or was he one of the lucky ones with a reserved occupation, seeing the trains and their occupants only as a source of irritation and intrusion, never thinking of the heartbreak and sorrow of recent partings they might conceal?

As the train gathered pace I longed to be back at Crin Cottage, enjoying a welcoming meal with my family all around me like the little scene I had just witnessed. I imagined our cosy kitchen, the oil light blue with the smoke from Father's pipe, the air thick with the smells of Mother's cooking. I could almost hear the banging of pots and the laughter of the girls as they washed up the dishes from the evening meal and the contented grunt of Gypsy curled up on her rug before the fire. Instead I was journeying back to whatever fate held in store for me and the uncertainty and horrors of a war by no means over.

That in itself was not without its problems either. Being absent without leave could be a capital offence given the right circumstances. Although I was confident that the charge would be dropped as soon as I rejoined my regiment, I was nevertheless filled with some misgivings regarding my future if for some reason it was not.

Soon it was dark and I settled down to a night of fitful sleep and tormented dreams on the crowded train. It was still only March and the night was cold and the train unheated. I awoke shivering with cold to a day of scudding cloud and occasional snow flurries, the blustering wind promising an uncomfortable time ahead as we crossed the Channel. The train had been shunted into sidings on a docks where a troopship, already making smoke and with a good head of steam, was berthed at an adjacent jetty.

Those carriages containing men under guard which by now had swollen to over a hundred were the first to embark, their occupants chivvied and bullied by the same armed MPs who had accompanied us from Newcastle. Once on board we were herded below to a stinking mess deck, still stale with the stench of vomit and sweat from the previous crossing and once inside, the iron, watertight doors were clamped shut behind us. Some men panicked at the prospect of being trapped in what might prove to be an iron coffin should the ship have been attacked by submarines, beating on the doors with their fists, pleading to be let out. Many had been in the trenches, had experienced the terror of hours huddled in underground cellars as a barrage crashed and exploded overhead, waiting for the one that had their name on it. Some had dug frantically at the earth with bayonet or trenching tool to drag men blue lipped and suffocated from collapsed dugouts which had become their graves. Now the claustrophobic affect of the airless compartment was too much for them. But nobody came. After several hours of waiting, the changing throb of the engines pulsating below our feet and the rolling motion of the ship told us we were under way. Now there was little else to do but pray, placing our lives securely in the hands of the seaman's God and, more practically, in the vigilance of the sleek grey destroyer we hoped would be weaving its protective web about us in the dark, dangerous waters of the Channel.

Chapter 18

I Rejoin my Unit near Vimy Ridge - March 1918

Anthem of doomed youth

What passing bells for those who died like cattle?
Only the monstrous anger of the guns,
Only the rifles stuttering, rapid rattle,
Can patter out these hasty 'orisons.
No mockeries now for them; no choirs; no bells,
Nor any voice of mourning, save the choirs,
The shrill demented choirs of wailing shells;
And bugles calling for them from sad shires

Owen

The scene that greeted me when we disembarked at Calais was one of utter confusion. Such had been the speed and territorial gains of the German advance in recent days that movements officers had little if any idea of the exact whereabouts and condition of many of the Allied divisions. The situation was so flexible that circumstances were changing by the hour as desperate defenders were either overrun or fell back to reform again for one last ditch effort against an enemy intent on taking all before it.

As soon as we had landed our guards ordered us to fall in with the other troops and once ashore, make the necessary arrangements to rejoin our regiments. It had been decided that individual commanders would take whatever action they though appropriate regarding returning offenders. Presumably our escorts considered it unnecessary to accompany us any farther, assuming that now they had delivered us to France there was nowhere else to go other than to stay and fight. Besides, this was already too close to the action for comfort for most of the MPs, and with every man on this side of the Channel liable to be pressed into service at the front, common sense plus a strong desire for self preservation dictated that a speedy return to Blighty on the next available ship should be expedited without delay!

Of course, for the more desperate of their charges there were other options, some of which would have been to chance all and go on the run in France, or even taking the first opportunity to surrender to the enemy. But the uncertainty of the situation as to who was holding what territory and the inevitable and dreadful sentence of a courts martial if caught, made neither option hardly worth considering. Furthermore, there was a rumour that the decision whether or not to prosecute the charges had been delegated to the local commanders of each individual's regiment. If this indeed was the case then it was reasonable to assume that, with the need for any man who could bear arms of paramount importance as well as the ever changing situation on most fronts, the odds were that most of the offenders were likely to "get away with it".

The town was crowded with troops all seeking information and the means to rejoin their regiments. Many were old hands returning back off leave or recovered wounded recently discharged from British hospitals. Scattered amongst them, conspicuous by the freshness of their uniforms and the bright shine on their boots, were the many erstwhile non-combatants that until now had been fortunate enough to hold down safe postings back in Blighty. Now they would be expected to take their chances with the rest of us in the line and within days would experience the hardships and horrors of the front, killing or being killed by an advancing enemy flushed with the success of their recent campaign. Gone forever was the so called "luxury" of a toughening up process for new arrivals in training camps like Étaples so for these men the first live round that whistled past their ears would have been fired by the enemy and had certainly been aimed to kill.

Despite those grave misgivings history would show that when it came to it, almost without exception, these men would not let their country down.

Many of the towns and villages which had been well behind our lines at the time of my last visit were now back in German hands. Albert had fallen and now it was German troops passing beneath the outspread arms of the hanging Virgin who offered up fervent prayers for her early destruction. This time they would be answered. On 22nd April, British artillery levelled to the ground both her and what remained of her tower, thus preventing its use as an enemy observation post. So ended the legend of the lady who, as many of the more cynical amongst us would maintain, was probably the only virgin left in town! And what of the legend, that when she fell the war would end? Six months later an armistice was declared and hostilities ceased. Was it only a coincidence or did fate really play its part? I will leave that to your own conclusions.

Every road into town was blocked with military transport either bringing wounded in or taking troops and equipment out. Fleets of commandeered French taxis and buses with crude red crosses daubed on their roofs disgorged injured men onto the quayside for shipment back to England before turning back for another load. With luck, for these the war was over as it certainly was for those for whom medical assistance had come too late. Amid the bustle on the quayside, several burial parties were going quietly about their business, stacking up the dead on handcarts to be taken for burial in mass graves outside the town. Troops milled around in confusion, their numbers varying from single individuals to complete sections as they sought to find the whereabouts of their regiments and the means of rejoining them. Crude notice boards with regimental names scrawled on them in chalk advised troop commanders to join the queue for further information on their movements.

I joined a small line of men waiting beneath a sign marked "brigades of the 11th division". When my turn came the movements officer manning the desk told me that as far as he knew the Northumberland Fusiliers and in particular units of the eighth regiment were still supporting the Canadians holding out on Vimy Ridge. Remarkably this was the only part of the line that had not broken. He advised me to link up with a section of the Dorsets who I eventually found, gloomily awaiting their transport in the ruins of what had once been a school. They were commanded by a very young second lieutenant from the Manchesters who was taking them as far as Hazebrouck before joining his own division farther to the east near Ypres. He was very nervous about the whole affair, explaining that this was his first time out, as it was for most of the men in his charge. He was still unaccustomed to the frequent detonations from artillery firing close at hand and throughout the journey kept involuntarily ducking his head at each explosion. Even my assurances that the guns were mostly ours and therefore the shells were all outgoing did nothing to convince him of his safety.

We waited for more than an hour until our transport arrived. This was in the shape of several decrepit lorries and vans, all of which had seen better days, a fact that soon became apparent when nearly all of them broke down at some point in the journey. Several had to be abandoned at the road side and their passengers distributed among the remainder so that, by the time we reached our destination, each lorry was filled to capacity with cramped and indignant travellers.

After a journey of less than fifty miles but lasting several hours in which we were often forced to make detours to avoid territory that scouts informed us was either under attack or already held by the enemy, our convoy lumbered into Hazebrouck, an impressive town of some size which at first sight seemed to have escaped the rigours of war. I stayed that night in a large house which had been commandeered as a military staging post and in the morning begged a lift from a party of Canadians and a section of Portuguese Pioneers as far as Souchez.[1] From there I travelled the remainder of the journey on foot. After many false trails I eventually located my Regimental HQ established in what had once been the village of Neuville St Vaast on the western slopes of Vimy Ridge and it was with some relief that I found my old CO, Captain Robinson, still in charge, finally dispelling any fears I had about the accusations regarding my extended leave. Fortunately it had been him who had received the original order resulting in me and other volunteers taking part in the scheme and he was amused but not surprised to hear the suspicion and disbelief with which it had been greeted. Apparently within a week of its issue the order had been rescinded, but of course it was too late by then as I was already back in England.

When I asked if it would be possible to rejoin my old friends in thirteen platoon, his reply came as a terrible shock.

"Williams", he said "I'm afraid that won't be possible. Unfortunately every one of them is dead!"

He explained that every member of the original platoon, more than twenty men in all, had been sheltering in a dugout which had received a direct hit from an enemy shell. There were no survivors. This news came as a severe blow to me as I had known most of them and counted many of them as my friends. I could certainly count myself fortunate that, had I not been on extended leave, there is little doubt that I would have died with them.[2] Of my dead friends, I would later learn that the trench system they had been occupying was the original German front line and was therefore "the wrong way round" to offer maximum shelter from incoming shells. To explain this, when occupied by the enemy the parapet or front of the trench would have faced the British lines and it was on this, the safer side, that the Germans constructed their deeper dugouts. In this way they were not exposed to direct hits and therefore offered greater protection, especially the high trajectory of mortar bombs. But since we had occupied them, attacks came from the opposite direction with what had once been the parados or rear of the trench now facing the enemy. In this way the mouths of the dugouts were directly exposed to incoming shells. My friends had been huddled in one of these, no doubt snatching a few precious moments sleep between duties, when they had died. Hopefully, and with the grace of God, they never knew what hit them.

This odd situation existed all along this part of the line with British and Canadian troops occupying former German front line trenches. It was said that a visiting high ranking officer had been scathing in his remarks regarding the construction of the trenches, demanding to know why the firing step and loopholes apparently faced the rear, away from the enemy. His embarrassment can only be imagined when it was explained to him that the trench in which he stood had until recently been manned by an enemy now entrenched in what had originally been their support lines and they were therefore in the opposite direction to where he was looking!

Before we left to join that part of the division still on duty at the front, the following day the odd assortment of men, including myself, who had been hurriedly collected together to form a new platoon, were briefed by Captain Robinson. He emphasised the importance of holding the ridge at all cost against an attack which was anticipated at any moment. This was because Sir Douglas Haig, contrary to the views of many of his junior commanders, was positive that the main thrust of the German breakout would eventually be aimed at Vimy Ridge and the rich coalfields of Bethune which it protected and was convinced that all the enemy activity to the south was merely a feint to disguise this, the main objective of their plan. But not for the first time, Haig had got it wrong.

As a consequence, dug in in well fortified positions in the miles of tunnels and natural caves that bisected the eastern slopes of the ridge, the Canadians waited in some numbers for this anticipated attack. Supported by units of the 34th Brigade recently relieved from its toils near Arras and with enough artillery to repel any but the most formidable attack, they scanned the lower slopes of the ridge for signs of an enemy that would never come. Local commanders were ordered to stay and fight to the last man, there was to be no retreat or surrender under any circumstances.

Thus it was that I found myself crouching in the remains of a German trench just below the crest of Vimy Ridge with a distinct feeling that maybe this time my luck was about to run out!

There was no question that I was back; the sights and smells all around me told me that. Looking down over the ruined landscape at my feet I could see dead men, British and Germans, scattered in the grotesque positions of death. Many had been there for weeks so that their rotting bodies had swollen and burst from the remnants of their uniforms and what had once been a face was now a pealing skull covered with a thick coat of flies which rose in clouds when disturbed. Not a tree or building had been left standing, the wooded slopes of the ridge smashed to matchwood with the ferocity of previous attacks. In the muddy waters of big shell holes, bodies floated face upwards, their white, bloated faces and clawing hands looking like the remains of drowned and putrefying frogs. Everywhere I looked was scattered the debris of war, tin cans, broken equipment, bandages, and over everywhere a constantly moving cloud of paper scraps blown to and fro on the wind. Over all there were the familiar smells of war, the overpowering odour of rotting flesh, the sickly sweet aroma of lyddite and the acrid stench of cordite, while in the trenches the usual smells of urine, sweat, and human waste from frightened, unwashed men, invaded the senses. These were the everyday smells and sights of war that I had known before and must learn to accept again.

When not on watch we were set to work improving our positions, digging new fire steps and loopholes in the ruined trenches or filling and stacking sandbags that a carrying party had brought up the line the night before. Once it was dark we went out in working parties laying new wire or repairing old in a furious fight against time to conciliate and strengthen our position against an attack which never came. Occasionally there would be a minor skirmish by enemy raiding parties or a token barrage from artillery sited well beyond our horizons. Once or twice the prevailing winds were such that the gas alarms were sounded as shells began to plop and fizz in front of us, spreading their yellow cloud of agonising death to anybody unlucky enough to be caught in its path. But by now we had been issued with the new gas respirators, replacing the urine soaked cloths which had so inadequately protected Tom and his comrades less than two years before. These offered ample protection against most attacks, only the danger of burns from mustard gas needed to be avoided, if it came in contact with exposed flesh. So we stood to, thrusting our hands deep into our pockets, holding our rifles between our knees, watching through the green tinted glass of the respirators for the enemy to emerge through the yellow fog. But they seldom came and when they did were easily repelled and soon the wind that constantly blew on the high slopes of the ridge cleared the gas away allowing us to escape from the sweaty, claustrophobic confines of the masks. But for several days after an attack, pockets of gas could lie in shell holes, staining the water yellow with its poison, setting a deadly trap for any unwary victim seeking cover there while under attack.

In the time I spent on the Ridge, the hours on night watch were by far the worst. Each of us would take turns to man the most dangerous positions, drawing lots as to which location each of us would occupy far out in no man's land. As evening fell we moved out into the saps leading towards the isolated forward listening posts, taking with us a rifle, a few bombs, a gas alarm and Very pistol. The gas alarm was used to signal the start of a gas attack, giving those behind us ample time to put on their respirators before the yellow cloud enveloped them but the need to fire the Very pistol had a much more sinister implication. This must only be done when a forward position was about to be over run, signalling to those manning the main trench that they could expect the enemy to be upon them in five minutes or less. Unfortunately, it also signalled the end through death or capture of the individual firing it.

As soon as the last man signalled he was in position, the saps behind us were blocked with cross barriers and razor wire. Intended to hamper the enemies advance, it also ensured there was no retreat for any sentry whose nerve might fail him at the last moment when faced with certain death.

Each minute spent out there in the dark seemed more like an hour, where every noise was amplified, every flickering, sinister shadow a possible enemy. At least the night was never silent, the continuous rumble of distant artillery firing along the line and the occasional stutter of a machine gun combining to keep me company. Occasionally a star shell would illuminate the night sky, casting its eerie light on the shattered landscape, further emphasising the threatening black shadows of a hundred shell craters, any one of which might contain a watching enemy. Soon it would splutter and die, turning the night so much darker than before so that sentries strained desperate eyes for any tell tale sign of an impending attack.

Eventually, after what seemed like a lifetime the sky would gradually lighten signalling the dawn when the familiar shapes of objects, so sinister in the night, came slowly into focus. At last the sun would rise on another day accompanied by the comforting sounds from the waking trenches behind me, and an assurance that in reality I had never been alone.

As soon as I was relieved I would run back along the saps, joined on the way by other sentries going in, the relief of surviving another night reflected in the loudness of their voices and happy faces.

"What the hell was that noise just after midnight, thought it was the end I did, very near shit myself!"

"You're getting soft old lad. Got bloody trench fever you have, seeing a bloody Hun in every hole", our relief and new found joy at just being alive echoing through the trenches in our laughter.

As we neared the main trench somebody would shout a warning that we were coming in, giving the password if ordered to. Too many men returning from raiding parties had been shot by a nervous guard just when they thought they had reached the safety of their trench.

The night would end as countless nights before with the obligatory stand-to followed by mugs of hot tea laced with rum. Sometimes we would fire a bit of morning hate just to let Jerry know we were still ready and waiting if he fancied a fight but usually we would just settle down to the tedium of another day as little cooking fires were lit all along the trench and breakfast got started. Soon the smell of frying bacon would mask for a moment the less appetising smells our noses had become accustomed to.

After eating it was time to find a place to snatch a few hours fitful sleep, usually curled up in one of the many ruined dugouts constructed by the enemy.

But all too soon the lengthening shadows would herald the coming of another night when fresh sentries would be expected to make their reluctant way out to their isolated posts where once more the lonely terror of the forward lookout's duty would begin.

Chapter 19

The Beginning of the End - April 1918

Returning
Sombre the night is.
And though we have our lives, we know
What sinister threats lurk there.
Dragging these anguished limbs, we only know
This poison-blasted track leads to our camp-
And a little safe sleep.
Rosenberg

Through information gathered from German prisoners of war and other sources, Haig was convinced that the attacks to the south were really only a diversion and that any attack worth its salt must be ranged against Vimy Ridge and the coalfields it protected. However, while our division was stationed there the major attack he predicted never materialised and, as history would show, never would. In reality, was this information on which Haig based this theory just a double bluff by the Germans to ensure that the Canadian Corps and a great deal of equipment remained out of circulation throughout the German final offensive? If it was, it certainly worked!

All around us the Germans were recording success after success as the battered and exhausted British forces fell back or were overrun in the face of overwhelming odds. But despite these successes, time was running out for the Germans for they knew that soon the Americans would be entering the war and despite having advanced more than forty miles in less than two weeks, they still had not managed to administer that final decisive blow that might lead to a British surrender. Until that time, pockets of resistance were hanging on for grim death, fighting rear guard actions, their commanders sending back runners almost by the hour begging for more ammunition, supplies and, most of all, reinforcements. When and if the latter eventually arrived, they were dismayed to find that the majority were mere boys, shipped out from England as soon as their basic training had been completed. Before now, nineteen had been the minimum age for conscription, but such was the need to replace the huge casualties sustained in the recent campaigns that the age limit had been reduced to eighteen.[1] From now on these youngsters would be expected to take up the fight for the remainder of the war. This they did, and did it well.

It had become the accepted policy that field commanders should no longer disclose the seriousness of the situation to their beleaguered troops, nor to keep them up to date with the circumstances as they unfolded. Indeed, such was the speed of the enemy advances that from their headquarters well behind the lines they knew even less regarding the overall position than we did! The adopted policy seemed to be "the less the men know about the gravity of the situation, the better they will fight" and if this was the case, then it was an insult to the tenacity and fighting spirit of the men under their command. As one of my mates commented, "We're just like a crop of bloody mushrooms, up to our necks in the shit and always kept in the dark", a sentiment we all heartily agreed with.

Both in the reserve trenches and in the line, rumours were rife regarding our isolated position on the ridge. True, the Canadians were still in position and backed by their heavy artillery we were confident that it could be held against almost any enemy frontal attack. But the disconcerting news that Armentières, the home town of that legendry mademoiselle of musichall fame had been evacuated and that enemy storm troopers were within five miles of Hazebrouck, was received with some dismay and apprehension. It was obvious to everyone that should those two British strong holds fall, the way would be open for this new breed of handpicked and specially trained troops to skirt around the ridge leaving us outflanked and isolated, and should that happen we would be left with no avenue for support or escape. It would only be a matter of time before well equipped enemy divisions following up would be able to mop up the remaining pockets of resistance, including ourselves, which the highly mobile and fast moving storm troopers had left behind.[2] On the face of it our future did not look very promising!

It was about this time that Haig issued his legendary Order of the Day to all British divisions still desperately holding on all along the line.[3] However, when it was read out to the exhausted troops it had the opposite effect to that which had been intended, for instead of acting as a rallying call to these battle weary men, wherever it was received its contents produced howls of ironic laughter and snarls of derision. In it he ordered them to "hold every position to the last man", something that many of them had been doing, unsupported and under horrendous conditions, for as long as they could remember. The order continued "With our backs to the wall and believing in the justice of our cause, each one of us must fight on to the end", the latter producing much sarcastic speculation and ribald suggestions as to exactly where he himself would be making his last stand. Most of it was unrepeatable but as one of our old hands was heard to remark while peering out from the flooded shell crater that was his only cover at the ruined landscape stretching out before him, "I don't see no bloody wall, in fact I don't see two bloody bricks still stuck together! If some kind soul would be good enough to point out this bloody wall I'm supposed to put my back to, I'll gladly get meself behind the bugger this very minute!"

Although we were usually spared from frontal attacks by raiding parties, the almost daily artillery bombardments delivered by the enemy were a constant ordeal, adding to our growing list of casualties. It was therefore a relief when we received orders that the battalion was to be sent back to Vermelles in order to rest and reorganise.

So we said goodbye to the Canadian Corps who had shared our discomforts on the ridge for the last two months, many of whom had become our good friends. They would remain there for a further three months before leading the decisive Allied counter attack and the eventual advance on the Rhine. It is a matter of history that the attack on the ridge, so clearly anticipated by Haig, never came[4]. It would not be until September that we would meet the Canadians again when our divisions would link up in a coordinated attack to the south of Arras and the Cambrai road, an action which would play a significant part in my future well being.

On the second of May our division formed up to march the short distance to Vermelles, situated only several miles south of La Bassée and to the north of Lens. However, the enemy's spectacular gains made even that difficult, forcing our already exhausted column of men to make a painful detour well beyond Lens, taking an extra three days of hard slog to achieve it. I remember little of that march, only the endless cobbled roads and my swollen and bleeding feet.

The routine was always the same, march for three hours then rest for one, my ungainly pack, rifle and equipment getting heavier by the hour, the chaffing straps gnawing cruelly into my shoulders until they bled. After a while each mile became a pain wracked blur, only instinct making me place one foot in front of the other, dropping instantly asleep wherever I fell when the order came down the line to fall out. Some never made it, collapsing from exhaustion as they marched before being taken away in one of several ambulances that accompanied us on the way. Simply out of desperation or the knowledge that they could go no further, others refused to move and were dragged away to who knows where by unsympathetic military policemen just as exhausted as they were. Somehow the rest of us made it, driven on mainly on a diet of bloody mindedness and a desire not to let the regiment or our officers down, who chivvied and encouraged us every mile of the way, either marching alongside us or riding equally weary horses.

On reaching Vermelles the company was billeted in the ruins of what had once been a large church and although most of the roof was missing it was a relief to be away from the icy wind that always seemed to blow along the exposed slopes of the ridge. In no time at all we had constructed improvised shelters from the ruined pews and priceless canopies that had once adorned the church. Rich oak panelling was ripped from the walls to be broken up and used as fire wood and altar candles, found by a scavenging party in the ruins of a store room, lit. Soon a building that only a few hours before had been just an abandoned shell had become a well organised billet. Once again the church rang to the sound of laughter from men who were just glad to be alive, while the plaintive notes of a mouthorgan, playing softly in the night, caused even those of us who had grown accustomed to the atrocities of war to shed a silent tear in the privacy of our billet. Somebody even produced an ancient gramophone and some records and soon the strains of the popular songs of the day, admittedly most of them were sung in French, floated through the ruins. We joined in with several renderings of the many trench ballads we knew, the obscene, bitter words often sung to the tune of well known hymns. The inevitable card schools were set up, the players oblivious to everything around them other than the content of their next hand. Probably for the first time in its history the church was filled with the appetising smell from a bubbling pot of Maconachie stew and frying bacon coming from the field kitchens set up by the cooks almost as soon as we arrived. For weeks in the trenches we had existed on a daily diet of bully beef and hard tack biscuits which, although if totally indigestible, burnt well, so made excellent fire lighters in times of shortages.

Too famished to wait for the food to cook right through, we tore into it with relish, savouring every mouthful, licking our mess tins clean and like so many Olivers, going back for more. By now we could eat almost anything, anywhere and to us that first meal in our new safe billet was the stuff of gods. After the dangers and hardships of the ridge we felt that this was heaven and I would like to think that God in his wisdom, knowing our desperate situation, would have approved of what we were doing in his house. The bible says "wheresoever two or more are gathered together, there shall be the house of God " and to twenty or more exhausted, footsore, lice ridden, hungry soldiers, it most certainly was.

For the first time since my return I received some letters from Mother and was relieved to read that all was well at home. She wrote that since I had left, my brother David had been home for two weeks and in that time he had coaxed Tom, still suffering from the effects of gas but improving by the day, to walk as far as Hodnet and back without assistance, something she had thought he would never manage again. Buoyed up by this good news, I went about my duties with added vigour.

During my time off I was able to carry out some much needed repairs to my kit as well as replying to Mother's letters. Later we visited a military bath house which had been set up in the centre of the town where I enjoyed the luxury of a hot bath, shared with a number of my comrades, the first I had had since leaving home. Afterwards we were issued with clean shirts and underwear, leaving the ones we wore, as well as our uniforms, to be decontaminated in the giant steam boilers set up for that purpose. Although the heat accounted for the adult fleas it did not kill their eggs which in time would hatch out to take the place of their deceased relatives, their constant itching guaranteeing to make our lives a misery.

But this euphoria proved to be short-lived. Within a few days of arriving we were once more in the front line, this time in the ruins of what had once been the town of St Elie, a small town which had once guarded the approaches to the Bethune – La Bassée canal. This had been taken some months before in hand to hand fighting and still contained hundreds of half buried, putrefying bodies, both military and civilian so that the sickly sweet stench of death was almost overpowering. The stench infiltrated and polluted everything and everywhere and at times was so strong it became unbearable. Finally, although we would have been safer in the ruined buildings and cellars of the town, the conditions there were so appalling and the danger of disease so great, that the line was extended to a new position in the fields beyond the town. Because of this, before doing anything else we had to quickly convert what had once been only a line of shallow rifle pits into more substantial trenches.

For the moment the enemy's advance had drawn to a halt, presumably while they regrouped and waited for their supply trains to catch up with them, but it was obvious from information gleaned from the trickle of enemy deserters that passed through our lines each day that the recent successes had cost them dearly in both manpower and equipment. In fact, it would appear that so much damage had been done that many of the elite divisions of handpicked men especially trained specifically for this offensive, were no longer functioning. For our part, while our enemy had no one left to turn to, we knew that if we could only hang on long enough we would soon be joined by the thousands of American troops who had already landed in France.[4] We also knew that, like a cornered animal with its back to the wall, it was only a matter of time before they were on the move again with one last dash for victory. Knowing this we burrowed feverishly into the ground, constructing hastily built defences, our shirts both soaked with the sweat of honest toil and the constant fear of being overrun which never left us, for have no doubt about it, we were all afraid. Fear was the constant, overwhelming reason why thousands of us survived and because of this, despite what has been written; during the war the accepted philosophy throughout the ranks was that it was much better to be a live coward than a dead hero! We lived with fear both day and night, hiding behind it like a protective shield until it became just another part of our chaotic, turbulent lives.

About a mile in front of us, the Germans manned their forward positions, their movements sometimes visible from where we lay. Between us stretched a moonscape of cratered fields, of blasted trees and the occasional ruined building. Usually in the early morning when the land was still shrouded in mist they launched speculative raiding parties against our positions, usually preceded by a mortar or medium artillery attack, which, if a favourable wind was blowing, included what had now become the inevitable crop of gas canisters. But with each attack our defences grew stronger as did our confidence so that when some sections of the Manchester regiment moved up to join us, our spirits really soared.

As each day passed and the news from the front improved, we began to realise that at last the scales of victory were slowly beginning to tilt in our direction and by delaying his attack the enemy was losing what advantage he had.

Sometimes enemy aircraft bombed or machine gunned our positions, flying parallel to our lines, placing the freshly dug, open trenches in their direct arc of fire. On the odd occasion these would be attacked by one of our aircraft and a dog fight would ensue and knowing that our tormentor now had his mind occupied with more pressing matters, we would watch from the comparative safety of our trenches, cheering on any success as it happened or cursing each failure, as the tiny aircraft wheeled and dived above our heads in what had become a dance of death.

On one occasion I was instrumental in registering a kill myself. At the time I was taking my turn as a gas guard and lookout, manning one of those dangerous, forward positions sited well in front of the line. Peering over the rim of the shell crater that provided my cover, I saw a German aircraft approaching from my right and the moment I saw it I realised it was different to the usual attackers as the tips of its wings were painted bright red. By that time everybody had heard about the Red Baron and his flying circus of scarlet painted aircraft, could this possibly be one of them? I feverishly wound the handle of the gas alarm, blowing my whistle at the same time, for some men were working in the open ground to the front of the trenches in an area totally devoid of cover. In seconds the aircraft had made its turn and began its run up the length of our trenches, firing its machine gun as it came. Fortunately those men nearest the trenches were able to dive for cover but others caught in the open ground were not that lucky as the tracing pattern of the bullets reached them as they ran. Safely out of the line of fire, I could only watch in horror as the death and destruction unfolded before me. First one man seemed to stumble then topple forward to the ground, another man with half his head blown away, staggered on for a few paces, a scarlet spray of blood spouting from his wound before crashing in a fury of thrashing arms and legs to the ground. Two more, caught only yards from the safety of the trench were caught in full stride, turning head over heels like shot rabbits as the bullets found their mark. By now the aircraft had reached a position behind and directly opposite me, flying about thirty feet above the ground, the coloured ribbons on the bombs he had now release fluttering towards the ground. From my position, I could clearly see the head and shoulders of the pilot above the rim of the cockpit, the sun reflecting brightly on the brown leather flying jacket he was wearing. Behind him, farther down the trench men were beginning to regain their composure, scrambling from cover to fire their rifles at the retreating aircraft, which, having completed his run, the pilot swung away to the right in a shallow climbing turn which took him just beyond were I lay. By now I too was ready and with my rifle supported on the rim of the crater I had him firmly in my sights as he passed in front of me. As the steepness of its turn increased, for a split second the aircraft seemed to hang motionless right above me so that most of the pilot's upper body and the back of his head were in full view. From a range of less than fifty yards, taking careful aim at the sun's bright reflection on the back of his jacket, I couldn't miss. As my first round found its mark his head flew backwards, this reaction only adding to the steepness of his turn and so exposing his body even further. My second shot was aimed where the first had been and this time, as the bullet hit home his body was thrown spasmodically forward, before pitching backwards once more, his head and arm hanging limply over the side of the cockpit. All down the line men were cheering and shouting, some firing shot after shot at the stricken aircraft as it described a lazy arc before crashing in the broken ground in front of us. For a few seconds it lay there, the apparently lifeless body of the pilot still hanging from the cockpit. Almost instantly there was a puff of smoke followed by a small explosion as high octane fuel spilled onto the hot exhaust and within seconds the engine compartment and one wing was engulfed in flames. At the same moment, the pilot seemed to regain consciousness, lifting his head then struggling with his harness, his one arm dangling uselessly by his side. We watched in horror as the fire took hold, the flames fanned by the wind quickly engulfing the forward section of the aircraft. Suddenly and to everyone's surprise, we saw that one of our officers had scrambled out from our trenches and, dodging the many shell craters in between, raced towards the fiercely burning aircraft. We immediately recognised him as Captain Lee, our second in command, who, it appeared, was intent on saving the trapped pilot whose desperate screams could now be heard above the roaring flames. Forgetting for a moment that the pilot was the enemy, all along the line men were cheering the Captain, willing him on as he raced to where the crashed aircraft lay. Suddenly the cheers changed to shouts of anger as a lone machine gun opened up from somewhere in the German positions far beyond the burning aircraft. Caught in the open and with little or no cover, a burst caught the Captain in full stride, his momentum carry him a few more yards before crashing heavily to the ground. For a moment he lay still, then to our relief we saw him roll sideways into a nearby shell hole. We furiously returned fire; firing like maniacs until the bolts of our rifles grew stiff with the heat, any thought of the stricken pilot completely forgotten, all the while screaming abuse at an enemy so far away they could not hear us nor could we see them. It was not until the Lewis gun sited farther down the trench jammed that the firing became at first more sporadic and then eventually stopped. In the broken ground between us lay the flaming wreckage of what had once been a man and his flying machine, now nothing more than a funeral pyre.[5]

Why did the machine gunner open fire that day? In a war in which by now no quarter was asked or given, there still existed a certain chivalry, a degree of honour and respect given and received on both sides. I would like to think, being so far away that he couldn't see the perilous situation the pilot was in, that his intention was to provide covering fire to a stricken comrade, allowing him to get back safely to his own lines rather than being captured by the running man the machine gunner perceived to be pursuing him. From his firing position so far away he would not have seen or known that the pilot was badly wounded and trapped in his burning aircraft and that his only chance of survival lay in the heroic actions of Captain Lee.

As for the heroic Captain Lee, feted as an hero, as soon as it was dark a stretcher party brought him in and he was immediately taken back to a clearing station, badly wounded but expected to survive.

And who was the anonymous pilot who died that day flying an aircraft with red painted wing tips? Certainly not the Red Baron for, also the victim of ground fire, he would crash and die only ten days later in the killing fields of the Somme.[6] But just for a moment, in that broken land on the outskirts of the stinking pile of rubble that had once been called St Elie, I thought that perhaps I'd become a part of history.

Chapter 20

Rest and Relaxation - May 1918

Song of the KSLI
We are King George's army,
We are the SLI.
We cannot fight, we cannot fxxx,
What effing good are we?
But when we get to Berlin,
The Kaiser he will cry,
Hoch, hoch, mein Gott,
What a bloody fine lot,
Are the boys of the SLI.
Sung to the tune of the hymn *"The church's one foundation"*

During our stay in the St Elie sector we were not continually in the line, about half that time being spent on relief. In the latter part of the war a system had been adopted that rotated units between the front and reserve lines. This meant that even when our division was on a tour of duty in the fighting zone, almost half the strength would be enjoying a period of rest, while on particularly difficult fronts the whole division might be relieved and taken back well beyond artillery range for an extended period of rest and relaxation. During this time, officers who were entitled to leave every six months as well as any of the lower ranks who in theory received but very seldom got ten days leave every twelve months, could hope to get away to England. On the twenty-fourth of April, having been relieved by the Kings Yorkshire Regiment, we went into divisional reserve at Mazingarbe. By that time we numbered only twenty-five officers and seven hundred and sixty-one other ranks from a peace time compliment of over two thousand men.

Even in our periods of relief we were never allowed to forget for one moment that we were in the army. Daily kit inspections were arranged and route marches in full battle kit the order of the day. All these things that we had readily accepted while under training now seemed so unnecessary and pointless here. Only a very few of our company were fresh out from England, most being seasoned veterans, each one desperate for a short spell of rest away from the depravations and dangers of the front. Needless to say, we had little time for the mock battles, fought in terrain that bore little or no resemblance to the actual conditions we faced during the real thing. To make matters worse these were often overseen by red faced majors who we suspected had never experienced a shot fired in anger themselves. There was infantry training, close order drill, bomb throwing and bayonet fighting, all of which many of us had experienced firsthand. What was the point of trying to explain that the sensation gained from sticking a bayonet into a straw stuffed dummy bore no resemblance to that of a human being? On the training ground, how was it possible to emulate the shrieks of pain, the fountain of blood and the sickening crunch as thrusting blade first hit, then penetrated, resisting bone? How it might prove necessary to shake the writhing body off the blade or even worse, blow it off with a bullet, then having done it, that your tunic and face might be spattered with a mixture of burnt cordite, steaming blood and shattered flakes of bone? How you would clear your eyes with a shaking hand before charging on to the next and possibly worse act of butchery. Only someone who had experienced this firsthand could adequately describe that feeling. Once the action was over and the red mist that swam before your eyes had cleared and the initial surge of elation at having survived another brush with death had gone, the sickening feeling of horror and disgust as the truth of what you had just done began to sink in?

We played football matches against other companies, "to retain the spirit of teamwork and reliance on each other", a philosophy that army life was based on and something most of us took for granted anyway.

How could it be any other way? There were so many occasions when you had only come through by putting your trust in the man next to you. Perhaps it had been a stranger who, for a few brief moments had been your only hope of salvation and, for just as many occasions, you had been his. Throughout the conflict, comradeship, the sharing of hardships and danger together no matter what the personal cost, were gladly acknowledged as part of our normal way of life.

During these brief periods of relief I was able to enjoy the occasional visit to one of the few villages nearby which were still occupied by civilians. Sometimes a group of us would manage to beg a lift as far as Vermelles or even Lens where, despite almost daily shelling from German artillery sited in the hills beyond St Elie, many bars and cafes still remained open. During rest periods we were often billeted with French families who despite what we had heard, were always very kind to us. We repaid their kindness with gifts of bully beef and the inevitable apple and plum jam which we had in abundance. They in turn gave us fresh milk and eggs, a welcome relief from the thick, sweet, condensed milk and powdered eggs that made up our rations while in the line. Gradually some farmers were returning to their homes and beginning to restore the land to its original fertile condition. It was early spring and the fine, warm weather ensured that each meal we ate included delicious fresh vegetables cooked as only the French know how. Some families still had eligible daughters living with them and there were always those amongst us, I won't say who, young and fancy free, who sadly repaid the kindness of their parents by trying to seduce their daughters!!! These were jealously guarded and shielded by anxious fathers from any amorous advances made by even the most determined Tommies, often against the secret wishes of their willing but frustrated daughters!

Fortunately, in the bars and estaminets of the town the gaudily dressed but predominantly middle-aged women that we met didn't suffer from the same lofty ideals, offering their services to anyone who had the cash to pay for them. Venereal diseases where a real problem, just one more to be faced in a world in which all the odds seemed to be firmly stacked against us making survival our overriding priority. Never far from our thoughts was the certain knowledge that in a few days time we might again be facing death in the line so that we lived each one to the full and let tomorrow take care of itself. We were given lectures, shown pictures on the subject, and told harrowing tales of the effect VD could have on the unfortunate victim. Figures were trotted out showing that more people had been hospitalised through VD than from trench foot, pneumonia and frostbite combined. Oddly enough, if given the choice between death and being maimed, most of us would have opted for the former, so catching the pox seemed to be the least of our worries and as such, we paid little or no attention to it. However, particularly in inclement weather given the choice of attending a lecture no matter on what subject was infinitely better than being on fatigues, but, like most other things in our lives, what we had just learned was not taken seriously and for much of the time attracted the predictable derisive and ribald comments and advice from the captive audience.

"Can't dip our bloody wicks now without the MO's approval, better take the bugger with us next time we go on the razzle so we can send him in first. Probably find a platoon of bloody sappers in there when he does, ready to blow his bloody balls off!"

We had seen the demonstration and heard the warnings so often before that at the appropriate moment the whole audience would yell out an indelicate rhyme describing the symptoms and the telltale discharge produced by that unfortunate disease.

"And the MO said squeeze and he squoze and a bubble arose like the snot from his nose, only ten times bloody greener"

That it was inevitable we would forget everything we had been told the moment the first glass of wine had been gulped down or a scantily dressed young lady caught our eye from across the room, was readily accepted by the MO and all his team! Anyway, their warnings had something of a hollow ring when perhaps the next time we were in town we realised that the chap sitting at the next table nervously negotiating a price with a hard faced but willing lady, was the same earnest young medic who only that morning had been delivering the lecture!

On paydays, with enough money in my pockets to burn and the knowledge that every day could be my last, I joined the crowds eagerly making their way into town. Outside, the pavements were alive with activity, crowded with uniformed men, some of the luckier ones with a pretty girl on their arm. There were officers and men representing all the Allied armies, reflected in the colour and styles of the uniforms that filled the streets. While the majority might be dressed in dusty khaki, there were also the French in their horizon blue and occasionally the darker blue of the Royal Flying Corps or Royal Air Force as it was now called since its establishment as an independent unit earlier that month. On each corner of the street or slowly patrolling their beat, the women of the night plied their weary trade, most of them sad, sidewalk cast offs, too old or haggard to be made welcome in even the most seedy of the bars, each of which was filled to bursting point with soldiers from every regiment and nationality. Each was a tiny part of the mad human frenzy determined to enjoy themselves at any price, and never mind the cost, for didn't the saying go that you couldn't take it with you and that there were no pockets in shrouds?

We suspected the French of lacking backbone and therefore not to be trusted since their mutiny earlier that year. Safe in the knowledge that they didn't understand, we had taken to calling them "kippers", accusing them of being, "two faced and having no blooming guts", while we called any airman not wearing wings "penguins", for as everyone knew, as ground crew they had a safe and cushy number often well behind the lines, suggesting, like the bird of that name, that they were "Full of shit, always flapping but never flying!" They took it all in good part and I'm sure they had an equally derogatory nickname for us. If they did I never heard it but I'm sure it would have referred in some way to "cannon fodder"!

While we were all on relief things were different. Here we were all brothers together, united with the single aim of enjoying the few hours of leisure we had coming to us. It was therefore not unusual to see a couple of French infantrymen sharing a bottle of wine with some Australian Gunners while at the next table English Pioneers were doing the same with several Mounted Riflemen, each wearing the insignia of South Africa in his hat. We also shared the few available women who formed a steady procession between the bar and the bedrooms at the back. I was older and more confident now so willingly took my turn with the rest, happily parting with a franc or two to buy the obligatory green drink entitling me to a dance or more. Sometimes it was five francs or sometimes more for her services, depending on the age and looks of the lady concerned. I loved the character of the bars, the rich, spicy fragrance of French tobacco, the smell of cheap perfume and the pungent smell of perspiring bodies, all combined together to form a unique and unforgettable atmosphere. Most bars had a tinny piano or, in the bigger ones, a noisy band banging out the popular tunes of the day sang in broken English by a sequined, buxom, beauty. Fortified by the contents of a bottle or two of cheap wine I could forget the fear and anxiety that was never far away at the front. There, the sure and certain knowledge of a violent and sudden death was never far from my thoughts. In the dimly lit, erotic atmosphere of a bar I needed no reminding that, while I was here enjoying myself, not so many miles away working parties and patrols would be out there in the dark, or anxious forward lookouts would be carrying out their lonely, nerve racking duties, knowing that at any moment a burst of machine gun fire, an exploding grenade or thrusting bayonet could leave them with the other sun bleached and rotting corpses that hung, like keepers' trophies, along the wire. But should they survive, in a few days time it might be one of them sitting where I now sat. Then it would be him buying drinks for the same lady who, at this very moment, was professing her undying love for me. Would they think of me as I took my turn, courting death in the pulverized, stinking, rat infested acre or two of land that we were expected to defend, even with our lives? I think not.

Admittedly most of the available ladies were well beyond their best. They served each client with a bored indifference, granting each one the allotted ten minutes of their time, cursing those unfortunate enough who, through drink or sheer fatigue, failed to rise to the occasion. Fortunately I never had that trouble for I was nineteen now and in my prime. Once fortified with enough bottled courage to the point where even the plainest of bar girls looked almost presentable and egged on by my equally frustrated mates, I did my duty and took my turn with the best of them! On blank weeks, with all my money gone, there was always the Christian Fellowships that had been set up in most towns. Here, for the price of enduring a sermon on the weaknesses of the flesh or the perils of the demon drink, it was possible to drink free coffee all evening or perhaps join in a sing song around the piano or pedal organ with those other unfortunates who found themselves in the same penury circumstances as me. Often to the discomfort of the resident padre, although these sessions always began with hymns, it would not be long before we would be substituting our own, sometimes rude, often bitter but always humorous words for the original more pious version

> *"The bells of hell go ting-aling-aling,*
> *For you but not for me,*
> *The herald angels sin-aling-aling,*
> *I'll be up there for tea!"*

Sooner or later there would be a few raucous choruses of, "It's a long way to Tipperary" or the more sentimental, "Keep the home fires burning", often sang in several different languages. Then men would fall quiet as the thoughts of those loved ones they had left behind came flooding back. Of course they were keeping each of our home fires burning, but what would we have given to be warming ourselves by them now.

The days and weeks wore on and like a giant pendulum the Michael offensive began to slow, reached its zenith, faltered for a moment and then fell back, but not before it had sent shock waves coursing through both the French and English governments. Before it did, for the first time in the war Paris had got a taste of death and destruction from German long range guns but even so, in the end the cost of their success had left the German divisions badly depleted and any that remained too exhausted to mount another major offensive against the British line. After much consultation they reluctantly decided to go back on the defensive, accepting for the first time that, "the enemy resistance was beyond our powers".

Slowly but surely we were regaining the ground we had lost and our enemies were once more on the retreat. Still the Allies had not played their major card. This we saw as the new legions of Americans who, our officers informed us, were expected to enter the war at any moment. If we could only hang on long enough they said, these might prove to be the one decisive factor that would lead to ultimate victory.

As it happened, when the Americans arrived they would bring with them an additional far more deadly yet fundamental weapon that would play a significant part in the Germans' eventual defeat.

In March, when the Michael offensive first started, the Americans had only 290 thousand troops in Europe and although they were willing and rearing to go they were as yet untrained and not ready to fight. By October their numbers would have swelled to more than 1.5 million.

The previous year an epidemic of what would become known as Spanish influenza had spread across the United States, carried there by the thousands of European immigrants flooding into that promised land.[1] Now the American soldiers carried the virus back with them and in late May, after their first offensive near Catigny, American prisoners of war came into contact with the Germans and in so doing passed on the deadly virus. Within weeks the already weakened German army was decimated with a major flu epidemic that proved to be more deadly than any conventional weapon employed by either side. Whole divisions were struck down with an illness that, for the old, the weak or the undernourished, had no known cure. Many of the troops from both sides, weak and exhausted from months in the line, had no defence against it. It is estimated that throughout the world over twenty-seven million died in the ensuing epidemic. Our troops did not escape unscathed either. While we were in reserve at Mazingarbe I was awarded my first stripe and took up the duties of section lance corporal. I had never been one for authority, preferring the anonymity I found in the ranks, but I soon realised that wearing the stripe had many advantages, opening doors that had previously been closed to me.

Once more I was pressed into service, this time assisting the medics at a clearing station sited in an old warehouse on the outskirts of the town. My duties included overseeing the stretcher bearers carrying in the wounded from the CCS[2] at Bully to the railway station at Mazingarbe, before seeing them safely onto the train for transporting back to the base hospital at Dieppe. My first and only brief experience of this kind of work had been in the mud at Passchendaele and on that occasion, in order to survive I had been obliged to revert back to my role of infantryman. Significantly, a large number of patients bore no war wounds but were victims of the flu epidemic that by now was also decimating our ranks. They came in their hundreds from all sectors of the front, pale skeletal men, gasping for breath like fish out of water. By the time they reached us many were so ill they were beyond saving. These lay quietly on their stretchers or makeshift beds, shivering in blankets and greatcoats despite the heat of the day, vacant eyes staring unblinking at the sky. Only their shallow, gasping breath, blowing tiny bubbles in the bloody flux that ringed their mouths or the minute flicker of an eyelid separated them from those already dead.

At the railway station a RAMC corporal had the unenviable task of deciding who should go and who would not survive the journey. Those that were able watched him with tortured eyes as he made his way slowly down the line, waiting in turn to be given their chance to either live or die. He was only a young man in his twenties and the onerous responsibility he carried showed in the haunted expression on his face. What sort of world was this where such a burden could be placed on somebody so young? Could it be right that he should be expected to take upon himself the mantle of God and decide at a glance whether a man should live or die?

He tied a label marked with their destination on the lucky ones, the others he passed quickly by with a tiny shake of his head. That was our signal to remove them from the line and carry them to a place out of sight of the others where they would be made comfortable and left to die. There were some with horrific wounds and others classified as walking wounded. Each was given a tetanus injection by another medic wielding a huge steel needle which closely resembled an icing syringe, and according to those unfortunates receiving it, was just as blunt!

Beyond the town, burial parties were digging graves, soon to be filled with the anonymous, gas-cape shrouded bodies of the dead. At each graveside a harassed padre went through the motions of an improvised burial service before hurrying on to the next, having no time or inclination to discover if the occupant was Gentile or Jew, Atheist or Agnostic. Each received the same brief service committing them to the grave and into the tender hands of whoever in life they had recognised as their God. While I was there I found one of my old comrades who had served with me on Vimy Ridge. A victim of the flu epidemic, he was one of the unlucky ones rejected as unable to travel. I pleaded with the corporal to change his mind but all to no avail. He explained that like so many others, my friend's condition was so advanced, that even if he survived the train journey, there was no chance that he would recover. To me it seemed so unfair. Here was somebody who had survived the war thus far only to die from what in other circumstances and to a fit young man might have proved to be nothing more than an everyday illness. I sat with him for a while and held his hand. Although he showed no sign of hearing, I reminisced about the happy times we had had and all the good friends we had left behind. After a while I realised he had stopped breathing. Reluctantly I allowed the burial party to take his body away, another broken link in the tenuous chain that led back to my beginnings.

Chapter 21
Attack on the Hindenburg Line - September 1918

A soldiers marching song
It's a long way to Tipperary, it's a long way to go.
It's a long way to Tipperary, to the sweetest girl I know.
Goodbye Piccadilly, farewell Leicester Square.
It's a long, long way to Tipperary, but my heart's right there.
Judge

The division remained in reserve at Mazingarbe or in the line at St Elie throughout July and August and on into early September. Little did we know but throughout this period, while still appearing to be consolidating their defences to the east of our position and engaging us in the occasional morning's 'hate', the Germans were also thinning out and in the process of implementing a limited withdrawal back behind the formidable wire belts and deep defences of the Hindenburg Line. Peering across the bleak landscape we would occasionally see tiny grey coated figures digging furiously at some half constructed trenches or hear them hammering home pickets in the dark of the night. If the sun was behind us and the light favourable, we might fire a speculative round or two in their direction, perhaps wagering our daily rum ration on the outcome of the shot, but while we were enjoying the luxury of this rare moment of inactivity and they busy with their tasks, neither side had any desire nor inclination to go looking for trouble. That is not to say that our senior officers would not have been happier had we occasionally "woken up the line a bit", but we were having none of it. So for the first time in many months I enjoyed a period of peace on what was now regarded as one of the quieter sectors of the line.

Throughout our stay the usual crop of rumours flourished, many even predicting the scale and location of the next phase of the campaign. Some were very specific, even describing in graphic detail the actual role our company would play. Throughout my time in the army it never ceased to amaze me where or from whom such rumours originated, for although seldom true, they often resulted in many sleepless nights and eventual disappointment for those gullible enough to believe them. Now, if what we were hearing was true, the next offensive would be the one that would see us all home for Christmas! How many times had I heard that before, and suffered the inevitable disillusionment as a consequence? But, as the saying goes, hope springs eternal, so just like everyone else I found myself hoping and praying that this time the rumours might prove to be true. Common sense still warned me not to pin too many hopes and expectations on what would surely turn out to be merely barrack room gossip and just another, "three blue lights" rumour[1] Admittedly things had seemed unduly quiet over the last few weeks but surely it was impossible that the Germans, until recently taking all before them, could have suddenly become so weak and dispirited that they were now in full retreat? Only a few weeks ago our commanders had been urging us to put our backs to the wall and fight, if necessary, to the last man, now, if rumour control could be believed the enemy were ours for the taking! But if I ever needed reminding to practice caution, I only had to recall those heady days of 1914 when so many of my friends, many long since dead, had volunteered to fight in a war which they had been assured "would be over by Christmas!" Nor could I ever forget the sensation of horror, shock and disbelief I had experienced when the realisation that on the Somme a combination of poor leadership, bad planning and inferior ammunition had managed to change an anticipated victory into a bloody defeat. The tens of thousands of brave young men who met their deaths that day had believed their officers when they said that after the barrage they would cross no man's land unopposed and were marching all the way to Germany. I had been fresh out of training then, naive enough to believe that everything I was told by an officer must be true so that I had envied those men their coming glory, bitterly regretting not being allowed to go with them. Following the wars greatest barrage, they too would have been confident of success right up to the moment they scrambled from their trenches only to be met by that murderous hail of fire. By then it was too late. Like lambs to the slaughter they obeyed their leaders, content to put their trust and eventually their lives into the hands of those men their military training had taught them to always believe. Unfortunately, often to my cost, since then too many bitter experiences had taught me and many thousand others that this would not always be so. Military historians offer an explanation but not a defence for the frequent but predictable incompetence often bordering on deceit that was shown by senior officers and was endemic in this war. They point out that command headquarters were sited so far behind the lines that those who staffed them were too remote to accurately judge the often changing situation for themselves. On the other hand, their junior officers, isolated from reality but sharing our hardships at the front, often knew less about what was going on than we did. The massacre on the Somme was the first but certainly not the last betrayal that I would experience during my service career. I count myself as one of the lucky ones but many thousands would pay for such dishonesty and incompetence with their lives.

There was no doubt that these latest rumours were making a great impression on the many new conscripts who had recently swelled our ranks, men not usually known for either their enthusiasm or co-operation so that suddenly a new air of purpose and optimism could be seen in everything they did. Predictably, the more experienced of us, those that they called "the old and the bold",[2] had heard it all before so wisely kept our council.

Understandably, these rumours were the main topic of conversation in every billet, bar and cafe, wherever men were gathered together. Certainly the details of the attack, accurate or not, must also have been known to the enemy who, once the main thrust of the Michael offensive had petered out, had retreated behind heavily protected defensive positions.

In a war where the need for secrecy warranted little importance, it was still sometimes possible for either side, merely by reading the European newspapers, to be fully aware of any impending attack well before it happened. Now well and truly into the war as a single unit commanded by their own officers and fighting their way tree by tree and snow drift by snow drift, through the gloomy forests of the Argonne, the Americans had discovered this to their cost in one of the first actions they fought. On that occasion a Swiss newspaper had had the audacity to publish the actual times and duration of their preliminary bombardment, resulting in the salvoes falling on positions that had been evacuated the night before. So much for neutrality!

Since then, the time and experience they had gained had been used wisely and now the battle lines were drawn which we hoped would lead to an Allied victory.

In August, after many months of inactivity guarding the Vimy Ridge and the coalfields of Bethune, our comrades the Canadians took the initiative and for the first time went on the offensive, leapfrogging our right flank and driving forward at great speed to take the formidable Siegfried Position in a single day. Then, presumably pausing only long enough to, "hang out their washing on the Siegfried Line", they pushed on to smash their way through the heavily guarded and previously invincible Wotan position. Now only the banks of the Canal du Nord lay between them and the extended wire belts of the Hindenburg line. This was a series of defences which had only been breached once before and then only briefly, by the Tank Corps at Cambrai, and at that time our leaders had been too astounded by their own success to exploit it! We would meet our Canadian friends again when we joined forces for the next phase of the campaign.

So the Germans watched and waited from behind the impregnable defences of their famous line, prepared to defend them to the bitter end with the same commitment and determination that they had shown in previous campaigns. .

On 20th September, 36th Brigade was assembled in a large field outside Versailles to be addressed by our commanding officer, Lt Col. Foord and this, we knew, could mean only one thing. The previous night he had assembled all his junior officers and NCOs at command HQ in order to acquaint every company as to how and where each aspect of the coming campaign involved them. Now those details would be spelled out to us. Here was the moment many of us had been waiting for with such keen anticipation for it was common knowledge that the latest big push was already underway and enjoying some success. Now we would learn what part our Brigade would play in the next phase. Would it be a "cushy" support role or like on so many other occasions, would the Fusiliers be expected to lead the charge? The CO began by explaining the present situation all along the front before going on to describe, then evaluate, each aspect of the plan in more detail. He even provided an approximate timetable when each phase would be put into action. For reasons of secrecy these plans had not been revealed, even to divisional commanders, until the last minute and because of this, as we could expect to be in action in less than seven days time, there would be little time to prepare. On a more positive note, due to this element of surprise our senior officers anticipated an early and overwhelming victory against an unsuspecting and ill prepared enemy! This bit of news sent a wave of laughter and derisive cheering through the ranks. What element of surprise, what secrecy? As the details of the plan had been revealed, each one of us had realised that they almost exactly matched the rumours we had been hearing for the last three weeks, and if we had heard them, then so had the enemy! Could this be the start of another debacle similar to the Somme, this time with us cast as the main players?

Fortunately, as he went into more detail, things began to sound much better. He had been informed that the Austrians, one of Germany's staunchest allies, were now out of the war and already suing for peace, while in Germany the civilian population was starving and demanding an end to the war, a fact that was known to her front line troops. Despite taking heavy casualties the Americans were taking all before them on the Argonne and the Canadians, itching for a fight after their prolonged stay on Vimy Ridge, had already turned their section of the formidable Siegfried Line and were now camped on the banks of the Canal du Nord. Now, as part of this plan, our Brigade would be supporting them during their next offensive. This time, the Colonel concluded, there was a real chance that this final "Grand Assault"[3] as he called the plan, would lead to ultimate victory.

The news that we would be supporting the Canadians was greeted with a spontaneous cheer from amongst our ranks for we had seen them in action on the Ridge and at Passchendaele and knew what they were capable of when it came to a fight.

We learned that the plan of attack would involve all available Allied troops and would be phased over three days. We would not be in action until the second day, 27th September, when our orders were "to co-ordinate with the Canadian Corps in an attack south of the Arras, Cambrai road and across the Canal du Nord". Unfortunately, because of their difficulty in crossing the canal, we would not be supported by the now customary large number of tanks associated with such offensives. Instead the enemy would be softened up by a massive barrage concentrated on the far bank throughout the previous night. This latest information brought groans of despair throughout the ranks for every recent Allied success had been led by tanks and now, just when we needed them most the most we would be facing our toughest obstacle without their support. If the Germans had machine gun posts dug in on that far bank, then we were in for a pretty rough crossing. Not many of us slept that night as the magnitude and danger of the task placed before us was contemplated and discussed in every billet.

The man lying next to me was beside himself with worry.

"Corp, you've been around a bit, with no bleeding tanks in support we haven't got a prayer have we?" he moaned, "And even if we reach the canal, how am I expected to get across when I can't blooming well swim!"

I must admit that this was not an unreasonable question and one it was hoped our leaders had considered while making their plans! Come to think of it, how were any of us going to get across, loaded down with heavy equipment and under fire from the far bank? To make matters worse, not just my questioner but many of us were unable to swim, a fact highlighted by my attempts at crossing the Severn during basic training! Unfortunately our knowledge of the local area was not sufficiently up to date to know that long sections of the canal were still under construction and therefore did not contain any water!

Admittedly the consequences didn't bear thinking about but I did my best to console my new friend who I'm sure would have had to have been very green not to detect the lack of conviction in my voice.

"Don't worry", I told him, "You stick close to me. The Canadians will go over first with us supporting them and the way them buggers fight there will only be a few stragglers left behind for us to mop up."

Although much younger than this man, I was flattered to think that he saw me as one of the "originals"[4] and therefore worthy of asking my advice. My reassurances must have gone some way to convincing him for it was not long before the night was filled with his contented snores. It seemed a lifetime since I sought similar advice and comfort from the old miner while experiencing the terror of my first bombardment, now still only aged nineteen I was looked on as an old hand! How I envied him his innocence!

As usual, on the night before any attack sleep never came easily to me so it was with some relief when reveille roused me to a wet and windy morning and I was able to lose my thoughts on other and more pressing matters.

By mid-morning on the 26th everything had been packed up and the division was ready to move. We fell in in columns of threes carrying full battle kit and supplies for three days, and on the command "quick march", swung away from the town that had been our home for the past few weeks. As we trudged along the muddy road I recognised familiar farms and villages where I had stayed. At some, the curious occupants came out to watch us go and in the towns people lined the streets, running beside us as we marched, some pressing sweets and fruit into our hands, others throwing flowers. As if by magic French flags had appeared at nearly every window and tattered Union Jacks were being waved. One old man even produced a bugle and blew a passable rendition of the charge while another played a tan-tivvy on a battered but highly polished coach horn. The optimism and enthusiasm of the occasion was so infectious that we joined in, breaking ranks to kiss and hug the pretty girls as if it was a victory parade, for to the French who had also heard and believed the rumours; it seemed to be just that. Were not all the signs of victory plain to see? Was it not true that it was more than a month since an enemy shell had fallen on their town? Hadn't they been told that people living behind the German lines had seen columns of dejected enemy troops on the move almost every night? They marched always in one direction, to the east. Now the British tommies were going too and although they saw us as their friends, like ourselves, they hoped against hope that we would not be coming back.

"Vive la Angletaire, vive le Tom-eee", they cried and we responded with, "Vive la France", followed by the only verse we knew of "Le Marseillaise", and a rousing chorus of "Rule Britannia". All at once the occasion took on such a carnival air that even we were convinced that victory could not be far away. Being filled with that hope and expectation put a new spring in our stride and we laughed and joked as we marched along those cratered and rubble strewn roads. But even where it was still intact the pave was hard and uneven under foot, causing men to stumble as they marched, cursing the stone blocks for the menace that they were. Many a marching man had broken an ankle, slipping on their irregular shapes; many more had been killed by flying blocks when the road had been hit by shell fire.

Remarkably we seemed to be the only troops on the road, a fact that I found surprising as I had expected there would have been a lot more men pushing Eastwards behind a retreating enemy. Once more I began to experience some doubts about the validity of our orders.

Our route took us well to the West of Arras so it was mid-afternoon before we reached our destination. No sooner had we arrived at Vis-en-Artois and before we could renew our acquaintance with the Canadians, we were told that there had been a change of plans and now our Brigade would move to Villers-lès-Cagnicourt, a mile or two to the north.[5] Here we would be accommodated in the assembly trenches overnight before moving up to the Buissy Switch, our jumping off point, in the morning. This at least was good news for it meant that with luck we would no longer be part of the frontal attack attempting to cross the Canal du Nord.

Although we were exhausted, any thought of sleep was impossible that night, the crowded conditions in the trenches making it difficult to find a place where there was enough space even to lie down. To make matters worse, just as it was getting dark the fine drizzle that had been falling for most of the day became a steady downpour, turning the bottom of the trench into a river of brown, muddy, water. Worse still it turned the ground in front of us into a slippery morass, filling the minds of those of us who remembered the dreadful conditions at Passchendaele with bitter memories.

It was always like this the night before an action. Some said it was unwise to sleep in case your troubled dreams reflected the fear and apprehension of the coming day while others fell almost immediately into untroubled dreams as if tomorrow was just another day. For myself, I could never sleep before an action.

In the quiet of the night a confusion of questions and doubts tormented my troubled mind, ensuring that even had I wanted to, any attempt even to doze would have proved to be impossible. Time after time I asked myself the question, would I survive the day? Would I be one of the lucky ones, coming through unscathed or with a wound not serious enough to be fatal? How many of these men, many of them my friends, would live to see another day? How many would be blinded, how many maimed? How many so badly mutilated that their bodies would never be found again? And perhaps the greatest fear of all was the constant, nagging fear of being afraid, of cowardice and when it mattered most, of letting both myself and my comrades down. In the darkest part of the waiting night, I'm sure that every one of us reluctantly came to the same inevitable conclusion, that in the morning many of us would have a rendezvous with death.

The night was alive with the sounds of many activities coupled with sporadic enemy shelling that was already causing some casualties. All through the night, other units were moving up to take their places in the assembly areas, while on the road below us came the constant racket of traffic as tanks and artillery moved cautiously along it in the dark. Just after midnight I heard the splash of marching feet and whispered orders as columns of men passed along the trench where I lay. In the light of a shaded lamp I recognised a familiar cap badge and realised to my delight that these were men of the 7th Shropshires. I called out to one of their sergeants who told me that they would be in action on our right flank with the Third Division and would mount the second wave of the attack behind the kilted Jocks of the Royal Scots Fusiliers.[6] Although I saw nobody that I knew, hearing once more the familiar Shropshire drawl and knowing they were close at hand was a great comfort to me that night. The following day, although suffering heavy casualties, they would take then hold their allotted section of that formidable defensive network known as the Hindenburg trench.[7]

Stand-to was sounded at four o'clock and a breakfast of porridge, washed down with mugs of hot sweet tea liberally laced with rum, was served to all hands where they stood at the firing step. Zero hour was not until 5.20 and although we were not expecting to be in action until later that day we spent the last hours cleaning then re-cleaning our rifles, checking equipment, sharpening knives and bayonets and all the other seemingly trivial activities that whiled away the time before the first wave went over the top. To experience this waiting is to understand how a condemned man feels as he counts the relentless ticking of the clock marking the last few hours of his life.

During this time we were ordered to fill in the usual field postcard, crossing out all but the, "I am well" column. These we left in our rucksacks along with other small personal possessions that we would recover if and when we survived the day. Should any of us not make it, the contents, minus the field postcard of course, would then be sorted and sent back to our dependants, so it was not unusual at times like this to see a number of the saucy photographs or other dubious articles so popular at the time, discarded around the trench, done to avoid embarrassing the folks back home when they discovered that the personal possessions of their dear departed contained little more than a pack of dirty postcards!

The attack was to take place along a front fourteen miles wide. I had accepted by now that this was to be the biggest and possibly one of the most decisive battles of the war, even so, I was surprised at the apparent restraints set out for those units taking part. The plan involved each battalion not doing the normal thing and pushing on once it had taken the objective allocated to it, but remaining where it was while other still intact supporting battalions leapfrogged through and on to the next objective. They in turn would repeat the manoeuvre until the final limit of advance set for the day had been reached. At that point no further advances would be made until reserve units and the necessary supply convoys were given time to catch up. In the meantime all the positions to the rear would be occupied by comparatively fresh troops in case of an enemy counter attack. For the many of us who had only known the static depravations and horror of trench warfare throughout the war, this would prove to be an entirely new experience.

As the time of the attack approached, the tension became almost unbearable as junior officers moved up and down the trenches giving last minute orders and encouragement to their men. Whispered instructions were given and runners sent doubling forward, ducking and diving, using any available cover to carry their orders to those men already in place in the forward positions. Punctually at zero hour a green flare marked the beginning of the action and all up and down the fourteen miles of the front a furious barrage was unleashed on the enemy positions. In my section, the first wave of the attack was to be led by units of the Canadian Corps and from where I lay the ground sloped gradually upwards so once again the enemy held the higher ground. After about ten minutes or so the barrage lifted then crept menacingly forward and as I watched, tiny figures swarmed from positions they had occupied under cover of darkness in rifle pits and scrapes well forward of where I lay. Now they spread out across the broken ground to closely follow the flashes and explosions that marked the passage of the barrage up the hill.

Soon the morning was filled with the rattle of rifle fire and the louder crump of grenades as the first waves began to engage the enemy. At a signal, at regular intervals other lines of men rose from cover to move resolutely forward up the hill, their bayonets flashing scarlet in the light of the rising sun. Already men were going down in great numbers under the hail of enemy fire as they dodged and weaved their way through broken wire entanglements and muddy shell craters that obstructed every foot of the way. There was no panic, no hurry, and no indiscipline. This was where the hours of training and comradeship would pay off. It was at times like this where the team spirit of men at war, vital for success, could persuade untried soldiers to overcome fear and logic and the instinct for self preservation and keep moving forward. When common sense and instinct urges them to dive for cover, it is very hard to ask men to stand up and face the enemy. This is especially so when all around them their friends are dying before their eyes. Now, keeping their spacing, only closing in to fill the space left by a fallen comrade, the Canadians moved resolutely forward to where the cloud of smoke and debris marked the line of the enemy position.

Somewhere back at command headquarters, in a vain attempt to preserve the surprise element of the attack orders had been issued that there must be," No hurrahs by divisions going forward!" during this phase of the attack. Despite that, faintly, above the din of the battle, we heard the cries of the attackers. "On Canada, on Canada," and their cry was taken up by a thousand others on the hill. Suddenly we were all cheering as the tiny figures, using bayonet and club, fell on the grey coated German soldiers who rose up to meet them from behind their defences. For a moment the whole dreadful spectacle was there for all to see as men hacked and clubbed, bombed and stabbed in a battle for life or death. For a few moments we heard as well as saw the noise of battle, the shouts, the curses, the shots, and the crash of bombs. Then, mercifully, the morning breeze blew a curtain of smoke across the whole terrible scene.

By now the barrage had lifted before moving on to beyond the German line, effectively boxing the defenders in. For them there was no escape. Gradually the smoke cleared and the firing subsided and soon only the muffled explosion of mills bombs flung into enemy dugouts, and the occasional crack of a rifle broke the silence. Suddenly, fluttering in the wind we saw the Canadian flag suspended from a bayonet hoisted above the parapet. Looking at my watch I was surprised to see that it was barely eight o'clock. Our first object, the Red Line, had been taken and up to now my platoon had not left our trench!

Soon after nine we received orders to move forward up to, then beyond, the Buissy Switch in the rear of the 11th Manchester Regiment. Leaving our cover we moved forward up the hill, the Manchesters leading the way. Our platoons followed about two hundred yards behind in column of route with each platoon spaced at one hundred yard intervals. Accordingly, W, X then Y platoons led the way while Z, my recently reformed platoon, took up the rear in front of HQ Company.

We pushed on at a good pace passing the dead and wounded from the first assault on the way. I saw medics offering what comfort they could to the wounded, applying rough field dressings to ghastly wounds which in many cases would result in the death of the victim long before he could be evacuated. As usual they went about their business with a smile and a word of encouragement for each man they treated. Already stretcher bearers were carrying men back in the direction from which we had come and walking wounded, sometimes in twos and threes, were helping and supporting each other back down the hill.

Reaching the trench only recently taken by the Canadians we were confronted with a scene straight from hell. Bodies were lying everywhere, sometimes piled three deep where machine gun positions had been. Many of the enemy had been killed by the fury of the barrage but others bore the unmistakable signs of having died at the business end of a bayonet or having their brains dashed out in the hand to hand fighting. In the bottom of the trench more bodies lay in the grotesque poses of death. Down there, amongst these bodies and sometimes walking over them, were the Canadians, seemingly oblivious to all the carnage they had created scattered all around them. Amazingly they were going about the business of securing the position as if it was just another day.

When first the Manchesters then ourselves came up then passed through them they stopped what they were doing to cheer us on our way.

"Go and get 'em you bloody Kitches,[8] it's that way to hell", they yelled, white teeth grinning from smoke blackened faces. "Let us know when you reach Berlin and we'll come up and drink your bloody health. In the meantime, our orders are to stop right where we bloody are, thank you very much!"

It was all good humoured banter and who could begrudge them their moment of triumph for they had already done far more than had been expected of them that morning. How great that sacrifice had been could be measured in the many hundreds of Canadian casualties that still littered the hillside. What would those of us who had fought at Ypres and on the Vimy Ridge have given to have had these tough, no nonsense fighters alongside us as we ploughed on into who knew what.

We went cautiously forward as far as possible until a burst from a German machine gun sent our forward scouts diving for cover. By this time we were beyond the crest of the hill so were able to see the flat plain at our feet, running away into the distance. Now it was possible to see the damage done by the German retreat. Here was senseless destruction at its worst, the systematic demolition of all possible cover or means of sustenance for any would be pursuers. All across the plain, pillars of smoke rose lazily into the air, each marking a burning stores dump, farm or orchard. Where crops had been planted, now there was only smouldering ash where fields of standing corn had been reduced to blackened squares. Any trees or even the remains of trees had been sawn off and burnt to eliminate their use as cover. Later we would find that even the wells had been poisoned and any buildings too sturdy to be easily reduced to rubble, booby trapped to maim or delay the unwary pursuer. About a mile away, among this destruction I could see the next German defensive line, the drifts of snow white clay and hastily constructed belts of wire clearly marking its position. Even from this distance it was possible to see that it was so far unshelled, un-bombed and therefore still very much intact. It was obvious that if we could see them, then the enemy could see us. Certain too that the infantry and machine gunners waiting in the comparative safety of their trenches would, at that very moment, be setting their sights and testing their aim across the open ground over which we must soon pass.

Zero hour for the Manchesters was timed at 11.30, with us due to jump off at midday so until then we held our positions waiting for the expected barrage to commence. The enemy were already in action with trench mortars falling amongst us causing some casualties. Fortunately many were hitting the open ground separating us from the Manchesters and it was with some relief that I realised that the enemy gunners had not yet found our range. It had been raining most of the day and while I watched, another heavy squall came scudding across the plain below us, blocking out our view of the enemy positions and their view of ours. At least while it lasted we were safe from their attentions. Fortunately, just as it cleared, shells went screaming over our heads as our own barrage opened up, the first well-aimed salvoes falling directly on the German lines and on the belts of wire. After a few minutes it lifted and rolled back to the position where the creeping barrage which we would advance behind would begin.

The technique of artillery firing bombardments had improved a great deal since my early days when almost as many casualties could be sustained from "friendly" shorts as by the enemy. With experience, the co-operation and understanding between infantry and gunners had become such that it was now possible to persuade even the rawest of recruits to advance in comparative safety. Hidden by the smoke and debris from a well-aimed barrage, attacking forces could be almost on top of the enemy defences before sustaining casualties.

Whistles blowing all along the line signalled zero hour and to a man the Manchesters rose up and moved forward towards the enemy. I watched each section rise and follow on until each one was on the move. Now it was our turn. Ahead of where I lay our three forward platoons were on their feet and advancing towards the enemy. Ahead of them the forward sections of the Manchesters were already forming up behind the pall of smoke. From somewhere within the smoke a red flare arched into the sky. This was the signal for the gunners to lift their sights and start the barrage creeping forward.

The ground began to level out as we reached the plain and almost immediately men began to fall as the enemy opened up with small arms and 77's firing high explosives and shrapnel almost at point blank range. It was a certainty that our casualties would have been so much greater had the German gunners not been blinded by the smoke and debris from the barrage. Fortunately, the restricted range also limited their use of gas shells.

It was clear that in our present position we were sitting ducks and the sooner we got across this open ground and reached the enemy the better.

"Come on lads", I shouted, breaking into a run, trying to catch up with the barrage which by now had come to a standstill, for I knew that where the fall of shot was now concentrating must be marking the enemy positions, still almost three hundred yards away. I could see groups of men each side of me, still drawn out in line of advance: now gaps were beginning to appear as more and more men went down under the murderous hail of machine gun fire. What was happening up front? I could see groups of men from our last two platoons still moving forward but all the Manchesters as well as our first platoon seemed to have disappeared from sight. Could they all be dead or just hidden by the smoke? In the last few minutes the barrage had stopped. This could only mean we were so close to the enemy lines, to continue would endanger our own men. Almost immediately, through the clearing smoke I saw the outline of an enemy trench about one hundred yards away. Now I saw what was left of the leading platoons of the Manchesters who had almost reached it, cheering as they ran, and as I watched they closed with the unseen enemy in the trenches below.

Everybody was running now, every mind focused on the white mounds of clay in front were already men were joined in mortal combat, fighting hand to hand in the confined space of the trench. It was not surprising therefore that I never saw the enemy aircraft approaching from my left until it was too late. It was firing as it came and already men were going down in its path. It was fortunate that as I ran I was reloading my rifle, working the bolt to push another round into the breach and because of this my rifle was at the port, slanting from right to left across my body and it was this that almost certainly saved my life. It all seemed to happen in a split second. First I heard the rattle of the aircraft's guns and saw the spurts of dirt streaking towards me as bullets struck the ground. Almost at the same moment I heard the sickening but unmistakable "thwack, thwack" of bullets hitting flesh and was aware of the two men on my left going down. I remember thinking "Jesus Christ this is it" as the high velocity round hit my right hand just as I levered another round into the breach. Had I not been doing that, the round that hit me would have surely killed me. As it was, the exploding bullet passed through my hand before detonating on the metal breach, showering my right side with metal splinters blown from the shattered rifle and the impact badly damaged my right hand, almost severing it from my arm.

The force of the blow knocked me off my feet and for a moment I lay where I was, feverishly trying to regain my senses. Gaining some composure, I quickly established that although quite serious, the wounds to my side were not life threatening and at that time were causing me little pain. However, it was quite obvious that the wound to my hand was extremely serious as blood was gushing from it in such large quantities that there seemed a real possibility I might bleed to death if it was not attended to without delay. My first priority was to find some cover as the air around me was still full of the whistle and crack of bullets. A few yards away I could see a still smoking shell crater so, taking my life in my hands I made a dash for it, ducking and weaving as I went. Once safely inside I had time to consider my position.

Even if I had been able to there was little point in going forward. From where I lay I could see that the fighting had intensified all along the enemy line and that more and more of our men were arriving, leapfrogging over the bodies of their fallen comrades to plunge with bayonet and bomb into the action. At the same time the enemy were bringing up reinforcements from their reserve trenches to the rear, so there seemed little prospect of an early victory or any help in that direction, while to go back the way I had come was also fraught with danger. I knew it was more than a mile back to our assembly area and a first aid post, besides, as I was already feeling dizzy due to the loss of blood, I felt certain I wouldn't make it that far. As I crouched there considering my next move I was showered with dirt and pebbles as somebody jumped down into the crater beside me. I vaguely remember seeing the face of a young soldier peering down at me and being aware that on his arm he wore the red cross of a medical orderly.

"Christ, you can't know how glad I am to see you", I muttered, "I think I've had my bloody hand blown off". Then everything turned hazy as first my world changed to purple and then black as I slipped away into a dead faint.

Chapter 22

The End of the Line - September 1918

"A Shropshire Lad"
With rue my heart is laden,
For golden friends I had,
For many a rose-lip't maiden,
And many a light foot lad.
By brooks too broad for leaping,
The light foot lads are laid;
The rose-lip't girls are sleeping,
In fields were roses fade.

Housman

It must have been the agonising pain in my arm that shocked me back to consciousness. Even so, I was still aware of a severe cramp in both my legs, while my arm, hand, and all down the right side of my body seemed to be on fire. On top of all that my head pounded unmercifully. Of course, without knowing it, a combination of shock, an acute loss of blood, plus a liberal dose of morphine meant that no matter how hard I tried I found it impossible to understand where I was or what had happened to me. Even so, despite my confused state of mind I was still able to recognise my surroundings and recognise the seriousness of the situation I found myself in. I was fully aware that I was lying in the bottom of a large shell crater, and a fairly recent one at that, for the reek of cordite was still heavy on the air. Adding to that, the broken earth all around me was still warm to my touch. I could also see that my right hand and arm were heavily bandaged up to the shoulder and, despite numerous layers of wadding, both were still bleeding profusely. My tunic and shirt had been ripped open, exposing my chest, and more bandaging had been applied from under which blood was also seeping. To my relief, apart from the pain from these wounds and a splitting headache, a tentative exploration of the remainder of my body confirmed that everything else seemed to be all there, in reasonable good order and functioning correctly.

Confused and disorientated, I tried to scramble to my feet only to discover that my head was spinning so violently and my vision so blurred that this proved to be impossible. It was fortunate that it was. Above my shelter the battle was still raging with the air alive with bullets, so to have left its protection at that time would have meant certain death. I shook my head, desperately trying to clear the mists that blurred my vision and threatened once more to enfold me but still my memory remained stubbornly blank and no matter how hard I tried I could not remember the circumstances that led to my being here. Only one thing was certain. Even in my shocked and confused state, it was obvious from all the noise and activity I could hear that I was close to and had probably been involved in some sort of action, but where and when remained a mystery. After a while, still losing blood and getting drowsier by the minute, I slipped once more to the bottom of the crater where, still clutching my injured arm to my chest, I drifted into a drug induced but pain free sleep.

It must have been several hours later before I awoke because now night was already falling and the crater was filled with shadows. Above my head the noises of the battle had diminished and instead of bullets, the sky was filled with stars. Now the only sound to break the silence was the rattle of a machine gun firing a long way off accompanied by the sullen thump of distant mortars. I was relieved to find that my head seemed clearer now so after some initial hesitation I decided it should be safe to leave my hiding place to take a look around. As I was about to move a startled voice caused me to gasp with alarm and grab for the bayonet still secured in its scabbard on my belt.

"Jesus Christ mate, you frightened me almost to death. I've been lying here alongside you for more than three hours thinking you were a corpse. When you moved I thought I was seeing a blinking ghost!"

Shaking with fear but relieved to hear that the voice was English, I peered into the gloomy interior of the hole where I could just make out the outline of a man. He was lying on his side, his head resting on his pack, and even in the fading light I could see that he too was heavily bandaged.

"Who the hell are you?" I demanded still unsure of the situation and embarrassed by my obvious fright. "Where am I and what the hell is going on?"

Using his rifle as a crutch he dragged himself painfully across the crater to crouch beside me.

"We both copped one in the attack" he explained, "You were already here when I arrived, being attended to by a medic. He bandaged us both up then left saying he would be back. That was hours ago so I guess the poor buggers bought one or he wouldn't have abandoned us like this. Reckon if we're going to get back to our lot we'll have to manage by ourselves", adding almost as an afterthought, "Christ knows if I can make it though in the condition I'm in."

He explained that he'd been hit by shrapnel in the head and both legs and like me had taken cover in the nearest available shell hole. Slowly my recollection of what had happened was coming back. I remembered being almost up to the enemy trenches and seeing the approaching aircraft. I even recalled the moment of horror knowing I'd been hit and my relief at seeing the medic then waking for a while and hearing the battle raging close by. As my mind cleared it suddenly dawned on me that should the attack have failed, we could now be lying only a short distance from positions still occupied by the enemy! I whispered a warning to my companion, urging him to be quiet. I need not have bothered for now he was lying very still with his face to the ground and appeared to have slipped once more into unconsciousness. Gingerly raising my head above the rim of the crater, I looked about me. All was quiet. I waited expectantly, anticipating at any moment the cry of a German lookout, evidence that I had been seen, but when none came I decided it was probably safe to explore further. Judging by the condition of my companion and my own need for urgent medical attention, time didn't seem to be on our side, for to stay where we were and hope to be rescued would surely mean certain death.

I had hardly eased myself above the rim of the crater when there was a bang and a wooosh as a flare arched into the sky, lighting up the surrounding area with its ghostly silver light. At the same time a bullet whistled perilously close to my head, causing me to dive for cover back to the bottom of the hole.

"Don't move Fritz, we've got you covered", yelled a voice with an unmistakable Lancashire accent. "Throw your rifle out, then come out of that hole with your hands up or I'll bloody well bomb you out. Shnell, shnell, pronto Fritz, your bloody wars over mate".

Not for the first time in my military career, I realised that I was being fired on by friendly forces. On this occasion I couldn't have been more relieved!

"Hold your fire you daft buggers," I shouted, "There's two of us here, both wounded and we're both as British as you are! For God's sake give us a hand out of this bloody hole before we bleed to death."

Even then they weren't sure. German soldiers had been known to play such tricks before, opening fire on unsuspecting rescuers as soon as they left their cover to offer help.

"What outfit are you from, we don't know who you are?" came the uncertain reply.

I had thought the man lying next to me was still unconscious but suddenly he scrambled groggily onto his knees. Now, in the dying light of the flare I could see he wore a sergeant's stripes on his arm.

"I know who you are though", he shouted back," and I never thought I'd be glad to hear your lousy voice Private Higgins, you stupid Scouse bastard. It's Seargeant Edwards here from 'A' platoon and some poor bugger from the Fusiliers. Now get your bloody fingers out and help us out of here!"

From then on everything was just a blur. Soon I was surrounded by concerned faces, and helping hands were lifting me gently out of the crater and onto a stretcher where medics cleaned then redressed my wounds before giving me another shot of morphine so that I slipped once more into a painless sleep.

I spent the next twelve hours in a twilight world drifting in and out of consciousness. Once I was aware of being in an ambulance and then on a train with nurses and doctors. At one time a concerned padre hovered over me. Fortunately I was too weak and ill to understand or care.

It was several days before I was sufficiently recovered to realise where I was. This I discovered was a base hospital in the French port of Boulogne where I remained for several weeks. Finally I was declared fit enough to travel and the next day was put aboard a steamer bound for England.

On arriving, having first been assessed for treatment, I was sent to a VAD in Wakefield where I would stay until Christmas and thanks to the skill and patience of the medical staff during that time I gradually regained the use of my arm and hand. However, there was an added legacy to my wounds. Because of my weak condition and poor life expectancy, the doctors at Boulogne had decided not to remove the shrapnel in the form of several pieces of rifle breach and bullet splinters still embedded in my body. Eventually their entry wounds would heal and I would carry these dubious trophies with me for the rest of my life.

The hospital at Wakefield might have been pretty sparse but to me it seemed like heaven. After so many months of deprivation, the luxury of a warm, safe bed and regular meals defied description. As part of my treatment and to encourage my wounds to heal, each morning I was placed in a warm saline bath. There I would lie for hours on end, perhaps reading the morning papers or simply relaxing in the comfort of the soothing water. Enjoying such luxury, there were several times each day when I had to pinch myself just to prove I was not dreaming.

Suddenly all the news in the papers was positive. All along the front the Germans were in retreat and suing for peace and I found myself regretting not being there to see it through to the end. To be in at the kill and able to celebrate the surrender with all my friends, toasting the health of those who had survived and the memory of those who hadn't, would have been a privilege indeed.

As it was there were great celebrations back at home. At eleven o'clock on the 11th November, all the church bells across the land rang out to proclaim the news that once more there was peace in Europe. Every street was thronged with people, everybody kissing and hugging each other like long lost friends. Strangers were shaking hands, children were singing and women were crying. Flags were flying from every mast and the day was proclaimed a public holiday.

Those of us who were well enough were allowed to go into the town, only to find ourselves feted as heroes. On a more sobering note, it was impossible not to see that the people who celebrated the peace that day were mostly women and children or old men for in a little more than four years the war had stripped our country of an entire generation of its young men.

All the pubs were open and landlords were serving free drinks to anyone in uniform. Curfew at the hospital was at five o'clock but by then we were past caring. The celebrations went on long into the night and it was not until the following morning after being paraded before Matron that we were made to realise the error of our ways. Feeling thoroughly hungover and still slightly tipsy, I apologised profusely for my actions, pointing out that it had been a very special occasion. My excuses cut no ice with that formidable lady who regarded total abstinence and good order as a normal way of life. As I received my punishment, it seemed ironic to realise that those of us who had been feted as heroes only the day before were treated as villains today. As a result, I wonder how many other veterans who survived the war, spent the day after Armistice on their hands and knees polishing what seemed to be several miles of hospital corridors!

At Christmas I was allowed home on leave and the celebrations started all over again. Of course my parent's joy was tinged with sadness at the loss of Jack, but the rest of us had somehow survived, scarred certainly, but by and large all in one piece and safely back home again. Other families were not so lucky. In Hodnet none of the three Jones brothers would return or Alex and Jessie Berry, both of whom I'd gone to school with. Their names and those of thirty-two others would be recorded for posterity on the monument raised in their honour in Hodnet churchyard.

But life had to go on and this year, with the signing of the Armistice, Christmas had the added incentive of ensuring that everyone enjoyed themselves. At home it was just like old times with friends and neighbours visiting throughout the morning. All insisted on drinking my health and shaking me by the hand, sufficient grounds for Father to get out the damson wine he'd been saving for just such an occasion. The home made beer also flowed like water so that later that day there was hardly a sober member of the family who sat down to the Christmas dinner Mother and the girls had prepared.

That evening I slipped away by myself and climbed to the place where Mother and I had stood on the day I enlisted. I was so much older and wiser now, grown cynical and hard by my experiences over the last three years. Standing there I suddenly realised that the war had robbed me of my youth, taking away those formative years that transform a boy into a man. Instead, still only nineteen, I had experienced sights and sounds so horrifying to be beyond description. Worse still I had become immune to them. Gone were the innocence and hope of yesterday, to be replaced with a confusion of feelings I would carry with me for the rest of my life. Now all that remained were the bitter memories of an old man trapped in the body of a youth. Standing alone in the darkness, shielded from my family by the privacy of the night, these pent up emotions suddenly spilled over and I sobbed uncontrollably for all that I had lost and all those things that could never be again.

As I stood there the bells at Hodnet began to ring out, calling the faithful to evensong. Forgetting my concerns I wiped away the tears and ran to join the rest of the family and together we walked through the frozen lanes to the little chapel in Paradise for the Christmas celebrations. Little had changed except that now there were spaces set aside in family pews that not so long ago had been filled. The pot-bellied stove was still coughing and belching in the corner and the oil lamps still filled the little room with their acrid smoke. The same minister, still determined to save our wayward souls, was prophesying our demise from the pulpit, assuring us that, should we not mend our ways we would surely be condemned to hell fire and damnation. Gone were the days when he could frighten me with lurid descriptions of hell for I had been there a thousand times before and, had he asked, could have described it to him in every horrifying detail. Hell was blood and guts and broken limbs piled on top of each other in a bombed out trench. Hell was the searing yellow smoke of gas that scalded men's lungs and the ever present stink of putrefying flesh. Hell was the dreadful fear of approaching death, cowering beneath a barrage, or the dying screams of a bayoneted man. Hell may not have been named on the map but I could tell him it was a place not so many miles away across the English Channel.

As my leave came to an end I decided that I would write and ask for a further extension. I had nothing to lose by trying, some conscripted men were already being demobbed and I considered that with my injuries it must only be a matter of time before I too would join them. Unfortunately there was a difference between many of them and me. I had not been conscripted but had volunteered for service and was therefore considered to be a regular and because of this military logic and bureaucracy saw things in a very different light. I was so convinced the authorities would see it my way that by the time I received a curt reply through the post denying my request, I had already overstayed my leave period by three days. Accordingly, adopting the attitude that I might as well be hung for a sheep as a lamb, I decided that I would not return until the following week and face the consequences then. In the meantime, I would not worry my family by telling them that I was already technically classed as absent without leave, still considered a serious charge even though the war was over. I had not taken into account the tenacity of the military authorities or the determination of the local constabulary. The following day Mother was on her way into Hodnet when she was accosted by a policeman who was a newcomer to the village and although on nodding terms with Mother, knew nothing about her family.

Greeting her with a polite good day he asked her if she knew the whereabouts of an old friend of mine, Ernest Edwards.

"Yes," Mother replied," I saw him yesterday in the village with his young lady. She's in the WAC you know. They're here on leave together".

Imagine her surprise to be told that in reality neither was on leave at all but had been reported absent and were therefore wanted by the authorities. She was even more surprised by his next enquiry!

"You don't by any chance know a Walter Williams do you, he comes from these parts and is also on the run!"

Telling me about it later, Mother admitted she almost died with shock.

Not knowing any better she disputed what he was saying, explaining that I was her son and that I was also on leave, recovering from my injuries.

"I'm afraid that's not so, Mrs Williams", he said, "I know that your Walter has been on leave but it ran out last week and now he's posted as absent. I've got no alternative but to take young Edwards and his girlfriend in. However, because your lad's only been gone a few days, I'm giving him the chance to be on the train back to his regiment by the morning. I'll be there to see he does or I'm going to have to come looking for him as well".

Mother wheeled the trap round in the road and drove furiously back home. I might have been almost twenty-one but even that was not old enough to escape the verbal lashing and boxed ears I received when she arrived. She was still of the old school where anybody in authority had to be obeyed. To have suffered the ignominy and shame of having the village constable tell her that her son was wanted by the authorities was too much to bear.

Painful memories of childhood days came flooding back as I waited for Father to come home, knowing that I had to endure the retributions all over again. I was not disappointed! Admittedly he stopped short of taking his belt to me but only just so it was a very chastened and dejected young man who sought an early refuge in his bed that night.

The next morning I was up at first light and at Hodnet station in good time to catch the eight o'clock train. As he had promised, the village constable was there to see me off and I took the opportunity to give him a wink of appreciation for his kindness. He knew full well that I was already in hot water and by him not returning me under arrest avoided me facing the extremely serious charge of desertion. If proven, this would ensure the prospect of several years in a military detention centre.

My journey was interrupted by many delays so it was early morning before I arrived at Newcastle. The weather was freezing, with snow lying inches deep on the ground so having spent the rest of the night huddled on a park bench I was glad when it was time to report to East Boldon Barracks.

I did my best to justify my absence to the orderly sergeant, explaining that I had applied for an extension but my leave had expired before I received the letter of refusal. Not unnaturally, he had heard it all before and proved to be unsympathetic to my cause. First I was charged with being five days absent without leave, then told to report to the quartermaster's stores, draw a rifle, full webbing and pack and be fallen in on parade by nine o'clock.

All the kit was second hand and in a filthy condition. The rifle was also thick with dirt with the white clay blocking its barrel suggesting that it too may have spent some time in France. It was hopeless. I did my best but by nine o'clock my efforts had hardly improved the situation at all. Once on parade I was joined by several other men including two sergeants who had also been absent but the fact that all of us were veterans of the war cut no ice with the young provost officer in charge of us. In fact if anything he seemed to hold that against us, reasoning that we were experienced enough to have known better.

While we were on parade my old Adjutant walked by and recognising me, stopped to ask about my health. "Glad to see you survived Williams," he said, shaking me warmly by the hand, "are you staying with us now the show is over or are you returning to civvy street?" but once he learned that I intended to apply for demob as soon as I could he seemed to lose interest, leaving me to my own devices. We fell in on parade and when the inspecting officer got to me I received the full fury of his tongue. Not given the chance to explain the shabby condition of my kit, I now faced a further charge of being slack on parade. My prospects were getting bleaker by the minute!

At the end of the inspection we were ordered to, "port arms", a drill that involved throwing the rifle up and across the body in two movements, while a third movement placed it on the left shoulder. Unfortunately, having been stood to attention throughout the inspection I had lost all feeling in my injured right hand, an in attempting to carry out the order I dropped my rifle with a mighty clatter, sending it spinning across the parade ground. By now the inspecting officer was trembling with rage, demanding to know what my problem was, unconvinced with the explanation regarding my injured hand.

"Fall out two men and march that man to the sick quarters," he screamed to the provost officer, "If the MO says he is fit to be on parade then charge him with casting away his arms and dereliction of duty".

The way things were going it looked as if I might be in DQs for the foreseeable future!

Fortunately, my prospects improved once the MO saw the condition of my freshly healed wounds and decided that I was certainly not fit to be on parade. In fact, he considered my condition to be so serious that I should see a Travelling Medical Board and, based on their decision, the possibility of a medical discharge from the army.

After that things moved quickly. Within a week the TMB decided that although my wounds were not serious enough to warrant a medical discharge, I should be released from service anyway. But not before the army had had its pound of flesh for there was still the little matter of the charge of being absent without leave to be dealt with. I was duly paraded before the commanding officer who, having heard all the facts still found me guilty. My punishment would be the loss of two days pay and I would be reduced to the ranks. The following day I was paraded before the company and once the charge had been read out, the CO stepped forward and ripped my solitary stripe from my sleeve. I can't say that I regretted parting with it, in hind sight it had never provided the opportunities I thought it would anyway!

The following day I took the train back to Shropshire and the camp at Prees Heath where I would eventually be discharged. So I left the army a private, just as I had been when I joined, but everything else had changed and my life would never be the same again. When the day arrived for me to go I had few regrets at leaving, knowing that I would miss the comradeship of army life and the many friends I had made, but little else.

Travelling home that night I lingered for a moment on the haunted road through Paradise. It was March and the ground was frozen hard, my way lit only by a winter's moon. On an impulse I started to run and, just as they had done when we were children, there were the echoes of ghostly footsteps following on behind. Could these footsteps really be the spirits of children our parents had told us had drowned in the frozen pools, or were they the spirits of those countless friends I had left behind in France? Alone on that deserted, moonlit road I told myself that they were and, happy with their company, was comforted by their presence. Wrapping my coat around me against the biting wind, I turned once more for home, knowing and hoping that perhaps the ghosts of the countless other young men who would not be coming home that night were walking beside me and watching over me. If that was the case then I knew that I was walking in the company of heroes and knowing that, I hope I travelled with their blessing.

Notes to Chapters

Chapter 2
Early Days in the Army

1. On the first day of September 1902, Walter's brother George died aged six. This must have been only months after the family arrived at Daneswell. Nothing is known about the cause of his death. No mention is given by Walter, even of his existence, other than to name him in the family tree.

2. The Canadian authorities were offering handsome rewards for any British worker prepared to emigrate and assist in opening up the new territories and those people with farming skills were particularly welcome. In January 1914 in a speech to Parliament on the Rural Exodus, the Liberal leader Mr Asquith said, "The very flower of our peasantry is being carried away to Canada. It is mainly the best class of worker who is going to work on the one million acres waiting to be cultivated".

3. Jack (John) Williams name is on the war memorial standing at the approach to Hodnet churchyard which records those locals who fell in both world wars.

4. Up to the beginning of 1916 all recruits had been volunteers, but after the terrible casualties at the Somme the numbers wishing to volunteer reduced at an alarming rate. As a result, an act of Parliament was rushed through making all men of nineteen or over report for registration and eventual conscription. In 1918 the age limit was reduced to eighteen where it would remain throughout the Second World War and on into the post war years of National Service. Conscription, like National Service, was eventually discontinued in 1960 when the Services returned to the pre 1915 era when all recruits had been volunteers.

5. In January 1916, battalion machine gun teams were brigaded into the newly founded Machine Gun Corps. The badge consisted of two crossed Vickers machine guns surmounted with the British crown. Thus came into existence the highly trained and formidable Machine Gun Corps which would eventually contain more than one hundred and sixty thousand men. It was disbanded in 1922, having been described as "a corps born only for war and not for peacetime parades". A memorial in Hyde Park erected in memory of those who died in the MGC which depicts a statue of "The Boy David" carries the following inscription: "Saul hath slain his thousands, but David his tens of thousands".

Chapter 3
First Days in France

1. At the outbreak of war Germany could put only thirty submarines to sea compared with the one hundred and forty-three of the combined Anglo-French navies. Being powered by petrol engines which were extremely noisy and with their flaming exhausts visible by night, they were particularly vulnerable to detection. Because of this their initial role was seen only as sea-going scouts but later in the war, like the tank and the military aircraft, they developed into efficient and deadly weapons of destruction, playing a major role in blockading the supply routes to the United Kingdom. Armed with both guns and torpedoes, their range of operations soon been extended to several hundred miles while their ability to stay submerged was now measured in hours. In February 1917 Germany's leaders decided to attempt to destroy Britain economically by sinking on sight all shipping bound there, whether Allied or neutral. In April 1917, on her first raid the submarine U93, acting alone, sank 27,000 tons of Allied shipping.

2. The gilded statue which surmounted the church tower, became known to the troops of both sides as the Leaning Virgin when it was knocked sideways by a German shell in 1915, after which it became a popular belief that when it fell it would signify the end of the war. Even as superstitions go this was most improbable, made even more so due to the fact that it was now being held up by steel wires put in place by French army engineers! Thousands of British troops gazed up at it as they passed through Albert on their way to the Somme. Both the tower and the statue were finally destroyed by British gun fire to prevent its use as a German observation post after the British withdrawal from Albert in 1918.

3. The exact number of horses used on both sides which were killed in the Great War is not known but conservative estimates put the number in the tens of thousands. Although senior officers were always mounted on horses, many of which were commandeered from the English landed gentry, the mule was more popular as a beast of burden. Steady under fire and prepared to go where many horses wouldn't, these sturdy animals were the unsung heroes

of the transport and artillery brigades. By the later stages of the war, so many horses and mules had been killed that they had to be imported from Canada and America.

Chapter 4
Early Experiences of Trench Warfare

1. At the start of the campaign the 36th [Ulster] Division consisted of the 107th, 108th and 109th Brigades, each Brigade containing units of the Irish Rifles, the Irish Fusiliers, and the Inniskilling Fusiliers. During the first day of the Somme they succeeded in taking the formidable Schwaben Redoubt on the Thiepval plateau, recognised as one of the toughest strongholds on the Western Front, but eventually had to pull back through lack of support. Earlier in the day units previously held in reserve had been sent forward to clear part of Thiepval wood. Finding themselves in open ground and coming under heavy machine gun and mortar fire, 107th Brigade accelerated their rate of advance. Unfortunately, having no one in authority to control them, they arrived on the second line ten minutes too early for the attack when the British guns, firing on time, opened up their barrage on this very ground. Pinned down in the open ground with nowhere to go they became victims of their own artillery. Two thirds of the Irish Battalions were either killed or wounded during that barrage. A memorial to the Ulster Division can be found in the rebuilt town of Thiepval.

2. The small holes or scrapes dug into the side of trenches and used by off duty soldiers to rest in were known as "funk holes". The word funk is unfortunate as it implies "avoiding doing something through fear" which in this case was not true. In fact the term dates from the South African wars and describes a dugout or other shelter. No disparagement of the occupant was implied by the civilian slang word "funk" meaning coward or cowardice.

3. During the war, miles of tunnels were dug by Mining Battalions recruited from the miners of British coalfields. Tunnels were dug under enemy positions, before being filled with high explosive. Others were used as forward listening posts, monitoring enemy conversations. Often tunnels from both sides were

only feet apart and on occasions actually met when a hand to hand fight to the death would ensue in the cramped, dark confines of the tunnel.

4. Sited in woodland behind the trenches along the Ancre and above the Somme, ranged against the enemy, the Allies mounted the following heavy artillery pieces:-

124 six-inch, 61 nine-point-two-inch, 12 twelve-inch and 6 fifteen-inch howitzers. These were complimented with hundreds of medium and small bore field artillery pieces.

At 7am on the morning of 24th June the order to fire was given and the first of thousands of 200 pound shells went spinning across the wire. The bombardment would continue almost nonstop for a further seven days, only lifting at zero hour on the first day of July. It was and still remains the greatest concentrated artillery bombardment ever fired.

Chapter 6
The Start of The Battle Of The Somme

1. The training camp at Étaples was sited just inland from Le Touquet, the site of many infantry based depots and military hospitals. Always known by the troops as 'Ee-tapps', it is best remembered for the cruelty of the instructors based there to the many thousands of returned wounded, released prisoners and new drafts out from home who suffered in their hands. Many years later, the Bullring and the man made punishment hill described by Walter, was the subject of a film starring Sean Connery about a detention camp sited in the desert entitled "The Hill". The rules prescribed that, "while undergoing Field Punishment No1, the subject may be attached for a period or periods not exceeding two hours in any one day to a fixed object, but must not be attached during more than three out of any four consecutive days, nor more than 21 days in all". Most men believed that their instructors and the military police stationed here were "base loafers" and were regarded as enemy number one by the fighting soldiers.

2. One of the many reasons for the failure of the Somme offensive was the inability of the artillery to 'cut' the belts of razor wire guarding the enemy

positions. This should have been achieved using shrapnel shells, a large number of which were actually surplus from the Boer War, but many failed to explode. When it became known at home, the scandal of the un-exploding shells was the subject of much bitter criticism in the British press and in Parliament.

3. The Battle of the Somme will always be associated with the apparently futile flinging of men across a no man's land of shell torn and blasted earth, against an enemy entrenched in impregnable defensive positions. Preceded by a weeklong bombardment calculated to have reduced the enemy to a pathetic shambles, the troops went 'over the top' on 1st July 1916 and walked to their deaths. Five months later the line had advanced seven miles at a cost of more than one hundred men killed for every yard gained. In November, when the winter rains finally forced a halt to the massacre, 101,873 Allied troops had been killed and a further 328,643 wounded. Another 44,458 were either missing or captured. A total of 23,080 officers were also killed wounded or missing during the campaign.

Chapter 8
The Clearing Station at Corbie

1. Due to the contaminated nature of the ground and the complete lack of even basic sanitary arrangements at the front, it was inevitable that almost every wound would become infected. Exacerbating this were infections caused by the many unburied and decaying corpses with which the troops were in daily contact and the ground being heavily contaminated from the frequent gas attacks. Many wounds became gangrenous, a condition where body tissues rapidly decay when the blood supply is cut off through disease or injury. This condition was inevitably fatal unless prompt medical attention was received. Successful treatment usually included amputation if the infection could be confined to a limb.

2. The death sentence was in force for mutiny, cowardice, desertion, murder, striking or disobedience, sleeping at or quitting a post and casting away arms. Three thousand and eighty men were sentenced to death but only 346, three of whom were officers, were actually executed. Interestingly, 91 of these had previously had their sentences suspended only to repeat the offence. Only two

British soldiers were executed for mutiny. Each sentence had to be confirmed by the Commander in Chief before it could be carried out and the signature of Haig appears on all but a few of the death warrants. Although he requested to do so, only the Australians refused permission for Haig to have any of their troops executed.

Chapter 9
Sent Home to England

1. Although in theory the charge of 'fraudulent enlistment', which included a boy 'mis-stating his age', could lead to prosecution, I can find no evidence that this was actually enforced. In fact, in April 1916 the answer to a parliamentary question regarding this stated that 'no such trial had taken place'.

2. During the first few months of the war it seems likely that many hundreds of young men falsified their age in order to join the forces. Of course at that time there were already youngsters serving as boy seamen and boy buglers and there seems to have been no efforts made to keep them away from the action. The youngest member of the forces known to have been killed during the war was a lad of only thirteen. Later in the war, after a scandal that rocked Parliament, efforts were made to return many of the men known to be underage back to the UK.

Chapter 12
Mud, Mud, Glorious Mud (Passchendaele)

1. Passchendaele ranked alongside the Somme as one of the worst military blunders with which this war would become synonymous. One general was reduced to tears when he saw the conditions Allied troops had been expected to fight in. "How could we expect men to fight in this?," he tearfully demanded, only to be told that he had not yet reached the actual battle field!

2. The Gheluvelt Plateau behind which sheltered the principal concentration of German artillery, was a promontory of low hills rising above the Ypres, Menin Road. One section, codenamed Tower Hamlets, was the scene of an attack by the Anzac Corps under the command of Lt Gen. Sir William Birdwood. The front line here was known as the Ypres Salient due to the fact that the line

bulged out into enemy occupied territory. This made it particularly dangerous as it allowed enemy artillery to be sited down both flanks of the bulge

Chapter 13
A Charge through the Forest

1. Many thousands of the bodies of men who died were never found. Their names are recorded on the hundreds of memorials scattered throughout France and Belgium. It was not unusual for wounded men to lie unfound on the battlefield for days, many dying from wounds which would have been treatable if they had been found in time. Almost one hundred years later bodies are being found in such a condition that their name and regiment can often be identified from scraps of uniform and the identity tags they were wearing.

Chapter 15
Home on Agricultural Leave

1. Field service caps softened by removing their wire frames were called "Gorblimey" hats. Early caps had ear flaps attached which when not in use could be buttoned on top. Gorblimey was a cockney expression used to ridicule the gaudy civilian caps popular before the war. Caps worn in this way were worn almost as a badge of honour, identifying the wearer as having served at the front.

Chapter 18
I Rejoin my Unit near Vimy Ridge

1. Portugal has for many years been one of Britain's staunchest allies, so it was not surprising that at the outbreak of the war it was one of the first European countries to offer assistance, putting two divisions into the field by 1916. However, by the time they were trained and fitted out, the government which had sent them had been replaced by one which had no interest in the war and was actively hostile to any co-operation with the Allies. As a result they spent much of their time in France supporting the Canadians in the Vimy Ridge sector where Walter would have been in daily contact with them. On 7th April 1918 and once more without the support of their officers who spent

much of their time in Paris on long periods of leave, they were in the line in an area to the north of Armentières when confronted by a massed enemy attack. Unfortunately their 1st Division chose not to fight but took off their boots, turned tail and fled, some of them expedited their escape on bicycles stolen from members of the British 11th Cyclist Battalion who were moving up to support them! Not highly regarded for their military prowess, these unhappy soldiers were universally known by the derisive nick name 'Pork and Beans', by other Allied soldiers.

2. While researching this book I have failed to find any other references to front line soldiers being released to carry out 'agricultural duties'. This doesn't necessarily mean that this was not so but when you consider the conflicting reception he received when he arrived in the UK, I suspect that it may have been an order whose meaning was wrongly interpreted by some local commanders. When he was in his eighties, Walter was invited back to RAF Shawbury and was feted as their guest of honour. In recordings made during his lifetime he described in great detail the time he spent ploughing between the huts, and some of the many friends he made at that time.

Chapter 19
The Beginning of the End

1. The minimum age for conscription was lowered to eighteen in early 1918 under an emergency act of Parliament. This became necessary because, by this time, most of the young men of nineteen or over were either fighting at the front or had already been killed or wounded

2. In anticipation of the planned counter attacks of 1918, the German army was completely reshaped during the winter and early spring of 1917/1918. This radical retraining plan was aimed at bringing the rest of the Infantry units up to the standard and mobility already demonstrated by the Special Assault Battalions, or Storm Troopers as they became known.

   The role of these fast moving and unconventional units was to carry the attack to the enemy, to seek out, attack, and where possible overrun any weak spots in the enemy defences, causing as many casualties and as much confusion as possible before passing on to their next objective. If a position proved to be too strong, the storm troopers would pass around it, going on to seek out a more vulnerable target. More orthodox troops following on behind, would then be used to eliminate these stronger pockets of resistance. Although storm troopers were handpicked from infantry regiments, they usually attacked with their rifles slung over their shoulders, leaving them free to throw the "Steilhandgranates" [hand grenades], which they carried both in their hands and in their belts.

3. On 11th April, Haig issued a special Order of the Day to those divisions still desperately holding the line in Flanders. It included the following words which amply illustrate the seriousness of the situation as he perceived it at that time.

"There is no other course open to us but to fight it out. Every position must be held to the last man: there must be no retirement. With our backs to the wall and believing in the justice of our cause, each one of us must fight on to the end." It is fair to say that the crisis was alleviated not by the hand of God but to the more mortal arrival and intervention of two additional British and one Australian Division!

4. With the knowledge that soon the Americans would be in the war and that the escorted convoy system now being implemented by the Royal Navy was enabling the British to survive the U-boat threat both in the Atlantic and in the Channel, the Germans decided that the time had come to seek out one final, decisive victory which would lead to an Allied surrender.

To this end Ludendorff produced three battle plans which he code named "George", "Mars" and "Michael", each directed at a different part of the line held primarily by the British. "Mars," considered by the Germans to be the most decisive plan, was aimed at Arras but included the formidable defences of Vimy Ridge. This plan, although the most telling should it be successful, was considered to be too difficult for the first assault, and too costly in men and machinery to deem viable. "George," while offering the best chance of victory, was aimed at the Flanders front where the boggy ground, churned up by months of nonstop shelling, would not be dry enough to ensure success before late April or early May. After much consideration, Ludendorff chose "Michael", an attack concentrated between Arras and La Fère on either side of St Quentin. This was planned to take place on 21st March. Much can be said of Haig's skill as a tactician that he too had reached the conclusion that any attack worth its salt must be ranged against Vimy Ridge and the coalfields which it protected. This conviction may have also been influenced by information gathered from German deserters. It must also be considered that this information may have been circulated as a double bluff, ensuring that the Canadian Corps and a great amount of ordinance remained their throughout the Michael offensive. Records show that Haig was so sure that Vimy was the real target and would eventually take the main brunt of the attack, that throughout the Michael offensive he was convinced that this and other attacks were mere decoys and the real offensive was yet to come.

With the benefit of hindsight we now know that, with the launch of "Michael", the proposed attack against Vimy was shelved indefinitely by the Germans and in the event, never ever materialised. In August 1998, almost eighty years to the day when the last offensive was fought on the slopes of Vimy Ridge, a British bomb expert was killed when a tunnel he was searching for First World War bombs collapsed. The day before, he had detonated a large number of still primed and active shells. To this day it is known that within the tunnels and caves that bisect the summit of the ridge there are still many tons of ordinance left from the war. Such is the scale of the task that although it is expected to go on well into the new millennium, it is felt that much of these still lethal explosives will never be recovered.

5. By the end of May there were more than 650,000 American troops in France. However, General Pershing, their commander under direct orders from the President, still continued to resist any requests for their entry into the war until they could fight as an independent National army under their own officers. The British anticipated that it would be weeks and possibly months before the American units would be sufficiently trained to enable them to take on that role. Until then all they could do was hang on and hope their intervention would not be too late.

In the event it was an isolated attack on Contigny on the 28th May that saw the first American offensive action of the war and later in June when they finally secured the much disputed Belleau or Bellow Wood at the cost of over 11,000 casualties.

6. Although radio communications had developed in leaps and bounds since 1916 it was used primarily well behind the lines at Corps HQ etc. In the line, telephone communications were still widely used but their exposed wires were subject to damage from shelling and were therefore considered unreliable. On the odd occasion, carrier pigeon and even messenger dogs were used with some success. But the most widely employed method of sending a message from one place to another was still by runner. Because of this, for the front line soldier, news received was mostly by word of mouth and was therefore days old and usually unreliable. To that end, a popular saying throughout the war was, "Don't obey the last order. By the time you receive it, it's probably out of date and has been rescinded anyway!" So you can imagine the excitement and speculation in many units up and down the line when the news filtered through that the Red Baron had been killed, probably by rifle fire from the ground. It was not uncommon for infantry to bring down the flimsy aircraft of the day and certainly Walter, remembering the aircraft with the red painted wings that he had downed only a few days before outside St Elie, would have been no exception. Imagine his excitement and that of his colleagues when they first heard the news, but history has shown that whoever the unknown pilot was who Walter brought down that day, it was certainly not the Red Baron, neither was he a member of The Flying Circus. That being so, an actual account of Walters kill is recorded in the war diaries written each day in the trenches, and can still be seen in the Public Records Office at Kew. It states:-

> *"April 12th*
>
> *At St Elies sector. Enemy gas shelling Vermelles. Battalion relieved 12th Manchester Regiment in the front line. Improving defences. Boche aeroplane brought down by our fire in No Man's Land between "K" Dump and "B....." [word unreadable] 78.*
>
> *Second in Command wounded by machine gun fire when crossing to it. Lt Col Foord 8bn Northumberland Fusiliers ".*

On Sunday 21st April, No 209 squadron of British Camels took off from Bertangles, north of Amiens, flying a high offensive patrol. At the same time Baron Manfred Von Richtofen, known by both sides as the Red Baron, took off with his squadron of brightly coloured Fokker triplanes, nicknamed The Flying Circus. Their orders were to carry out routine reconnaissance work and to protect several German two seaters doing observation work.

The two forces met over the Somme and a dog fight developed between the Red Baron and a British aircraft flown by a novice pilot. The Camel was pursued at low level along the Somme across British lines held by the Australians who opened fire with rifles at the pursuing aircraft. Suddenly the Red Baron, once the pursuer, now became the pursued when he was attacked from above by a Canadian pilot, Captain Roy Brown, who fired a diversionary burst at the red aircraft before turning away. Suddenly the Fokker lost altitude going into a low dive before crashing into no man's land near Vaux-Sur-Somme. The pilot had been killed by a single shot fired from below and to his right side. He was still only 26 years old and had been credited with 80 Allied "kills". Much has been said about who killed the Red Baron. At the time Captain Brown was given the credit and awarded a medal as a result. Later, war historians cast doubt on this as the angle of the fatal shot so clearly showed that it had been fired from the ground. In 1997 new evidence was put forward showing that the only person firing at the time from the necessary angle and range was an Australian, Sergeant Cedric Basset Popkin, who had claimed the kill at the time. Certainly it seems most unlikely that he was killed by Brown who, in his report, stated that the Fokker dived vertically into the ground, indicating that the pilot was already dead. Witnesses on the ground however stated that the aircraft crashed in a shallow dive and the pilot was able to switch off the engine before he died. Such was the notoriety of the Red Baron that within hours of his crashing all the fabric had been torn from his aircraft by souvenir hunters! Consequently, any evidence of shots hitting the plane from behind and above was lost. The following day the Red Baron was buried with full military honours by the British.

Chapter 20
Rest and Relaxation

1. There is still much speculation regarding the origin and type of influenza which decimated the world between the spring of 1918-19. To this aim, eighty years later in 1998, research was carried out on the bodies of several seamen victims whose bodies had been buried and therefore preserved in the permafrost of the Arctic.

   Throughout the world the epidemic claimed at least twenty-seven million victims. In Europe alone more than ten million died during the year in which it lasted. This can be compared with the 1,066,468 men enlisted from across the Empire who were killed or died of wounds during the course of the war.

   So far no one knows precisely where the epidemic started although at the time it was thought to have been in Spain, hence the name "Spanish Influenza". Another theory is that it started in America whose troops then brought it over to Europe. Wherever it started it found a sound bedfellow in the rat and lice infested trenches of France as it did in the unsanitary environs of India where it is claimed 16,000,000 or more died in the first nine months of the epidemic.

2. Casualty Clearing Stations [CCS] provided the first line of medical attention to the wounded and were usually sited just far enough behind the front line to be beyond even the longest ranged enemy guns. Treatment provided was only rudimentary, often by medics with only fundamental training in first aid. The primary aim of CCS's was to evaluate the seriousness of the patient before either patching him up and returning him to the front or sending him on to base hospitals or to England for further treatment. Inevitably many of the wounded died and were buried near the CCS. After the war many of these places became war cemeteries, some taking on the name of the original CCS sited there. These cemeteries are easily recognisable because most if not all of those interred there are identified with their name. Those cemeteries sited near battlefields and therefore containing unrecognisable remains have many headstones identifying those buried there as 'known only to God'.

Chapter 21
Attack on the Hindenburg Line

1. This was an age when superstition and folklaw still played a major part in the everyday lives of the fighting men. Many, like the story of the Hanging Virgin, predicted the end of the war, and seem to have been accepted as plausible by many of the men. Another popular superstition was that the declaration of peace would be signalled by the appearance of "three blue lights". As the war progressed and optimism was replaced by cynicism, "three blue lights" came to be accepted as anything that was unbelievable. With the arrival of the Americans the more popular and more explicit, "bullshit" would take its place.

2. A popular military saying is that, "there are old soldiers and there are bold soldiers but there are very few old, bold soldiers" the implication being that if you expected to survive the war you kept your head down and never volunteered. Those veterans who could boast of having survived several campaigns, no matter by what means, were afforded a certain grudging respect by the less experienced soldiers, earning the ambiguous but affectionate title of "the old and the bold."

3. The Grand Assault was the title given to the campaign that started on 26th September and involved all three Allied armies in combined attacks all along the German front. For the first time in the war the old philosophy of a "spirit of offensive, direct and brutal," so much admired by Haig but so costly in manpower was set aside for one of convergent attacks on all sides. The strategy of Grand Assault would mark the end of the old style trench warfare forever.

4. An "original" was the proud nickname adopted by an original member of the company, a veteran and a survivor who it was assumed knew all the tricks and "skives" and was therefore somebody well worth sticking close to.

5. Kitches, short for Kitchener's, was the nickname given to British soldiers by both the Canadians and Australians and referred to members of the original Expeditionary Force.

6. The Canadians, in accordance with the original plan, did lead the attack on that section of the Canal du Nord to the east of Vis-en-Artois, and subsequently crossed it. There is a military cemetery sited there and a memorial to the almost 10,000 troops killed in that and earlier campaigns fought in this region.

7. At zero hour the 1st Royal Scots Fusiliers had led the offensive and taken the "Whitehall and Ryder" sections of the Hindenburg trench. An eye witness account of the next phase of the campaign and the part played by the 7th Shropshires is as follows:

"By this time the British gunners had lifted their fire to the next German trench 400 yards up the slope and already the 7th Shropshires were coming through us and deploying beyond. They went forward at a walk behind the barrage, their rifles aslant, and we watched them reach and enter the area of the German counter-barrage. Many fell but the rest went steadily on, almost lost in the dust and smoke of the shell fire. The German SOS drew steadily back and when the air cleared we saw the Shropshire men in possession of the trench, and our men rose and cheered them".
Denies Rites, 2nd in command, 3rd Division. Taken from his book, "Trekking On".

More than 5,000 men serving with the Shropshires were killed during the First World War. Many more fatalities were recorded from Salopians serving with other regiments and in the navy and air force.

8. The following extracts from the war diaries kept by Lt Col Foord and available for inspection in the military records office at Kew, catalogue the final days of Walter's war.

Sept 20th 6pm.
"Division to co-ordinate with the Canadian Corps in attack S of Arras-Cambrai road across Canal du Nord"
Sept 22nd 9am.
"Brigade to move to Vis-en-Artois on 26th".
Sept 26th
"Slight change of plans. Battalion marched to Villers-lès-Cagnicourt and looked over accommodation in Buissy Switch.
Strength 21 officers, 681 OR's".
Sept 27th logged @ 5.20am

"Zero hour. Heavy barrage preceded attack by Canadian Corps. South of Arras-Cambrai road. Hardly any retaliation from the enemy. 8am, Red Line captured".

9-15 "Battalion moved from Buissy Switch @ about 200 yards in rear of 11th Manchester Regiment in column of route, platoons at 150 yard intervals in following order:- Y,W,X,Z and HQ Company. Number of POW captured is approx 200 with 2 large Howitzers, 2, 4.2's and some half dozen M.G's.

Casualties Officers O.R's

Killed 2 14 Wounded 2 85

Missing nil 15

Walter was one of the eighty-five other ranks listed as wounded.

Index

BV - #0040 - 090124 - C0 - 216/138/13 - PB - 9781909644229 - Gloss Lamination